Hard Labor

Hard Labor

Cesare Pavese

Translated by William Arrowsmith

The Ecco Press
26 West 17th Street, New York, N.Y. 10011
Distributed by W. W. Norton, 500 Fifth Avenue, New York, N.Y. 10110

Lavorare stanca © 1943 Giulio Einaudi editore, Turin.
English translation, introduction, and notes originally published
in 1976 by Grossman Publishers, New York. © 1976 William Arrowsmith.

Copyright © 1979 by The Johns Hopkins University Press

Manufactured in the United States of America

Cover photograph: Courtesy of the photographer, Russell Lee

The Johns Hopkins University Press, Baltimore, Maryland 21218
The Johns Hopkins Press Ltd., London

Library of Congress Catalog Number 79-2371
ISBN 0-8018-2180-0

Library of Congress Cataloging in Publication data
will be found on the last printed page of this book.

Contents

ix **Introduction**

	Antenati		**Ancestors**
2	I mari del Sud (1931)	3	South Seas
8	Antenati (1931)	9	Ancestors
12	Paesaggio I (1933)	13	Landscape I
14	Gente spaesata (1933)	15	Displaced People
16	Il dio-caprone (1933)	17	The Goat God
20	Paesaggio II (1933)	21	Landscape II
22	Il figlio della vedova (1939)	23	The Widow's Son
24	Luna d'agosto (1935)	25	August Moon
26	Gente che c'è stata (1933)	27	People Who Were There
28	Paesaggio III (1934)	29	Landscape III
30	La notte (1938)	31	The Night

	Dopo		**Afterwards**
34	Incontro (1932)	35	Encounter
36	Mania di solitudine (1933)	37	Passion for Solitude
38	Rivelazione (1937)	39	Revelation
40	Mattino (1940)	41	Morning
42	Estate (1940)	43	Summer
44	Notturno (1949)	45	Nocturne
46	Agonia (1933)	47	Death Agony
48	Paesaggio VII (1940)	49	Landscape VII
50	Donne appassionate (1935)	51	Women in Love
52	Terre bruciate (1935)	53	Sultry Lands
54	Tolleranza (nov. 1935)	55	Tolerance
56	La puttana contadina (1937)	57	The Country Whore
58	Pensieri di Deola (1932)	59	Deola Thinking
62	Due sigarette (1933)	63	Two Cigarettes
64	Dopo (1940)	65	Afterwards

Città in campagna	City in Country

68	Il tempo passa (1934)	69	Time Goes By
70	Gente che non capisce (1933)	71	People Who Don't Understand
74	Casa in costruzione (1933)	75	House under Construction
78	Città in campagna (1933)	79	City in Country
82	Atavismo (1934)	83	Atavism
84	Avventure (1935)	85	Love Affairs
86	Civiltà antica (1935)	87	Ancient Civilization
88	Ulisse (1935)	89	Ulysses
90	Disciplina (1934)	91	Discipline
92	Paesaggio V (1934)	93	Landscape V
94	Indisciplina (1934)	95	Lack of Discipline
96	Ritratto d'autore (1934)	97	Portrait of the Author
98	Grappa a settembre (1934)	99	Grappa in September
100	Balletto (1933)	101	Ballet
102	Paternità (1933)	103	Fatherhood
104	Atlantic Oil (1933)	105	Atlantic Oil
108	Crepuscolo de sabbiatori (1933)	109	Sand-Diggers' Twilight
112	Il carrettiere (1939)	113	The Teamster
114	Lavorare stanca (1934)	115	Hard Labor, Getting Tired

Maternità	Motherhood

118	Una stagione (1933)	119	A Season
120	Piaceri notturni (1933)	121	Night Pleasures
122	La cena triste (1934)	123	Sad Supper
124	Paesaggio IV (1934)	125	Landscape IV
126	Un ricordo (nov. 1935)	127	A Memory
128	La voce (1938)	129	The Voice
130	Maternità (1934)	131	Motherhood
132	La moglie del barcaiolo (1938)	133	The Boatman's Wife
134	La vecchia ubriaca (1937)	135	The Old Drunk
136	Paesaggio VIII (1940)	137	Landscape VIII

Legna verde

140	Esterno (1932)
142	Fumatori di carta (1934)
146	Una generazione (1934)
148	Rivolta (1934)
150	Legna verde (1934)
152	Poggio Reale (1935)
154	Parole del politico (ott. 1935)

Green Wood

141	Outside
143	Workers of the World
147	A Generation
149	Revolt
151	Green Wood
153	Prison: Poggio Reale
155	Words from Confinement

Paternità

158	Mediterranea (1934)
160	Paesaggio VI (1935)
162	Mito (ott. 1935)
164	Il paradiso sui tetti (1940)
166	Semplicità (dic. 1935)
168	L'instinto (febb. 1936)
170	Paternità (dic. 1935)
172	Lo steddazzu (genn. 1936)

Fatherhood

159	Mediterranean
161	Landscape VI
163	Myth
165	Paradise on the Roofs
167	Simplicity
169	Instinct
171	Fatherhood
173	Morning Star

Appendice

177	Il mestiere di poeta (1934)
185	A proposito di certe poesie non ancora scritte (1940)

Afterword

190	Postscript I: The Poet's Craft
199	Postscript II: Notes on Certain Unwritten Poems

204	**Translator's Notes**

Introduction

In 1941 Pavese was asked by an editor to provide a brief *résumé* of his life:

> You want my autobiography. . . . I was born in 1908 at Santo Stefano Belbo (Piedmont), and I live in Torino. I'm a bachelor; I've been constantly occupied in doing translations from English and American (I insist on the distinction) . . . seventeen books all told—including Melville's *Moby-Dick,* Joyce's *Portrait of the Artist,* Defoe's *Moll Flanders,* Faulkner's *The Hamlet,* Gertrude Stein's *Three Lives,* etc. In 1936 I published *Lavorare stanca,* a book of poetry which went unnoticed. . . .[1]

Nine years later, in 1950, Pavese had nine novels behind him (including *Among Women Only, The Devil in the Hills,* and *The Moon and the Bonfires*);[2] a handful of personal love poems (very different from *Lavorare stanca*); his masterpiece, *Dialogues with Leucò;*[3] a batch of critical essays;[4] and his brilliant (posthumously published) diary, *Il mestiere di vivere.*[5] In May 1950, at the peak of his career, he was awarded Italy's most coveted literary honor, the *Premio Strega.* Then, three months later, in the aftermath of still another miserably unhappy love affair, he committed suicide in a hotel room near the station—dying like a stranger in the city where he had spent most of his life and where he was living at the time.

In the spring of 1935, a year before *Lavorare stanca* was published, the Fascist regime suppressed the journal *La cultura,* of which Pavese had been acting editor. Jailed on the vague charge of "anti-Fascist activities," he was sentenced to three years of *confino* (detention, not imprisonment) in the tiny seaside village of Brancaleone in distant Calabria. For a lonely urban intellectual like Pavese, the sentence was a shattering estrangement from home, his life and work, his few friends, and himself. ("Roman" Ovid, banished to Tomi on the Black Sea, could not have been more isolated and displaced.) He served only seven months of his sentence, but those months were personally and professionally critical. In alien Brancaleone the solitary, unstable Pavese paid in person, paid again—but this time in absolute loneliness and anguished self-discovery—for the austere clarity of his poetry. Completed in his Calabrian exile, *Lavorare stanca* is, unmistakably, an act of radical personal culture—the beautifully disciplined product of almost four years' obsessive, solitary labor in which the poet named himself and his world by bringing his personal demons firmly, though briefly, under the control of his art.

The poetry is also cultural in a larger sense. Apart from the section entitled "Green Wood," *Lavorare stanca* contains no political poetry, not a shred of ideology. Yet the book is clearly a political and a cultural act. Negatively, for instance, the Fascist experience of the twenties and thirties is perhaps remembered in the title (cf. Notes, p. 212), but also in the tone, in the bleakness of some of the poems and the atmosphere of weary, suffering silence. Positively, it is present as the poet's radiant reaction to Fascist misery, in Pavese's laconic compassion and piercing sympathy. When Mussolini came to power in 1922, Pavese was a boy of fourteen; in a poem like "A Generation" (written in 1934, looking back to 1922), Pavese makes us feel the hopeless torpor, the tight-lipped, oppressive silence of a generation lived wholly under Fascism:

Boys are still playing games in the fields
where the streets end. The night is the same as always.
You pass the fields, and you smell the smell of grass.
The men in prison are the same men. And the women
are still women, still making babies and saying nothing.

In the terse, apparently toneless lines, Pavese packs the tension and frustration of twelve long years of "saying nothing"—the different but converging silences of a generation's shame, misery, mute courage, prison, hypocrisy, and conformity. This shared silence is the poem's "imaginative link" (cf. Postscript I, p. 190), a "resemblance" which the poem *narrates*. The silence derives in part from general complicity, a common shame, but the same reticence—slow, painful, elliptic—is also the sign of words beginning to form, of emerging confession. Quietly, unobtrusively, almost (it seems) unconsciously, the poet breaks the Fascist silence. Out of silence, the poem *speaks*. About silence.

Many Italian poets of the time, confronted with Fascism, chose conspicuous silence or withdrew into a sad "hermetic" inwardness (another, more literary, way of "saying nothing"). Pavese, like others, resisted; both his poetry and his translations of American authors were—and were understood to be—overt acts of literary rebellion against the regime. But his resistance was not merely negative defiance of official culture; it was an intense effort to rethink or create a valid Italian culture of his own. Fascist Italy was a caricature to which no truly civilized Italian could give his assent. But there was another Italy—ancient, humble, local—above all his own Piedmont, with its millennial peasant culture and its coarse, honest speech, untainted by Fascism or bourgeois refinement. And far away, beyond Italy and Europe, lay exotic America where Pavese thought he saw, rising like some continental Piedmont, a vigorous new culture, a language and literature whose genius was energy of spiritual purpose. Taken together, Piedmont and America pointed to a renewed, manworthy Italy. Hence Pavese's early experiments in prose and verse with Piedmontese dialect; hence, too, his missionary translations of American literature (above all, his classic rendering of *Moby Dick*), meant to quicken an Italy which had become "fossilized and barbarized." In *Lavorare stanca* Pavese tried, by using Piedmont and America as vertices, to triangulate a new, original (or perhaps forgotten) Italian poetry.

For this purpose realism was not enough, and certainly not the scrannel European variety. The poet's task was larger: to apprehend the miracle of the concrete, to find, as Melville had, "the spiritual meaning in every fact." To do this the poet had to stand open to the world and to others, to make his poetry *reveal*—the emphasis is Pavese's: *fervore di chiarezza rivelatrice*—the spiritual, mythical "presence" which things do not "express" but *are*. Hence the serious poet must reject the verbal and philosophical constraints of tradition, whether mandarin, Fascist, or simply *signorile*. The new poetry required a radically "new symbolism" (in Pavese's practice almost the opposite of conventional symbolism) and a new language: hard, colloquial, direct, but also austere and reticent, devoid of rhetoric, spurning all bookishness and decorative learning. The ultimate purpose of this new poetry was to replace Fascist (and traditional) culture with a new, noble (but unprivileged) indigenous culture.[6] This new culture would reconcile (as Fascism had divided): nation and province; city and country, "language" (Tuscan) and "dialect" (Piedmontese); literate and illiterate; the concrete object and its numinous or spiritual "field." It was a wild, sublime, impossibly Whitmanian project. The poet's mission was literally to create his culture from scratch or to incarnate its noblest meaning in his striving; if he could not create culture, he could at least make poetry out of the intent (as Pavese thought Whitman had done). In Whitman, Pavese found not so much influence as affinity, a common taste for the sublime and unlimited aspiration. The point is crucial to an understanding of Pavese's life and work. Despite his low-keyed, self-effacing style and his temperamental shyness, nothing is more central to Pavese than his intense, vaulting ambition and his transcendental passion. The sublime, "the boundless dream," ran in his blood; he wanted to ennoble everything he touched. Hence, we may suppose, his unrelenting efforts to curb his language, to rid it of that rhetoric which, unimpeded, would run riot, especially in a language like Italian.

When *Lavorare stanca* was published in 1936, the response was glacial silence. How could it have been otherwise? It is an astonishingly original book—so original that, forty years after its appearance, Italian critics have still not caught up with it. It was also rebellious work, strong poetry, written directly across the coarse grain of Fascist taste (and the fine grain of mandarin taste). Still worse, the author made no secret of his sympathy with "barbarous," democratic America. But the book's great, glaring offense was its impiety to tradition, its outright rejection of mandarin metrics, style, subject matter, and form. In the American view, a certain rudeness toward tradition is, at least in young writers, regarded as a promising sign; tradition, we like to think, should, for its sake and ours, be roughed around a bit. Not so in Italy, where purity of style and formal elegance are inculcated as the poet's highest duty; where "the high sound of the high dream" has always been venerated, and imitation of classical models has too often meant academic embalmment; where the aulic style achieves distinction, it sometimes seems, in direct proportion to the distance it manages to put between itself and ordinary life *(la vita vissuta)*. Admittedly, I oversimplify.[7] But the fact is that Italian, like Latin, is a mandarin literature, and writers are allowed to tap the energy of common life and speech only on condition that they conform generally to traditional norms of elegance and nobility. Writers who offend are literally drummed out of the literature. Until quite recently even so great a writer as Svevo was dismissed as provincial because of his Triestine Italian, and Silone is still being patronized as "vulgar" (because, as I heard one Italian critic snort, "The man writes peasant—*cafone*—Italian").

Pavese's offense was perversity. By education a mandarin himself, he had written flagrantly, barbarously "Americanizing" poetry. It was willful affront to literary tradition, not to Fascist taste, that counted against him. No true *letterato* would have regarded Fascist style, with its bombast and trumpery classicism, as anything more than a vile caricature of "good taste." But it is distinctly difficult to imagine a mandarin of the old school (Emilio Cecchi, say) reading *Lavorare stanca* with anything but lively contempt or bored indifference. Pavese's subjects (peasants, hobos, whores, etc.) were precisely those which tradition kept discreetly veiled or distanced; in the aristocratic preserve of poetry they had no place. The understated, almost prosaic Pavese line, meant to be murmured rather than chanted, sounded harsh and coarse to ears trained on Leopardi and Carducci. So, too, did Pavese's "flat" style, his ascetic diction, dialectal phrases, and colloquial cadences. So the book was simply put aside, ignored with the well-bred, disdainful silence which, in polite society, attends some unfortunate but unimportant breach of manners. The Italy of the thirties was too massively, pompously complacent even to notice that, for all its apparent barbarism, Pavese's work was, by *any* standard, utterly clear and honest poetry, beautifully functional, and written with amazing sureness of touch.

Certainly *Lavorare stanca* must have looked very strange to the closed, xenophobic Italy of the thirties. How new, in actual fact, was it? Remarkably so, I am convinced. There were, of course, important negative influences, like D'Annunzio, and one can perhaps detect here and there the influence of poets like Gozzano and the more realistic *crepuscolari*. In prose, of course (always much more open to innovation than the mandarin bastion of poetry), there was the exhilarating example of Verga and his successors, and regionalist experiments with dialect were common. Even in criticism there were noisy protests against mandarian torpor and Italian isolation, above all in the provocative manifestoes of movements like Marinetti's Futurism. Here, for instance, is that remarkable chameleon, Giovanni Papini, writing in 1908 in a vein uncannily close to Pavese two decades later:

> We—and I mean especially we Italians—are too literary and well-mannered. We are gentlemen even toward the earth, which has no need of politeness, and in our poetry, which suffers from overeducation. . . . It is not enough to open the windows; we must move out of the house, out of the city; we must feel and love things intimately—delicate things but soiled things too. We must express our love without regard for anyone, without fine words, without cramping meters, without too much respect for venerable traditions, proper conventions, and the stupid rules of polite society. We must regain a little of our barbarity, even our savagery, if we want to rediscover Poetry. If Walt Whitman cannot teach us at least this, there is no point in translating him and talking about him so much.[8]

Bracing salutary words, or so at first one thinks. Then, rereading, one notices that Papini is in fact hedging ("without *too much* respect for venerable traditions" is a giveaway) and that the appeal is couched in precisely the "fine words" it exhorts the reader to abandon. Papini is advocating revolt, not practicing it, and in this his protest is typical of the period. Yet the craving for change, for a new realism and a new poetry of the Italian earth, is nonetheless there, working like a slow yeast. But for twenty years the new poetry was a cause without a rebel of the requisite will and talent. And when at last a poet appeared—*with* talent, ready to "regain a little . . . barbarity"—the response was, predictably, a fastidious, intimidated silence. Both the 1938 and the (revised and augmented) 1943 editions of *Lavorare stanca* were pointedly ignored. Even after the war, when Pavese was an established writer, and in prose and film neorealism was the dominant movement, the ban against Pavese's poetry was still in effect.

Why? In part perhaps because Pavese the novelist had eclipsed Pavese the poet. But why had the poet been so totally eclipsed? Pavese thought he knew. In 1946, in (an unpublished) answer to the innuendoes of his critics, he wrote in defensive exasperation:

In the days when Italian prose was "an extended conversation with itself" and poetry was "a suffered silence," I was conversing, in both poetry and prose, with peasants, working men and women, sand-diggers, prostitutes, convicts, and kids. I say this with no idea of boasting. I liked those people then, I like them now. They were like me. A man doesn't boast that he loves one woman more than another. If he boasts about her at all, it is to say that he has treated her with clarity and candor. This is what I tried to do [in my work]. . . . Did I? Critics said that I imitated American writers, and the innuendo was that I had betrayed Italy. . . . But Italy in those days was estranged from herself, barbarized, fossilized. She had to be wakened from sleep, to clear her lungs, expose herself to all the spring winds blowing out of Europe and the world. . . . We discovered Italy—*that* is the point—by searching for words and human beings in America, Russia, France, and Spain. And this passionate identification, this sympathy with foreigners, involved no betrayal whatever. . . .[9]

No need to read between these irritably lucid lines. In Pavese's judgment, *Lavorare stanca* had been written off for reasons that had nothing whatever to do with the merits of the poetry. Now, forty years after its first appearance, the book is still being ignored for much the same extra-literary reasons—as a treasonably disloyalty to Italian tradition. Amnesty—or, at the very least, serious reassessment —is surely in order.

Any educated American reader, told the *Lavorare stanca* was "Americanizing" poetry, would register plain incredulity. Which perhaps proves nothing. But the fact remains that there is no trace whatever (apart from a reference to whaling in "South Seas") of direct or literal imitation of American work. Nor, so far as I can see, is there any significant influence of American forms, styles, or idiom. Such influence as there is, in fact, looks more like profound affinity. The chief affinity, as I suggested earlier, was what Pavese took to be the cultural mission of American writers and the tragic themes implicit in that mission. In contrast with Fascist Italy, America may have seemed Arcadian: sane, lively, wholesome, innocent. But America was above all else *active* culture, *active* poetry at its ancient *mission civilisitrice*. To the gigantic project of creating a culture from scratch, American writers brought, Pavese believed, an apposite *aretē*. "To possess a tradition," he wrote à *propos* of Melville, "is less than nothing; it is only in searching for it that one can live it." Americans, remembering Daisy Miller, Pound soaking up Kulchur at Rapallo, Gertrude Stein in Paris, and T. S. Eliot at Lambeth Palace, may smile. But Pavese's America was not that of the expatriates, but the noisy, sprawling, vulgar, turbulent America of the "boundless dreamers," Whitman and Melville. In later writers like Dreiser, Lewis, Sherwood Anderson, and Edgar Lee Masters, Pavese thought he saw Whitman's realistic heirs, working out in prose and verse the tragic implications, individual and social, of the Dream. In this view there was passionate projection as well as oversimplification; but the evidence, after all, was there, in assertion if not always in achievement. Pavese paid American writers the supreme compliment of taking them *au pied de la lettre*, and never more so than when they spoke illimitably and transcendentally (i.e., like Americans). The driving energy of American life, the electrical crackle of American speech, were also immensely attractive. But what really took Pavese's eye and mind was what he thought to be a conscious new poetics, an American "symbolism," in which the uninhibited energy of physical life incarnated transcendental purpose and meaning. Americans, he thought, had made *words* behave like *things*; they had heroically named their world into life. If this last belief was largely an illusion (as it surely was) it is an illusion that tells us that Pavese brought at least as much of himself—and Italy—to American literature as he took from it.

In 1947, years after he had renounced his faith in American literature, Pavese read Matthiessen's *American Renaissance*, and the old enthusiasm returned long enough for him to set down his richest statement of what America had meant to him:

Around 1930, when Fascism was beginning to be "the hope of the world," some young Italians happened to discover America in their books. . . . For several years those young people read, translated, and wrote, with a joy of discovery and revolt that infuriated the official culture; but the success was so great that it constrained the regime to tolerate it in order to save face. Was it a joke? *We* were the country of resurrected Romanism, where even geometers studied Latin, the country of warriors and saints, the country of Genius by the grace of God; and how did these low-class types, these provincial businessmen, these upstart multimillionaires, dare give us a lesson in taste, getting themselves read, discussed, and admired? The regime endured it with clenched teeth. . . .

The expressive wealth of [the Americans] was born . . . from a severe and already century-old desire to compress ordinary experience in language, without anything left over. From this motive sprang their continuing effort to readjust language to the new reality of the world, in order to create, in effect, a *new* language, down-to-earth and symbolic, that would justify itself solely in terms of itself and not in terms of any traditional complacency. . . .

At this point American culture became for us something very serious and valuable; it became a sort of great laboratory where with another freedom and with other methods men were pursuing the same job of creating a modern taste, a modern style, a modern world that, perhaps with less immediacy but with just as much pertinacity of intention, the best of us were also pursuing. That culture seemed to us, in brief, an ideal place of work and exploration—sweaty and anguished exploration —and not merely the Babel of noisy efficiency, of crude neon optimism, which deafened and blinded the naïve. . . .

In those years American culture gave us the chance to watch our own drama develop, as on a giant screen. It showed us a furious fight, conscious, unceasing, to give a meaning, a name, an order, to the new realities and to the new instincts of personal and social life, to adjust to a world dizzyingly changed the ancient meanings and the ancient words of man. . . .[10]

A remarkable statement, not only for what it says, but for what it does not say. "The ancient meanings and the ancient words of man. . . ." Ultimately, I think, it will be recognized, even in Italy, that Pavese's poetry is strikingly original; that it is not an American "sport" but deeply (often perversely) Italian work; that the greatest Italian and classical writers are constant and pervasive presences. So too, for that matter, are Baudelaire, and Proust, and Bergson, and Nietzsche. There is more Homer, for instance, in "South Seas" than Whitman or Melville. The project of creating a new culture, a new poetry, is at least as Vergilian and Dantesque as it is Whitmanian. Pavese's realism owes far more to Dante, Boccaccio, and Sacchetti than it does to Lewis or Dreiser. As for Dante, his influence is everywhere; positively, in Pavese's clawlike talent for seizing his object; negatively, in the principled refusal of figurative meaning. Again, Leopardi is a much more potent presence here than Anderson—yet there is not, so far as I know, a single echo of Leopardi anywhere. The paradox should not surprise us. As Harold Bloom has shown, it is the deepest obligations which are, by the stronger poets, the most vigorously suppressed. Pavese, a strong poet, could admit his debt to Greek Homer or Italian Dante (reluctantly), the Elizabethans (freely—they were past and alien), Vico (a philosopher), or the Americans (handsomely—foreigners again). But the challenge posed by Leopardi's triumphant, lifelong meditation on loneliness and death was too formidable to be acknowledged. (All his life Pavese contended with Leopardi; his *Dialogues with Leucò* is unmistakably intended to confront and surpass Leopardi's prose dialogues, the *Operette morali*). It was because the Americans, as foreigners, posed no threat to Pavese that their influence could be acknowledged (at least until the exaggeration of that influence threatened to eclipse the poet's achievement and originality in his own language).

From a traditionalist Italian viewpoint, Pavese's poetry may look barbarous or vulgar, but it has absolutely nothing in common with conventional *tranche de vie* realism or Italian neorealism either, with their homely intimacy and gritty addiction to the pettier human verities. Pavese's realism is austere, disciplined, restrained, and aristocratic, as precise and real as a razor, but also breathtakingly metaphysical in its aspiration to disclose the whole object, above all that radiance which ordinary realism ignores or strips away as so much worthless husk. Its aim is avowedly awe, revelation:

> In subject-matter, I wanted to confine myself within a given frame; I have tried for a concrete, finite presence. A true revelation, I am convinced, can only emerge from stubborn concentration on a single problem. . . . The surest, and the quickest, way for us to arouse the sense of wonder is to stare, unafraid, at a single object. Suddenly—miraculously—it will look like something we have never seen before.

That passage happens to come from the foreword to *Dialogues with Leucò*, but it applies without exception to everything he wrote. Poetry was *par excellence* the great craft of clarity; it began in darkness, confronting the chaotic and unknown, and proceeded to revelation. "The act of poetry," he wrote, "is an absolute will to see clearly, to reduce to reason, to know. . . . The poet can only say he is done when his clarity is evident to everybody, when it is common property, and in it can be recognized the general culture of his time."[11] The poet's ability to perform his Whitmanian mission of creating culture was, in fact, grounded in his passion for clarity, his power of revelation.

I emphasize the point for the simple reason that readers, for many reasons, good and bad, seldom associate realism with revelation, though the poetics are at least as old as Sappho. Hence the chances of misreading or under-reading are peculiarly high. But especially with a poet like Pavese. Not only has his name been linked, through his own criticism and translations, with names like Dreiser and Lewis, but he is generally viewed as a novelist and *prosatore* rather than a poet (quite despite the fact that his novels are based upon the same revelatory realism as his poetry and for that reason have usually been under-read). The reader, expecting realism in its simple or novelistic form, is likely to be blinkered by his own "set," blind to the presences looming and shining in Pavese's world of things. Or, still worse, he will read in the approved poetic manner, with the mindless modern expectation of "layered" meaning and Empsonian "depth" beneath a literal or narrative "surface." Finding none, he will promptly conclude that there is nothing there to repay his interest, nothing but "ordinary" realism. He will be wrong.

An aristocratic realism: austere, reticent, reserved. Is the poetry, then, simply the mirror of the man, a man who wrote as he talked, with weighted words and weightier silence? In actual fact, Pavese was proud of his (Piedmontese) taciturinity:

> Silence is a family trait.
> Some ancestor of ours must have been a solitary man—
> a great man surrounded by halfwits, or a poor, crazy fool—
> to teach his descendants such silence.

But his reticence went deeper; his solitude, if not absolute, was radical—a fact of his nature, often professionally fostered. Even with his few close friends he could be maddeningly reserved, sitting with them in a café for hours, never saying a word, then abruptly stalking off, leaving them to wonder what they had said to offend him.[12] His literary solitude was often nothing but intense, proud, helpless loneliness. But if his isolation needed friends, his pride and shyness (especially with women) made him keep them at a distance, where, he hoped, they would understand his loneliness without asking him to leave it. In return, he was thoughtful and affectionate, a kind and self-effacing friend. He prized his meditative solitude, his own rich inward life, but he lacked the true hermit's vocation; all his life he wanted a home, a wife, children, even while knowing that he needed solitude more. Of these temperamental ironies and cross-purposes, nobody was more aware than Pavese, always an acute—indeed frequently ruthless—critic of himself, as his own third-person analysis makes clear:

> Now P.—who is clearly a solitary because he understood when he was growing up that nothing worth doing is done except at a sharp remove from the world's business—is the living martyr of his own opposed needs. He wants to be alone—and he *is* alone—but he wants to be alone in a circle of friends aware of his loneliness. . . .[13]

It is an accurate, typically clear-sighted self-portrait: a radically divided man whose nature is everywhere crisscrossed by ironies and ambiguities; a man who, out of his own self-division, was determined either to achieve integration or, by intensifying the ironies, to make his tension creative.

It is also (as the phrase "living martyr" suggests) ironic self-dramatization. But there is no self-pity; the irony may be faintly mocking, but it has a pride of clarity. Denied a fully human life, Pavese perceived himself as doomed to the tragic stage, an actor "speaking his part on a gigantic stage."[14] The impoverished reality of his human life required the compensation of the sublime, of a noble passion worthy of his suffering; the part *had* to be tragic and the theater huge. As for his actor's part, Pavese insisted that he played it to the hilt—seriously, passionately, absolutely (*terribilmente sul serio*). He *was* what he played, and he played for keeps, all the way, transcendentally. Indeed, it was precisely this transcendental passion which had divided him against himself, which had made him, *he* thought, modally a poet:

> P.'s fundamental tendency is to assign to his actions a significance that transcends their effective meaning, to make his days a gallery of absolute, unmistakable "moments." The result is that, no matter what he says or does, P. is torn [*si sdoppia*], divided. Even while seeming to take part in the human drama, he is inwardly aiming at something else; he is already moving in a different world, which appears in his action as symbolic intent. This trait, which looks like duplicity [*dopiezza*], is in fact a necessary reflex of his power to be—in the presence of a piece of paper—a poet.[15]

Self-division was, in short, both curse and blessing. Pavese's solitude was incurable, circular. He exacted so much of reality that the demands literally unfitted him for the "ordinary" world; his consequent estrangement only exacerbated his loneliness, which in turn made his demands more intransigent. The only way out was to cut the circle, accept his estrangement, and live in the tension as best he could. Poetry bound him to the world but also estranged him from it. His transcendental passion *made* him a poet by metaphysically "displacing" him, cutting him firmly off from others; the poet was "in the world but not of it," sentenced to solitary labor. Or so it seemed. But this very displacement was the source of a compensatory power— the poet's unique capacity for a "double vision"[16] of the single object, a capacity which enabled him to name the world anew and thereby create a common world, a culture. ("The poet can only say he is done when his clarity . . . is common property . . . the general culture of his time.") The poet transcended himself by transforming the world, transforming it for others. In the transformation of his task, the poet was also transformed into the culture-hero or tragic hero, by his labors transcending himself on behalf of all. It was a role which, with ironic amusement at its grandeur, Pavese could live with. Fantasy too was a poet's power.

So Pavese purposively set about making poetry out of his own self-division. At times he seems almost to exploit it like so much poetic capital, with a schematic rage, everywhere finding antinomies, polarities, and "opposed needs." But the basic division was undeniably there; all Pavese did was to elaborate, refine, explore, and clarify it, according to his credo. At one pole was the Turin he loved, the city where, as intellectual and Marxist activist, he spent his *working* life (he drove himself obsessively, writing, thinking, reading); at the other pole was the country of his beloved Langhe hills and the *paese* of Santo Stefano Belbo, where he was born and spent his childhood summers ("To the boy who comes in summer/ the country is a land of green mysteries . . ."). Never poised, constantly veering and shifting, Pavese lived his real and imaginative life between these two poles, shuttling back and forth in an almost dialectical rhythm (summed up in the book's remarkably comprehensive title; cf. Notes, p. 204). The city stood for consciousness, purpose, commitment, will, heroic striving, and hard work (see "Discipline" and "Ancient Civilization"). When work and purpose staled and the body rebelled against the will's compulsions, Pavese "lit out" (like the boy in "Outside," a typical Pavese figure) for the hills and Santo Stefano, to wander around the countryside, loafing and walking with peasant friends ("South Seas"), getting drunk ("Time Goes By"), or just lying on the ground and staring at the sky (Pavese's persistent symbol of the infinite, framed usually by a contrastingly "small window"). The country meant release into natural mystery and the unknown "wild" ("The Goat God," "People Who Don't Understand," "Landscape I"), the anonymous, bookless world of the recurrent seasons and the "peasant's calendar," of instinct and the unconscious, of myth and "sacred time." If the city dialectically implied the country, so the country pointed back to the city ("City in Country," "Landscape V"). These two central polarities attracted and generated fresh, complicating pairs: words versus silence; freedom versus destiny; man versus boy; woman versus man; Olympian versus Titan; decadence versus barbarism. Finally, each set of polarities was also inflected so that it would produce its own informing spectrum of tonal positions. If the contrasting at times seems schematically Nietzschean or Spenglerian, the contrasts were nonetheless lived, grounded in Pavese's real Piedmont and blooded by his experience.

Even his basic poetic stance reflects his awareness of the antinomies that had shaped him and his decision to shape *them*. Thus he consciously counters his own mandarin training (and perhaps bent) by a deliberate, sometimes strained populism (common language, dialectal cadences, and so forth); the resultant tension is what gives *Lavorare stanca* its tone of "barbarous elegance" (or vice versa, depending on one's viewpoint). Hence, too, at the other pole, his deep distrust of his own primitivism and primitivism generally (cf. "The Goat God"; few primitivists have ever been warier of their premises than Pavese). And, finally, there is the charged "polar" geography of contrasted landscapes—hills, sea, ocean, streets, windows opening on fields, woods, sky—which the reader finds throughout Pavese's work, a complete, complex, mainly Piedmontese "world" whose imaginative actuality is reminiscent of Hardy's Wessex. The map is not difficult. The attentive reader of poems like "Landscape I," "People Who Don't

Understand," or "House under Construction" will quickly find his way simply by looking first for the broad lines of division, then observing how Pavese animates and populates his world with contrast and movement. Familiarity helps, of course, but each poem (story and novel) creates its own internally complicating and revealing map. The more the reader knows of the terrain, the more Pavese's landscapes "open up," constantly revealing new vistas by juxtaposing old features with new angles of vision, refining and enlarging. In this respect his work is a true *oeuvre*, a body of organically developing and related themes. The reader who knows only one novel or "dips" into the poems will miss the complex, cumulative power of the corpus. But the best access to "Pavese country" lies through *Lavorare stanca*. Here Pavese confronted his divided nature and reduced it to order, incarnating this order, elaborated by the imagination, in an apposite poetic "world," so comprehensive that all his subsequent work seems to be contained in it. Here, by willed clarity, Pavese created himself as a writer.

This will to clarity was for Pavese the poet's crucial, enabling courage. The poet had to *know*. But clarity depended not only on the bright order of the intellect but on instinctual clarity, too, a persistent openness to the mysterious "presences" out there, looming in the structure of "things." What was needed was a balance, a tension, a rhythm which contained both clarities. Excessive clarity of either kind —too pure, too uninflected by the other—was fatal. A poet could die of too much conceptual clarity; too many "presences" at full power could kill. The absolute zero-city, with its imperatives of work and purpose, was ultimately as fatal as the pure, instinctual wilderness of zero-country, with its annihilation of consciousness in the eternal, mythical "moment." To a revelatory realist, naturalistic "city-time" had to be corrected by "sacred time"; otherwise, there was no revelation. The poet's task was to *comprehend*—to include as well as grasp—both extremes, to fuse the poles in a poem and make a "concrete finite presence."

But balance was elusive, both for man and writer, but above all for the man. If writing (*il mestiere di scrivere*) was hard, exhausting labor, it was child's play compared with "the craft of living" (*il mestiere di vivere*—the accurate title of Pavese's diary). Apart from his editorial duties, the world of human "others" was one in which Pavese was both acutely uncomfortable and pathetically out of place. He could live in it only by forcing himself to "adapt," which he stoically and willfully set about doing. Real adaptation was out of the question; all his life he envied others what he thought was their effortless adaptation to the world, their marvelous ability to move in their environment like swimmers fitted to the water. So he worked at it, puzzling it out, piecing this formidable world together, trying to possess (and, if possible, incarnate) its human otherness by intense, meticulous observation.

The result was his own form of realism, which did not come to him naturally, but from his need to possess the world by observing it as other men, wholly immersed in living it, could not. Because he was "displaced," the poet could be "objective," and the consequence of objectivity was sympathy—a higher human objectivity. Pavese's sympathy is, I think, nothing short of uncanny. In the act of observing others, he seems not so much to usurp the objects of his perception as to merge with them in an identity that transcends and enlarges the original projection. He has the translator's gift, at peak power, of psychic emigration. And his realism is almost erotic (*questa amorosa simpatia . . .*), so completely does he fuse with what he perceives (see "A Season" or "Atavism"). The observation is compassionate because detachment and need, objectivity and projection, are strangely but powerfully combined in it. Hence, I think, the wistful candor of his gaze, and the dislocated and generic tenderness with which he treats what he sees; hence, too, the sad, studious awe which, like a Chinese Kafka, he brings to bear on a world he could not personally possess. There are times when Pavese's poetry gives his reader (certainly his translator) the sense of desperate, straining tenderness toward a world that eludes his grasp—the tenderness of a man going blind, for what he still sees or remembers seeing. There is real transcendence here in the power to impersonate others, but there is also deprivation and the anxiety of willed and therefore precarious attachment. Hence that intense, comprehensive energy of vision, a quiet but hungry eye that narrows to take in particulars and then dilates, to seize the presences those particulars intend.

The problem was those presences and their power over him. In the zero-country of instinct and those presences he was preternaturally at home. The human world had to be willed, but the presences came crowding in of their own accord; the "abyss" was all to near. Confronted with the abyss and its presences, Pavese felt an overwhelming vertigo, like the boy in "City in Country":

> The arbor hangs in empty air,
> the valley is miles below. The boy can't look down
> any more, he knows he'd feel like jumping. So he looks up,
> and the wonderful clouds are gone . . .

All he could do was to pull back and "look up," at the sky, the world. Throughout his life he teetered at the edge, torn, looking down, pulling back; finally the abyss took him. (The extraordinary fact of his life was not his suicide, but the fact that he managed to resist it as long as he did.) The temptation was, again, transcendence, the hunger to destroy the pain of consciousness by literally becoming the abyss. Against the presences that menaced him, Pavese's only protection was his art of clarity, his power to *name*. But at this point it is important to let Pavese speak for himself:

> Lying stretched out on the ground, I sometimes feel a violent shock, a jolt that sweeps me away like a river in flood, as if it wanted to pull me under. A cry, a smell, is enough to snatch me up and whirl me who knows where. I become rock, rotting fruit, dampness, dung, wind. . . . I strain like a tree or a wild animal which once was a man but has lost the power of speech. I no sooner succumb than I pull back, resisting. Why? Because I know that this is not my nature. . . . I speak of a present temptation. I stand stock-still, oblivious, looking at a landscape. The sky is clear, there is a brook in front of me, a wood. And suddenly a frenzy seizes me—a frenzy not to be myself, to become that field, that sky, that wood, to find the word that translates everything, down to the very blades of grass, the smells, even the emptiness. I no longer exist. The field exists. My senses exist, jaws gaping to devour the object. . . . It is a crisis, a revolt of the higher faculties which, deceived by a shock to the senses, imagine they will gain by surrendering themselves to things. And these things then seize, overwhelm, and engulf us like an angry sea, in their own turn as unpossessable and elusive as foam."[17]

Serious—deadly serious—words. Pavese is not—need one say it?—speaking metaphorically or dramatizing his plight; he is describing precisely the crisis of transcendence which ended in his suicide. Finally, he became revolted by the obscenity of describing—clarifying—his own feelings of vertigo and resistance, the recurrent agony of verbalizing a tension he no longer had the will to seek. The last words in his diary are these: "No words. An act. I won't write any more."

At least one third of these poems deal with love, sex, or related subjects like fatherhood. The abyss, for Pavese, had a woman's face, and his presences more and more came to resemble Furies. In sex, for whatever psychical or physical reason, he could not hold his balance, nor, it seems, his own. Here he was totally vulnerable. There was no escape; instinct nailed him to the cross.[18] "A man doesn't kill himself," he wrote in his diary a few months before his death, "for love of *a* woman, but because love—any love—reveals us in our nakedness, our misery, our vulnerability, our nothingness."[19] With everyday human relations, with colleagues, friends, *compagni*, he could manage to cope in his capacity as editor, activist, or friend. But *serious* sexual love, transcendent love, swept him off his feet, confronting him with the abyss and its engulfing presences. He desired love—but he dreaded it too. Hence his ambivalence toward marriage, which he feared and craved (cf. "Hard Labor, Getting Tired"), and his many transient sexual encounters, whose lack of *noble* seriousness left him feeling humanly unappeased and humiliated. In love, he was, as in so many things, absolute; it was all or nothing. *"Aut Caesar aut nihil,"* he said punningly, mocking his own unconditionality. To a woman he loved, he wrote about himself:

> P. plays his erotic role to the hilt, first because of his fierce need to escape his own loneliness; second, because of his need to believe absolutely in the passion from which he suffers, from fear of living a simple physiological state, of being merely the protagonist of a trivial love affair [*un'aventuretta*]. P. wants what he feels to be *noble*, to symbolize a nobility in himself and things.[20]

It would be wrong to treat these words as simply an expression of sexual disgust or self-hatred or his erotic poems as merely so many sublimations. Pavese's erotic absolutism, his craving to ennoble reality so that lover, beloved, and the world all reveal their energizing presence or "god," is his basic stance to life itself and the source of his *furor poeticus*. He had no wish to escape from sex; he wanted to humanize it and spiritualize it, just as his poetic realism aimed at making things declare their divinity, but without losing their status as real things.

In this sense the erotic poems are incantations, spells designed to summon the presences that obsessed him and make them reveal themselves (cf. "Morning," "Summer," "Nocturne," "Landscape VII"). But they are also apotropaic, intended to ward off these same presences by an act of *controlling*, clarity, and thereby to protect himself from their otherwise unlimited power. "Does the imagination dwell the most/," asked Yeats, "upon a woman won or woman lost?" For Pavese, a true nympholept in the great Italian tradition, it was always the woman lost, the fatal *she* of his life and work—*la donna dalla voce rauca* ("the woman with the husky voice"). On her his imagination dwelled obsessively. He had loved her to distraction, and she had later—with harsh and terrible words, it seemed to Pavese—rejected him. That is all that really matters.

Her presence—voice, gestures, memory, poise, radiance—fills the poems. Other women, her successors in Pavese's erotic life, are simply her recurrent incarnations. She becomes all women, a presence that fills the physical world; she is mountain, hills, forest, sea, storm. She is the earth itself, the unassimilable "other," Pavese's possessive but unpossessable *she*, whose *eyes*—combining mother, wife, and fury—follow him everywhere, relentless, demanding:

Those unknown eyes were strange, moist with sudden life,
they burned like flesh on fire. All the womb's
sweetness, throbbing with desire, blazed
from those eyes. The secret blossomed out like pain,
like blood. Everything went huge and scary, terror seized
the boy. Sky and trees were shining, a quiet light.

On soft summer nights, the boy sometimes cried
a little, sobbing to himself, inside, like a man.
Now, the man's alone. Another time, another sky.
Remembering, it all comes back now, all the terror
of that deep, probing look the woman imposes
on the boy. And he sees those eyes again . . .[21]

Those eyes are everywhere accompanied by a voice (*la voce rauca*), whose huskiness is, like sexual passion, ambivalent—soft and sweet but also guttural, raspingly harsh. Huskiness expresses the very nature of the voice, which is everlasting incipience: the primal whisper of the "time of origins" and a green, animistic Chaos (cf. "Landscape IV," Pavese's "Venus Anadyomene"). Perpetual pleasure is in it, suspended, poised "holding in air," like Dante's Earthly Paradise (*l'etterno piacer, tutto sospeso*). At least in the poems, this voice never quite reaches articulate words because it expresses a world whose single, sheeted coherence has not yet been divided by words or broken into "objects." It is not in fact a speaking voice at all, but the subvocal seething of the abyss, a living, breathing "presence," always forming, gathering. Not only does it issue from the absolute past of mythical and sacred time, it *is*, present and future too, the very being of memory. If the voice is always about to speak, it is also hoarse and faint with long disuse (like the voice of Dante's Vergil: *chi per lungo silenzio parea fioco*). It is instinct, too, and the unconscious, the "oceanic" voice (cf. "Lack of Discipline") which haunts the city, undermining its daylight certainties and making streets and houses seem unreal. The very intensity and persistence with which Pavese invokes this voice tells us, by backward inference, that he lives in the fallen world of words:

If the voice spoke, if anything jarred this barely
breathing silence of always, the sound would be pain.
The gestures would all return, the pain would be back,
pointless, jarring. The jangle of time would begin.[22]

By the "jangle of time" is meant profane, worldly time, with its pain of consciousness, memory, the nausea of recurrence, and the deadness of a reality of things whose informing presence has vanished. The world, in short, in which Pavese had to live after *la donna dalla voce rauce* spoke her final, fatal words of rejection.

But *she* was all women, and her rejections were as recurrent as Pavese's capacity to fall in love. Each rejection precipitated a crisis. This is why the late poems (those written between 1937 and 1940) are almost all, in one way or another, erotic invocations of *la donna dalla voce rauca*. In the early and middle poems (1932–1936) her "voice" or its equivalent is a constant, pervasive presence (e.g. "Encounter," written in 1932). But only very rarely is she the exclusive, or even the focal, center of interest. And, for the most part, the poems of these years are beautifully poised expressions of Pavese's knack for keeping his metaphysical balance and making his poetry serve his own therapeutic purposes. But late 1936 brought the end of "a long period of optimism and self-confidence" (Postscript II, p. 200), and the beginning of a long professional and personal (i.e., erotic) crisis, exactly corresponding in time to the late poems of *Lavorare stanca*. No matter where one looks, the rage for transcendence is overwhelming, as Pavese's world of things and people disappears in a flood of engulfing presences and incarnate landscapes ("Summer," "Morning," "Nocturne," etc.). There is no loss of poetic power; if anything, the new poems lean toward virtuosity. There is a strangely abstract sensuousness, and the absent dimension of "things" is compensated for by richer assonance and intricate repetitions in which one can hear the incantatory music of the poetry of *Death Will Come and It Will Have Your Eyes* already forming. Like the earlier erotic poetry, these new poems are real spells, designed to compel "presences"; but the spells are no longer apotropaic. The wild zero-country of chaos which was once, as in "The Goat God," perceived as humanly destructive, is now seen as the desirable but unattainable "other," which one could possess only by *becoming*, by literally dying into, it (Pavese's version of Dante's *transumanar*). The purpose of the poet's artistic control seems to be personal *loss* of control—a deliberate surrender to the presences which now, through the poetry, invade and possess the poet. These late poems are unmistakably suicidal.

Lavorare stanca was precious to Pavese. Not only because it was his first book, on which he had lavished his labor and created himself as a writer, but because it was, in his judgment, his best. Hence he was deeply hurt by the icy reception it received. He might have coped with outright hostility; cold, sustained silence was another matter, exacerbating his personal and professional insecurity. He was too humanly vulnerable, too isolated, to draw indefinitely on his own inner resources. Because his writing constituted his whole effective relation to the world of men, he needed praise,[23] needed to know that he was not, as a writer as well as a man, completely alone, that there was somebody "out there," listening if not applauding. The jacket-band he personally dictated for the 1943 edition ("One of the most isolated voices in contemporary poetry") speaks eloquently of the effect on Pavese of the failure of the 1936 edition, but the tone is, typically, an ironic, defiant hermit pride rather than self-pity. In his Postscript II (p. 199), the attitude toward his poetry seems dismissively gloomy, but it was written at the time when he had decided to abandon poetry for prose, and should be read in the light of that decision. Artists rarely change careers without having to repudiate the past or declare it officially "over." But Pavese's later comments show that, apart from occasional misgivings, he remained stubbornly, adamantly convinced that *Lavorare stanca* was not only his best work but among the finest Italian poetry of the time. In 1946, just four years before his death, he wrote, summing up his career:

> I am convinced of the fundamental, lasting unity of what I have written or shall write. By which I don't mean autobiographical unity or unity of taste, which is nonsense, but a unity of themes, vital interests, the monotonous stubbornness of a man convinced that he made contact with the real world, the eternal world, on the first day, and all he can do is revolve around this huge monolith, chipping away at it, working at its pieces, studying them in every possible light. By this I mean to say that my most "successful" work, the work which "in itself is witness to the character of my art," is, up to the present, *Lavorare stanca*.[24]

And finally, in the year he died, he made his boldest claim of all: "*Lavorare stanca* is a book that might have saved a generation. (I'm not joking.").[25]

Pavese may have been mistaken (I doubt it), but he was not joking. *Lavorare stanca* is pioneering work of startling boldness and freshness. As a *first* book of poetry, appearing in the doldrums of the Italian thirties, its ambition and originality cannot be exaggerated. With cool, quiet sureness, it breaks abruptly with almost a century of literary tradition: a book manifestly intended to inaugurate a new poetry and a new literary generation, Pavese's generation. In France, England, and elsewhere, a tired established literature had been roughly displaced by rebellious, innovating "moderns"; why not then in mandarin and Fascist Italy too? *Lavorare stanca* is the poetry of his reforming purpose—rebellious, pioneering poetry with the functional clarity of a mission to perform.

Clarity of literary mission combines with Pavese's intense personal passion for clarity. The result is a ruthlessness with himself and his work that will not let him pause long enough to explore its implications. In a few short years he mastered at least three distinct kinds of poetry (the austere narrative style of "South Seas"; then the remarkable technique of his "image-poem," and the final style of the erotic invocation), any one of which would have taken a gifted poet a decade to exploit. In part this was temperamental restlessness, but it also comes from Pavese's driving, obsessive need, reminiscent of Rimbaud's, to press his talents and time to the limits, to define himself by constantly moving forward. The goal was clarity, always clarity. He literally could not stop. No sooner had he begun to savor the delights of virtuosity than his very facility became problematic. Virtuosity implied complacency and repetition, a practiced, rote clarity, *troppo studiato*. Again and again he scrapped his conquests, reworking his poetics radically as he wrote, then moving on to a new perceptual plateau. (The two postscripts to the book—"The Poet's Craft" and "Notes on Certain Unwritten Poems"—are extremely revealing accounts of his "poet's progress," from excited discovery to doubt to disillusion, then back to discovery again, and his passion for clarity at any cost.) Poetic talent is probably rare at any time, but the real rarity is urgent, *disciplined* talent and moral clarity. It is this craving and capacity for controlled clarity, not some "experimental" fervor, that makes Pavese's poetry important and original.

For Pavese the great central mission of poetry was revelation. Poetry was not so much remembering as clear-sighted *naming*: the crucial Adamic act by which the poet (and through him, other men) might possess and humanize the world of the "given" (or god-given). The poet's clarity, his ability to name things well, with names that did not kill or truncate, was therefore "an accuracy with respect to reality"; and the accuracy of his names was decisive for the poet and the human culture which his language incarnated. A badly named world was a disaster for the world and everything in it, for men a cultural catastrophe. Who, looking at Fascist Italy or, for that matter, modern Europe, could doubt that the world had been named by a tribe of botchers and hacks? The remedy was heroic poetry and an integrating clarity of vision which might name the world afresh, as it still could be, or else rename it as it truly was before being botched and broken. Once, as in the poetry of Homer or Sappho, it had been a single, sentient, inspirited world, a place fit for human habitation. Now, it had been shattered into innumerable antinomies of spirit and matter (corresponding, one hardly needs to add, to Pavese's polarized world of country and city, sacred and profane, "presences" and "things"). Wherever one looked, "mere oppugnancy" ruled a world of spiritless things or thingless spirits. Mostly the old "presences" had vanished or, disguished as instinct, sex, the unconscious, violence, and the other secularized "powers," had gone underground. "Things" were not only sundered from spirit but even from themselves, and then subdivided into "surface" and "depth," "inner" and outer." Worse, these fractured things "existed" in a world of pure, mechanical click-clack time and uninformed sequence. "Now," as the sacred ground of the present, had been banalized; the divinity *in* things had moved to the fringes where it turned into "aura" and finally illusion, the last animistic relic of a desacralized world. There was also the reverse distortion, rarer but no less disfiguring, whereby "ordinary reality" (i.e., *la vita vissuta*, ordinary speech, etc.) was systematically emptied of meaning or demoted into phenomena and shadows, and narrative time was annulled by a sacramental Now and its human poetries.

By the poet's accurate naming, these sundered worlds could be reunited, the world could be given back its own lost reality. Things, accurately named, could be themselves again and not mere "signs" of other, "higher" things. Redeemed by the poet's "double vision of the single object of the senses," the alienated "presences" would flood back; things would have their old divinity again. Human time, mortal measure, would also return. The poet does not "remember" time in the ordinary sense of "remember"; he sees things with awe— things revealed as if for the first time—and he thereby *becomes* memory itself, with the power to reveal the timeless "now" forever "waiting," immanent in the time of "things." By narrating "before" and "after," the poet narrates the experience of transience but also its meaning, that immanent "now." Human time is transience punctuated by "eternal moments"—moments when men *become* memory themselves by leaving time and living in a dimension of immortal clarity and meaning. And meter is the measure of mortal time and transience.[26] By narrating it as it is lived—in the time of "things," illuminated by timeless, mythical meaning—the poet names a reality which physically and temporally corresponds to the tragic tension (brutal and divine) of human life. And finally, this rightly named reality, by reciprocal action, refreshes the language by which it was named into life.

This *résumé* of Pavese's complex and fluctuating poetics is admittedly an extrapolation, sketchy and impressionistic; but it gives, I think, the gist.[27] Regrettably, Pavese never worked out a coherent statement of his aesthetics, and, apart from a group of late essays on myth and poetry, his views must be inferred from his criticism and practice. But, in one form or another, revelatory realism was the basic stance of all his work, both poetry and fiction (which for that reason differs *toto caelo* from Italian neorealism). But so far as the reader of *Lavorare stanca* is concerned, what matters is the recognition that very unusual demands are being made of him. Revelation, of course, is something we no longer expect, or perhaps even want, from poets, any more than we expect a character in a poem to reveal the universal traits of the species. Yet this is precisely what Pavese gives us. His characters, like the woman in "A Season" or the boy in "Atavism," are as much generic as individual portraits—incarnate "destinies," the universal looming in the individual (". . . a complex of actions, thoughts, and relationship which compose a destiny, organized according to a rhythm which is this destiny itself, the active movement of the character's soul").[28] To moderns this notion of character as expressive destiny is very strange, very Greek, indeed; even stranger is the idea, central to Pavese's work, that rhythm and meter are the temporal movement by which, *narrated*, this destiny is revealed. This, we like to think, is not the way poets (or anyone else) should talk, much less write. But Pavese's structure and techniques correspond to this revelatory purpose. Thus a Pavese poem (or novel) is not the familiar Empsonian object with its layered, ambiguous, and polysemous structure. It is instead a dynamic unfolding, along a single narrative level. Revelation takes place in two complementary ways: positively, by the staggered release of meaning by the poem's narration of its "imaginative links" (see *Postscript I* for Pavese's account of this important technique); and negatively, by the gradual, crafted release of the meaning packed but suppressed in the poem's ellipses and silences. Pavese's reticence, in this resepect, is structural technique, and the power of his poems to reveal is usually in direct proportion to what has been deliberately suppressed in its ellipses.[29] The poem, in short, by verbal chiaroscuro, recreates the process by which the poet's darkness was first transformed into clarity and understanding, i.e., revelation. But this revelation is successful only insofar as it discloses the object or situation in its single entirety; quite consciously, I think, it sets out to frustrate the reader's expectation that the object be revealed as a sign or symbol of something else, that it show us, that is, a "deeper *level*" of meaning. Hence the reader conditioned to the pleasures of "layered" poetry is apt to find a Pavese poem flat, lacking in the polyvalent richness he has learned to demand. The problem, however, is not the poem but the reader's poetics, the routine critical insistence on polysemous structure and meaning. A Pavese poem asks just the opposite; it is the exact reverse of allegory (hence Pavese's quarrel with Dante). And its chief purpose is to make the object reveal the world it implies, to give back to the world the splendor of its own being, the richness of being *itself* and not some other thing.

This, I believe, is the key reason for Pavese's rejection of Italian and (apart from the Elizabethan dramatists) modern European poetic tradition. Ever since Dante, that tradition has accepted—and widened, as a matter of principle—the gulf between words and things, spirit and matter, pure form and common experience. It was by virtue of its vivid contrast with this tradition that, to Pavese's hungry eyes, the American achievement was so liberating and instructive. Free of cramping European constraints, those mythical Americans of his lived in a vibrant, vigorous, emerging culture; newly human themselves, they were, if not autochthonous, at least close to the earth. Like the strong poets of Vico's heroic age, they named their world, they made it humanly habitable. Writers like Melville and Whitman must have lived close to "things"—"things" as they were in Homer's Greece, still filled with their ancient "presences"; there was no other explanation of their work and purpose. In *this* America, Pavese supposed, words and things, "things" and "presences" had not yet yawed fatally apart. Galvanized by its poets and their energy of spiritual purpose, the new American language surged with the exuberance of "things" themselves; American writers, he thought, had the uncanny knack of using words so that they released the spiritual charge of the "things" they denoted. Ignored or repressed (as in Fascist Italy), that explosive charge was bound to vent itself in violence, excess, brutality. American culture was healthy because its writers could still reach and reveal this unconscious life, because they had broken down the barriers between "things" and words. For the Italian writer the task was not to imitate these Americans, but to establish on Italian earth an analogous Italian literature, a new poetry.

Again and again Pavese returns to the essential American achievement—a sense of the world, *this* world, *here, now*, in which objects were reunited with their "field," and the polarities reconciled in an enabling human (therefore inherently tragic and noble) tension. "The message of the Americans," he wrote, "is a sense of the mysterious reality under the words."[30] The Americans, he believed, had a "tendency to find a spiritual meaning in every fact";[31] they were obsessed by the desire "to arrive at a language that would so identify itself with things as to batter down every barrier between the common reader and the dizziest symbolic and mythical reality."[32] Again and again he remarks on the "wholly American idea of a mystic reality incarnated and imprisoned in the word, that disturbing realm of the subconscious life which is still, down to the present moment, the most vital contribution of America to culture."[33] As for Whitman, he had created a wholly new form of symbolism (i.e., revelatory realism): "The new symbolism of Whitman meant, not the allegorical structures of Dante but a different verbal reality, a sort of double vision through which, from the single object of the senses avidly absorbed and possessed, there radiates a sort of halo of astonishing spirituality."[34]

This "new symbolism" was precisely the quality which differentiated American from European realism—this American ability to hold tenaciously to ordinary reality while constantly intuiting the metaphysical "presences" behind it:

While a European artist (an ancient) will always maintain that the secret of art is to construct a more or less fictive world, to deny reality in order to put another, hopefully more significant, world in its place, a modern American will always tell us that his ambition is entirely to attain to the true nature of things, to see things with virgin eyes, to arrive at "that ultimate grip of reality" which is alone worthy of recognition. It is a sort of deliberately acclimatizing of oneself in the world and in America. . . .[35]

Here is the whole difference between American "realism" and that of Europe. In the twentieth century, when they [the Americans] return to talk of "realism" in self-conscious derivation from the naturalistic French model, the matter will be clearer: the realism of Lee Masters, of Anderson, of Hemingway, will variously seek the whole man, that second reality which underlies appearance; it will seek to "name" things in order to release from them their explosive spiritual charge, and for this reason it will not be appropriate to speak of province or *tranche de vie*.[36]

Here, in these essays on American writers (for the most part written just when he was composing *Lavorare stanca*), the central, governing idea of Pavese's essays is clearly, repeatedly, and obsessively articulated. Whether the qualities he observed in American culture were really there or simply the passionate projection of his own poetics and mission is debatable. But no matter how one decides, it cannot, I think, be doubted that what Pavese saw in the Americans with such intensity was in fact the essence of his own poetics and poetic vision, and that *Lavorare stanca* is his effort to create an analogous Italian poetry. And that, for my present purposes, is all that matters.

America was important to Pavese above all because it was *there, in the present*—living evidence, to his mind, that a nobler human culture could exist in the present and the future as well as the ancient past. Later, after the war, Pavese became disillusioned with American culture. In part this disenchantment was political, the reflex of a Marxist in Cold War Italy. But no less important was Pavese's growing conviction that American writers themselves had betrayed or lost the "boundless dream" of Whitman and Melville. "The young Americans," he wrote sadly in 1947, "have undergone an interior process of Europeanization; they have lost a great part of that tragic candor that was their destiny."[37] But if Americans were no longer loyal to the earlier promise, the great Greeks and Romans were still there, still "naming" their radiantly genial reality, as exemplary as always.[38] Disillusioned with his America, Pavese returned after the war to the classics with which he had first started out and with which he could still live, his poetics intact and strengthened by the encounter.[39] These "classicizing" years are those in which he wrote his "mythological" masterpiece, *Dialogues with Leucò*,[40] his essays on myth and poetry, and his richest novel, *The Moon and the Bonfires*, with its starkly revealing contrast (or confrontation) between an archaic-contemporary Piedmont and a nightmarishly bleak America. But whether the locale is America or Piedmont or Greece, the quest is always the same: a world in which ordinary objects possess or reveal a radiant divinity in their own right, and the ancient inspiriting "presences," rightly, accurately named, by poets of clear, comprehensive human vision, come flooding back in beauty and power, not to curse but to bless. Finally, it is worth remembering now, perhaps, that Pavese once took that world, those poets, and their poetics, to be American.

Translating Pavese is rewarding but ticklish work. Low-keyed understatement and tight-lipped terseness are familiar enough, in fact a modern poetic "manner." True reticence, language in which silence represents awe in the presence of mystery, a respect for what cannot be uttered, is much rarer. A hard, sparse, reticent verse, grounded in real speech and clear, compassionate observation, which aims at fusing things with their spiritual "presences," a poetry of *this-worldly* revelation—this is a poetry (and a poetics) we no longer possess. It may be a mirage, but I firmly believe it is not. In any case, it was what I consciously aimed at in trying to translate these poems.

The strategies of translation are, for obvious reasons, rarely interesting to readers; all I can say is that my strategies with these poems—metrics, idiom, cadence—were improvised in accordance with what I understood to be Pavese's aim generally and from poem to poem. It is for the reader to judge of my success or failure. I will only say that, as I translated, I found myself again and again veering between a realism which obscured the "mystery" it intended, and a "mystery" which engulfed the object being observed; the problem was finding and holding the proper tension. At first I found this disconcerting; later it came to be reassuring since it made me feel that I was, as translator, reliving the poet's experience in writing his poem.

I sought help wherever I could find it, and I was uncommonly lucky. My chief debt is remembered in the dedication. Without Stephen Berg's extraordinary affinity for Pavese's poetry (and his uncanny knack for intuiting it even through the barrier of my various drafts), his enthusiastic support (letter after letter chock-a-block full of suggestions, criticisms, and comments), this translation would probably never have been completed. Gertrude Hooker cast a scrupulous Italianist's eye over every version, gently querying and guiding, constantly insisting that I meet the letter and spirit of Pavese's Italian, preventing me from God knows how many gaffes and errors of nuance. (There are doubtless many more, but they are all my fault, nobody else's.) Simone Di Piero gave me the quite invaluable help that only a fellow translator (and fellow poet) can give, scores of closely argued letters full of incisive critical comment, candid, bracing, discerning; I owe him much more than I can say. And there were others, too. Luciano Rebay and Roger Shattuck both read a different score of poems and commented helpfully on each. From Italy Elena Croce, *traduttrice anche lei*, cheered me on. In Vermont my farmer-neighbor and friend, Charlie Buss, taught me most of what I know of the landscape of rural labor, the tough intractability of *la vita contadina* on which any true poetry of earth, like Pavese's, is based. And there were dozens of people, colleagues, friends, friends of friends, whom I pestered constantly for scraps of curious information—Piedmontese dialect terms, Italian depression slang, nuances, idioms. Finally, I am deeply grateful to Ann Dargis and Adrienne Leinwand, who typed the successive versions—in some cases dozens of them—without a word of complaint and sometimes even with pleasure.

Notes

1. Letter to Giambattisto Vicari, December 13, 1941, in *Cesare Pavese: Lettere 1924-1944*, ed. Lorenzo Mondo (Turin, 1966).
2. *The Devil in the Hills* and *Among Women Only* are available (with *The Beach* and *The House on the Hill*) in good translations by R. W. Flint (*The Selected Works of Cesare Pavese* [New York, 1968]).
3. Trans. William Arrowsmith and D. S. Carne-Ross (Ann Arbor, 1965).
4. *La letteratura americana e altri saggi* (Turin, 1951). The essays dealing with American literature, accurately translated by Edwin Fussell, are published in Cesare Pavese, *American Literature* (Berkeley and Los Angeles, 1970).
5. Published in English in an undistinguished and unreliable version under the title *The Burning Brand* (New York, 1961).
6. So Pavese believed in 1933: "The truth is that, for new America as for old Europe, nothing is born of nothing; and that, especially in the sphere of poetry, nothing notable is born unless inspired by an autochthonous culture. . . ." "John Dos Passos and the American Novel" in Pavese, *American Literature*, p. 106.
7. Among the exceptions is a group of younger writers known as Gruppo 63—Sanguinetti, Balestrini, Porta, Guiliani, and others—who have made programmatic explorations into new, spoken poetry. Among the *prosatori* the names of Celati, Balestrini, and Manganelli come to mind.
8. "Walt Whitman, poeta," *Nuova antologia*, June 16, 1908. I owe my knowledge of Papini's statement to Donald Heiney, who cites it in his valuable study, *America in Modern Italian Literature* (New Brunswick, N.J., 1964).
9. "L'influsso degli eventi," published posthumously in *La letteratura americana e altri saggi*, pp. 246-47.

10. Pavese, *American Literature*, pp. 196-98.

11. *La letteratura americana*, pp. 330-33.

12. Cf. Natalia Ginzburg. "Ritratto d'un amico" in *Le piccole virtù* (Turin, 1963), pp. 26-34.

13. Letter to Fernanda Pivano, October 25, 1940, in *Cesare Pavese: Lettere 1924-1944*. The document is essential to anyone concerned with the mesh of Pavese's life and work.

14. Ibid., p. 573.

15. Ibid., p. 572.

16. "The new symbolism of Whitman meant, not the allegorical structures of Dante but a . . . sort of double vision through which, from the single object of the senses vividly absorbed and possessed, there radiates a sort of halo of unexpected spirituality." Pavese, *American Literature*, p. 185.

17. From a late essay entitled (revealingly), "Professional Disease" ("Mal di mestiere"). *La letteratura americana*, pp. 317 ff.

18. The figure is Pavese's: "This fierce craving for a home and life he will never have is vividly clear in a proud sentence uttered one day by P. . . . 'The only women worth marrying are those we can't trust ourselves to marry.' Everything is here: the vamp and the fury, the wife and the invincible dream. To this dream P. is as it were crucified [*incrociato*] . . . P. has a vivid imagination and he has only to imagine himself in a painful image to feel the physical agony of it. . . . Years ago, he carried this image of the cross in his nerves *for two or three months on end*. . . ." Letter to Fernanda Pivano, October 25, 1940.

    For the image of the (sexual) cross in his poems, cf. "Fatherhood" (p. 103), where the word *inchiodato* (literally, "nailed") is, for reasons of English idiom, translated "riveted."

19. *The Burning Brand*, March 25, 1950.

20. Letter to Fernanda Pivano.

21. "Revelation," p. 39.

22. "The Voice," p. 129.

23. In his self-analytical letter to Fernanda Pivano, October 25, 1940, Pavese wrote: "But drama means audience. Here is P.'s obscene and unconfessed flaw. When he was a student . . . he felt himself so neglected and unapplauded that he deliberately threw himself down in the street among a group of friends with the sole aim of being the center of attention. . . . Later, over a long period, P. achieved his own stoical *ataraxia* by absolutely renouncing every human bond but the abstract one of writing."

24. *La letteratura americana*, p. 248.

25. Letter to Mario Motta, January 23, 1950.

26. An important point in Pavese's poetics—and poetics generally—for which I am indebted to Simone Di Piero.

27. From the perspective of the seventies, Pavese's poetics seem at times identical with phenomenology. But I can find almost no evidence that P. was more than indirectly familiar with Heidegger et al.

28. Pavese on Edgar Lee Masters' *Spoon River Anthology*. See *American Literature*, p. 172.

29. A crucial point in Pavese's poetics. See, for instance, Italo Calvino's perceptive remarks about the novels: "Every Pavese novel revolves around a hidden theme, around something unsaid which he wants to say but can only say by keeping it silent. Around it he weaves a texture of visible signs and spoken words; each of these signs in turn has a secret aspect of its own . . . which matters more than the visible one, but its real meaning lies in the relation which links it to what has not been said." *Révue des études italiennes* 12 (1966): 107 ff.

30. *The Burning Brand*, January 8, 1949.

31. Pavese, *American Literature*, p. 184.

32. Ibid., p. 180.

33. Ibid., p. 155.

34. Ibid., p. 185.

35. Ibid., p. 124.

36. Ibid., pp. 184-85.

37. Ibid., p. 193.

38. Here, for instance, is Pavese's characteristic comment on Vergil's *Georgics*: "They aren't beautiful because they feelingly describe the life of the fields . . . but because they imbue the whole countryside with a secret mythical reality. They go beyond appearances; they reveal even in the act of studying the weather or sharpening a scythe, the vanished presence of a god who has done it or who has shown men how to do it." Letter to Fernanda Pivano, June 27, 1942.

39. In 1949 we find P. recommending to a young writer his own spiritual odyssey: "The best means of discovering yourself is faraway people and places. I got my feet on the ground with *Paesi tuoi* and *Lavorare stanca* only after I had lived through the wildest passion for the South Seas (nineteenth-century Oceania and twentieth-century America). In those distant places and things, I literally discovered myself. . . . You have no idea what profound riches can be discovered in our Greek and Latin classics when you encounter them on your way back home from the American or German or Russian twentieth century. . . ." Letter to Nicola Enrichens, June 23, 1949.

40. See Pavese's letter to Paolo Milano, January 24, 1948: "I won't conceal from you the fact that my ambition in writing this little book was to become part of the distinguished Italian tradition of leisurely humanistics, from Boccaccio to D'Annunzio. Being the greatest barbarizer of our literature . . . it was a luxury I had long thought of allowing myself." "Barbarizer" is of course bitter irony; so too is the reference to traditional humanism, which Pavese intended not to join but to supersede, above all in its relation to Greek antiquity.

Antenati • Ancestors

I mari del Sud

a Monti

Camminiamo una sera sul fianco di un colle,
in silenzio. Nell'ombra del tardo crepuscolo
mio cugino è un gigante vestito di bianco,
che si muove pacato, abbronzato nel volto,
taciturno. Tacere è la nostra virtú.
Qualche nostro antenato dev'essere stato ben solo
—un grand'uomo tra idioti o un povero folle—
per insegnare ai suoi tanto silenzio.

Mio cugino ha parlato stasera. Mi ha chiesto
se salivo con lui: dalla vetta si scorge
nelle notti serene il riflesso del faro
lontano, di Torino. «Tu che abiti a Torino...»
mi ha detto «... ma hai ragione. La vita va vissuta
lontano dal paese: si profitta e si gode
e poi, quando si torna, come me a quarant'anni,
si trova tutto nuovo. Le Langhe non si perdono».
Tutto questo mi ha detto e non parla italiano,
ma adopera lento il dialetto, che, come le pietre
di questo stesso colle, è scabro tanto
che vent'anni di idiomi e di oceani diversi
non gliel'hanno scalfito. E cammina per l'erta
con lo sguardo raccolto che ho visto, bambino,
usare ai contadini un poco stanchi.

Vent'anni è stato in giro per il mondo.
Se n'andò ch'io ero ancora un bambino portato da donne
e lo dissero morto. Sentii poi parlarne
da donne, come in favola, talvolta;
ma gli uomini, piú gravi, lo scordarono.
Un inverno a mio padre già morto arrivò un cartoncino
con un gran francobollo verdastro di navi in un porto
e augurî di buona vendemmia. Fu un grande stupore,
ma il bambino cresciuto spiegò avidamente

South Seas

for Augusto Monti

Late one afternoon we walk along the flank of a hill
in silence. In the shadows of early evening,
my cousin is a giant dressed in white,
moving calmly along, his face browned by the sun,
not speaking. Silence is a family trait.
Some ancestor of ours must have been a solitary man—
a great man surrounded by halfwits, or a poor, crazy fool—
to teach his descendants such silence.

This afternoon my cousin spoke. He asked me
to climb the hill with him: from the crest, on clear nights,
you can see the glow from the lights of Torino
shining in the distance. "You live in Torino, I know . . ."
he said haltingly, "but you're right. Spend your life
a long ways from home. Make good, have a good time.
Then when you come back home, like me, at forty,
everything's new. These hills don't change.
The Langhe hills will always be here."
He said a lot, and he doesn't speak Italian,
but the drawling local talk, a dialect like the rocks
of this hill, so rugged and hard that twenty years
of foreign idioms and sailing foreign seas
haven't made a dent. And he climbs the path
with that look of concentration I remember seeing as a child
in the eyes of peasants beginning to tire.

For twenty years he knocked around the world.
I was still a baby, not yet walking, when he left.
They spoke of him as dead. Later, I heard the women
talking about him as if he were a character in a story.
The men, more matter-of-fact, just forgot him.
Then, one winter, a postcard came addressed to my father
(who had died by then), with a great big greenish stamp
showing ships in a harbor, and a message wishing us
a good harvest. Nobody knew what to make of it,
but the boy, much bigger now, breathlessly explained

che il biglietto veniva da un'isola detta Tasmania
circondata da un mare piú azzurro, feroce di squali,
nel Pacifico, a sud dell'Australia. E aggiunse che certo
il cugino pescava le perle. E staccò il francobollo.
Tutti diedero un loro parere, ma tutti conclusero
che, si non era morto, morirebbe.
Poi scordarono tutti e passò molto tempo.

Oh da quando ho giocato ai pirati malesi,
quanto tempo è trascorso. E dall'ultima volta
che son sceso a bagnarmi in un punto mortale
e ho inseguito un compagno di giochi su un albero
spaccandone i bei rami e ho rotta la testa
a un rivale e son stato picchiato,
quanto vite è trascorsa. Altri giorni, altri giochi,
altri squassi del sangue dinanzi a rivali
piú elusivi: i pensieri ed i sogni.
La città mi ha insegnato infinite paure:
una folla, una strada mi han fatto tremare,
un pensiero talvolta, spiato su un viso.
Sento ancora negli occhi la luce beffarda
dei lampioni a migliaia sul gran scalpiccío.

Mio cugino è tornato, finita la guerra,
gigantesco, tra i pochi. E aveva denaro.
I parenti dicevano piano: «Fra un anno, a dir molto,
se li è mangiati tutti e torna in giro.
I disperati muoiono cosí».
Mio cugino ha una faccia recisa. Comprò un pianterreno
nel paese e ci fece riuscire un garage di cemento
con dinanzi fiammante la pila per dar la benzina
e sul ponte ben grossa alla curva una targa-réclame.
Poi ci mise un meccanico dentro a ricevere i soldi
e lui girò tutte le Langhe fumando.
S'era intanto sposato, in paese. Pigliò una ragazza
esile e bionda come le straniere
che aveva certo un giorno incontrato nel mondo.
Ma uscí ancora da solo. Vestito di bianco,
con le mani alla schiena e il volto abbronzato,

that the card came from an island called Tasmania,
with blue blue water all around it, seething with sharks,
in the Pacific Ocean, south of Australia. His cousin,
he added, must be a pearl-fisherman. And tore off the stamp.
Everyone had his own opinion, but in the end they said,
if he wasn't dead already, he couldn't be long for this world.
Then they all forgot him, and a long time passed.

God, how long it's been since those childhood days
when we played at Malay pirates. The time it's been
since I last went swimming and almost drowned,
and shinnied up a tree trying to catch a playmate
and broke the branches and ruined the fruit, and gave
my rival a bloody nose, and then got a beating for it—
God, the water that's gone under the bridge!
Then other days, other games; another kind
of blood, the shocks and wounds that come from facing other,
more elusive rivals: thoughts, desires, dreams.
The city taught me fear, an infinity of fear.
A crowd, a street, sometimes a thought I saw
on somebody's face, have made me shake with terror.
My eyes still feel the hard, cruel light cast
by the endless streetlights on the tramping feet below.

After the war was over, my cousin came home.
One of the few, a giant of a man. He had money too.
His relatives whispered, "Give him a year at best.
He'll be flat broke by then, and moving on again. You'll see.
Good-for-nothing never came to a good end yet."
My cousin has a stubborn jaw: he bought a ground-floor shop
and somehow managed to convert it into a cement garage
with a blazing red pump out front for pumping gas,
and a great big sign by the curve on the bridge.
Then he hired a mechanic to handle the cash
while he roamed around the Langhe hills, smoking his pipe.
He married about then. Picked a local girl,
but blond and slim, like one of those foreign women
he must have met when he was knocking around the world.
But he still went out by himself. Dressed in white,
hands behind his back, his face browned by the sun,

al mattino batteva le fiere e con aria sorniona
contrattava i cavalli. Spiegò poi a me,
quando fallí il disegno, che il suo piano
era stato di togliere tutte le bestie alla valle
e obbligare la gente a comprargli i motori.
«Ma la bestia» diceva «piú grossa di tutte,
sono stato io a pensarlo. Dovevo sapere
che qui buoi e persone son tutta una razza».

Camminiamo da piú di mezz'ora. La vetta è vicina,
sempre aumenta d'intorno il frusciare e il fischiare del vento.
Mio cugino si ferma d'un tratto e si volge: «Quest'anno
scrivo sul manifesto:—*Santo Stefano*
è sempre stato il primo nelle feste
della valle del Belbo—e che la dicano
quei di Canelli». Poi riprende l'erta.
Un profumo di terra e di vento ci avvolge nel buio,
qualche lume in distanza: cascine, automobili
che si sentono appena; e io penso alla forza
che mi ha reso quest'uomo, strappandolo al mare,
alle terre lontane, al silenzio che dura.
Mio cugino non parla dei viaggi compiuti.
Dice asciutto che è stato in quel luogo e in quell'altro
e pensa ai suoi motori.

        Solo un sogno
gli è rimasto nel sangue: ha incrociato una volta,
da fuochista su un legno olandese da pesca, il cetaceo,
e ha veduto volare i ramponi pesanti nel sole,
ha veduto fuggire balene tra schiume di sangue
e inseguirle e innalzarsi le code e lottare alla lancia.
Me ne accenna talvolta.

        Ma quando gli dico
ch'egli è tra i fortunati che han visto l'aurora
sulle isole piú belle della terra,
al ricordo sorride e risponde che il sole
si levava che il giorno era vecchio per loro.

he haunted the fairs in the mornings, cagey and shrewd,
haggling over horses. Afterwards he told me—
when his scheme fell through—how he'd gotten the idea
of buying up every last working animal in the Belbo valley
so people would have to buy cars and tractors from him.
"But the ass, the real horse's ass, was me," he used to say,
"for dreaming up the scheme. I forgot one thing:
people in these parts are just like their oxen. Dumb."

We walk for almost an hour. The crest is close,
and the rushing whine of the wind gets steadily stronger.
Suddenly, my cousin stops and turns: "This year," he says,
"I'm going to have my handbills printed with this legend:
*Santo Stefano is always first and best
in the holiday feasts of the Belbo valley.* And we'll make
the people of Canelli *admit* it." Then he starts back up the path.
All around us in the dark is the smell of earth and wind,
lights far off in the distance: farms and cars,
you can hardly hear them. And I think of the strength
this man has given me, wresting it from the sea,
from faraway countries, from silence, always silence.
My cousin doesn't talk about the traveling he's done.
All he says, dryly, is that he's been here or there,
and thinks about his motors.

One dream, only one,
still burns in his blood. He shipped out once
as stoker on a Dutch whaler called the *Cetacean*,
and he saw the huge fins flying in the sunlight,
he saw the whales turning and running in a wild froth of blood,
and the boats giving chase, and the great flukes rising and thrashing
          out against the harpoons.
He mentions it at times.

But when I tell
him how lucky he is, one of the few people who've ever seen
dawn breaking over the loveliest islands in the world,
he smiles at the memory, saying that when the sun rose,
the day was no longer young. They'd been up for hours.

Stupefatto del mondo mi giunse un'età
che tiravo dei pugni nell'aria e piangevo da solo.
Ascoltare i discorsi di uomini e donne
non sapendo rispondere, è poca allegria.
Ma anche questa è passata: non sono piú solo
e, se non so rispondere, so farne a meno.
Ho trovato compagni trovando me stesso.

Ho scoperto che, prima di nascere, sono vissuto
sempre in uomini saldi, signori di sé,
e nessuno sapeva rispondere e tutti eran calmi.
Due cognati hanno aperto un negozio—la prima fortuna
della nostra famiglia—e l'estraneo era serio,
calcolante, spietato, meschino: uno donna.
L'altro, il nostro, in negozio leggeva romanzi
—in paese era molto—e i clienti che entravano
si sentivan rispondere a brevi parole
che lo zucchero no, che il solfato neppure,
che era tutto esaurito. È accaduto piú tardi
che quest'ultimo ha dato una mano al cognato fallito.
A pensar questa gente mi sento piú forte
che a guardare lo specchio gonfiando le spalle
e atteggiando le labbra a un sorriso solenne.
È vissuto un mio nonno, remoto nei tempi,
che si fece truffare da un suo contadino
e allora zappò lui le vigne—d'estate—
per vedere un lavoro ben fatto. Cosí
sono sempre vissuto e ho sempre tenuto
una faccia sicura e pagato di mano.

E le donne non contano nella famiglia.
Voglio dire, le donne da noi stanno in casa
e ci mettono al mondo e non dicono nulla
e non contano nulla e non le ricordiamo.
Ogni donna c'infonde nel sangue qualcosa di nuovo,
ma s'annullano tutte nell'opera e noi,

Ancestors

Bewildered by the world, I reached that age
when I punched the air with my fists and cried to myself.
Just listening to men and women talking,
not knowing what to say, isn't much fun.
But I got over that too. I'm not alone any more.
If I don't know what to say, I make out anyway.
When I found myself, I found friends.

I found out I had lived, before I was born,
in tough, sturdy, independent men, masters of themselves.
None of them knew what to say, so they just kept quiet.
Two brothers-in-law opened a store—the first luck
my family ever had. The outsider was stuffy,
tightfisted, cruel, and mean: a woman.
The other man, our man, used to read novels in the store—
people talked about *that*—and when customers came in,
they'd hear him answer gruffly, no,
there wasn't any sugar, he was out of Epsom salts,
he was all out of everything. Well, later on
our man helped his partner, who went broke.
Just thinking of folks like that makes me feel stronger
than looking in the mirror and rippling my muscles
or trying to twist my mouth into a tough smile.
One of my grandfathers—he lived a long time ago—
found he was being cheated by one of his farmers,
so he went to work in his own vineyards, right in the middle of
        summer,
just to see the work was done right. That's how
I've always lived. I always had an honest face,
a face you could trust, I always pay cash down.

In our family women don't matter.
What I mean is, our women stay home
and make children like me, and keep their mouths shut.
They just don't matter, and we don't remember them.
Every woman adds something new to our blood,
but they kill themselves off with work. We

rinnovati cosí, siamo i soli a durare.
Siamo pieni di vizi, di ticchi e di orrori
—noi, gli uomini, i padri—qualcuno si è ucciso,
ma una sola vergogna non ci ha mai toccato,
non saremo mai donne, mai ombre a nessuno.

Ho trovato una terra trovando i compagni,
una terra cattiva, dov'è un privilegio
non far nulla, pensando al futuro.
Perché il solo lavoro non basta a me e ai miei;
noi sappiamo schiantarci, ma il sogno piú grande
dei miei padri fu sempre un far nulla da bravi.
Siamo nati per girovagare su quelle colline,
senza donne, e le mani tenercele dietro la schiena.

just get stronger and stronger, so it's the men who last.
Oh, we've got our faults, and whims, and skeletons—
we, the men, the fathers—and one of us killed himself.
But there's one disgrace we've never known:
we've never been women, we've never been nobodies.

When I found my friends, I found my own piece of land—
land so worthless a man's got a perfect right
to do absolutely nothing, just dream about the future.
Work isn't good enough, not for my friends and me.
Oh, we can break our backs all right, but the dream
my fathers always had was being good at doing nothing.
We were born to wander and ramble these hills,
with no women, our hands folded behind our backs.

Paesaggio I

al Pollo

Non è piú coltivata quassú la collina. Ci sono le felci
e la roccia scoperta e la sterilità.
Qui il lavoro non serve piú a niente. La vetta è bruciata
e la sola freschezza è il respiro. La grande fatica
è salire quassú: l'eremita ci venne una volta
e da allora è restato a rifarsi le forze.
L'eremita si veste di pelle di capra
e ha un sentore muschioso di bestia e di pipa,
che ha impregnato la terra, i cespugli e la grotta.
Quando fuma la pipa in disparte nel sole,
se lo perdo non so rintracciarlo, perché è del colore
delle felci bruciate. Ci salgono visitatori
che si accasciano sopra una pietra, sudati e affannati,
e lo trovano steso, con gli occhi nel cielo,
che respira profondo. Un lavoro l'ha fatto:
sopra il volto annerito ha lasciato infoltirsi la barba,
pochi peli rossicci. E depone gli sterchi
su uno spiazzo scoperto, a seccarsi nel sole.

Coste e valli di questa collina son verdi e profonde.
Tra le vigne i sentieri conducono su folli gruppi
di ragazze, vestite a colori violenti,
a far feste alla capra e gridare di là alla pianura.
Qualche volta compaiono file di ceste di frutta,
ma non salgono in cima: i villani le portano a casa
sulla schiena, contorti, e riaffondano in mezzo alle foglie.
Hanno troppo da fare e non vanno a veder l'eremita
i villani, ma scendono, salgono e zappano forte.
Quando han sete, tracannano vino: piantandosi in bocca
la bottiglia, sollevano gli ochi alla vetta bruciata.
La mattina sul fresco sono già di ritorno spossati
dal lavoro dell'alba e, se passa un pezzente,
tutta l'acqua che i pozzi riversano in mezzo ai raccolti
è per lui che la beva. Sogghignano ai gruppi di donne
e domandano quando, vestite di pelle di capra,
siederanno su tante colline a annerirsi al sole.

Landscape I

for Pollo

The land up here isn't worked any more. It's all barren
ground: bracken and bare rock.
Work's no use up here. The peak is so scorched
the only cool thing is your own breathing. The real work
is the long haul up the hill. The hermit climbed here once,
and he's been here ever since, recovering his strength.
Goatskins are what the hermit wears,
he stinks of animals and tobacco, a musty smell
that's seeped into everything: ground, bushes, cave.
Once you lose him, he's hard to spot—the color of burnt
bracken. Visitors who make the long hard climb up
collapse on a rock, panting and soaked with sweat, and find him
lolling on the ground, breathing deeply,
staring at the sky. One thing he's managed to do
is let his beard grow, a few straggling reddish hairs
over his dark sunbrowned face. He drops his dung
in a kind of clearing, where it dries in the sun.

There are long green slopes on the hill and deep ravines.
The path through the vineyards brings up a bevy of giggling
city girls, dressed in violent colors, to celebrate
the she-goat and yodel back down to the valley below.
At times, a row of baskets piled with fruit appears,
but going down, not coming up. Doubled over, the peasants
haul them home on their backs, sinking from sight in the leaves.
The peasants have too much to do, no time to visit the hermit.
Day in, day out, up, down, they climb the hill,
and work like hell with their hoes. When they're thirsty,
they take a swig of wine. They put the bottle to their lips,
they raise their eyes to the scorched peaks, they drink.
The day's still young when they're on their way down,
beat from working since dawn. If a beggar stops them for wine,
well, there's plenty of water stored away in the cisterns,
so help yourself, friend! They hoot at the girls coming up:
Hey, girls, where's your goatskins? Why don't you get yourselves
        a hill,
squat on one of these hills and toast yourselves brown in the sun?

Troppo mare. Ne abbiamo veduto abbastanza di mare.
Alla sera, che l'acqua si stende slavata
e sfumata nel nulla, l'amico la fissa
e io fisso l'amico e non parla nessuno.
Nottetempo finiamo a rinchiuderci fondo a una tampa,
isolati nel fumo, e beviamo. L'amico ha i suoi sogni
(sono un poco monotoni i sogni allo scroscio del mare)
dove l'acqua non è che lo specchio, tra un'isola e l'altra,
di colline, screziate di fiori selvaggi e cascate.
Il suo vino è cosí. Si contempla, guardando il bicchiere,
a innalzare colline di verde sul piano del mare.
Le colline mi vanno; e lo lascio parlare del mare
perché è un'acqua ben chiara, che mostra persino le pietre.

Vedo solo colline e mi riempiono il cielo e la terra
con le linee sicure dei fianchi, lontane o vicine.
Solamente, le mie sono scabre, e striate di vigne
faticose sul suolo bruciato. L'amico le accetta
e le vuole vestire di fiori e di frutti selvaggi
per scoprirvi ridendo ragazze piú nude dei frutti.
Non occorre: ai miei sogni piú scabri non manca un sorriso.
So domani sul presto saremo in cammino
verso quelle colline, potremo incontrar per le vigne
qualche scura ragazza, annerita di sole,
e, attaccando discorso, mangiarle un po' d'uva.

Displaced People

Too much sea. We've seen too much of the sea.
Late afternoon—the colorless water stretches dully away,
disappearing into air. My friend's staring at the sea,
and I'm staring at him, and neither says a word.
That night we end up drinking together at the rear of a tavern,
each of us alone in the smoky haze. My friend has dreams
(dreamt in the roar of the sea and just as monotonous)
where the water between the islands is only a mirror
of hills spilling seaward, flecked with waterfalls and flowers.
His wine is like his dreams. He stares at his glass and sees himself
stacking great green hills on the valley of the sea.
Hills are what I like, and I let him talk about the sea—
the water's so clear you can even see the stones.

All I see is hills, their long, clean, flanking lines
everywhere, far and near, filling my earth and sky. But my hills
are harsh, with terraces and vineyards men have sweated to build
on that scorched ground. My friend accepts my hills, but wants them
covered with wild fruit and flowers, just for the joy of peeling
off that green skin and finding girls, more naked than fruit.
No need for that. My dreams are harsh, but they have a sweetness
all their own. Suppose tomorrow, bright and early, we took a trip
to my hills. We could stroll through the vineyards and, maybe,
meet with a couple of girls, dark brown, ripened by the sun,
we could strike up a conversation, we could sample their grapes.

Il dio-caprone

La campagna è un paese di verdi misteri
al ragazzo, che viene d'estate. La capra, che morde
certi fiori, le gonfia la pancia e bisogna che corra.
Quando l'uomo ha goduto con qualche ragazza
—hanno peli là sotto—il bambino le gonfia la pancia.
Pascolando le capre, si fanno bravate e sogghigni,
ma al crepuscolo ognuno comincia a guardarsi alle spalle.
I ragazzi conoscono quando è passata la biscia
dalla striscia sinuosa che resta per terra.
Ma nessuno conosce se passa la biscia
dentro l'erba. Ci sono le capre che vanno a fermarsi
sulla biscia, nell'erba, e che godono a farsi succhiare.
Le ragazze anche godono, a farsi toccare.

Al levar della luna le capre non stanno più chete,
ma bisogna raccoglierle e spingerle a casa,
altrimenti si drizza il caprone. Saltando nel prato
sventra tutte le capre e scompare. Ragazze in calore
dentro i boschi ci vengono sole, di notte,
e il caprone, se belano stese nell'erba, le corre a trovare.
Ma, che spunti la luna: si drizza e le sventra.
E le cagne, che abbaiano sotto la luna,
è perché hanno sentito il caprone che salta
sulle cime dei colli e annusato l'odore del sangue.
E le bestie si scuotono dentro le stalle.
Solamente i cagnacci più forti dànno morsi alla corda
e qualcuno si libera e corre a seguire il caprone,
che li spruzza e ubriaca di un sangue più rosso del fuoco,
e poi ballano tutti, tenendosi ritti e ululando alla luna.

Quando, a giorno, il cagnaccio ritorna spelato e ringhioso,
i villani gli dànno la cagna a pedate di dietro.
E alla figlia, che gira di sera, e ai ragazzi, che tornano
quand'è buio, smarrita una capra, gli fiaccano il collo.
Riempion donne, i villani, e faticano senza rispetto.
Vanno in giro di giorno e di notte e non hanno paura

The Goat God

To the boy who comes in summer the country
is a land of green mysteries. Certain plants
are bad for the she-goat: her paunch begins to swell
and she has to run it off. When a man's had fun with a girl—
girls are hairy down there—her paunch swells with a baby.
The boys snigger and brag when they're herding the nannies,
but once the sun goes down, they start looking nervous and scared.
The boys can tell if a snake's been around, they know
by the wiggling trail he leaves behind him in the dust.
But nobody knows when a snake is sliding through the grass.
There are nannies who like to lie there in the grass, they lie
right down on top of the snake, they like to be suckled.
Girls like it too, they like being touched.

When the moon rises, the nannies get skittish,
and the boys have to round them up and prod them home. Otherwise,
the wild goat goes berserk. Rearing up in the meadow, ramping,
he gores the nannies and disappears. Sometimes girls in heat
come down to the woods, at night, alone;
they lie in the grass and bleat, and the wild billy comes running.
But once the moon is high, he goes berserk, he gores them.
And that's why the bitches bay in the moonlight,
because they've caught the smell of the wild goat leaping
on the hill, they've sniffed the smell of blood.
And the animals in the stalls start quivering.
All but the hounds, the big ones, they're gnawing at their ropes,
and one, a male, breaks loose and tears off after the goat,
and the goat spatters the dogs with blood—hotter, redder
than any fire—until they're all crazy drunk, wild
with blood, dancing and ramping and howling at the moon.

At dawn the dog comes home, savaged and snarling,
and the bitch is his reward. The peasants kick her to him.
If the boys come home at dark, with one of the nannies missing,
or a girl goes roaming at night, they're punished, beaten.
They make their women pregnant, the peasants, and go on working
just the same. Day or night they wander where they like.

di zappare anche sotto la luna o di accendere un fuoco
di gramigne nel buio. Per questo, la terra
è così bella verde e, zappata, ha il colore,
sotto l'alba, dei volti bruciati. Si va alla vendemmia
e si mangia e si canta; si va a spannocchiare
e si balla e si beve. Si sente ragazze che ridono,
ché qualcuno ricorda il caprone. Su, in cima, nei boschi,
tra le ripe sassose, a villani l'han visto
che cercava la capra e picchiava zuccate nei tronchi.
Perché, quando una bestia non sa lavorare
e si tiene soltanto da monta, gli piace distruggere.

They aren't afraid of hoeing by moonlight, or making a bonfire
of weeds and brush in the dark. And that's why the ground
is so beautifully green, and the plowed fields at dawn
are the color of sunburned faces. They harvest the grapes,
they eat and sing. They husk the corn, they dance and drink.
The girls are all giggling, then one girl suddenly remembers
the wild goat. Up there, on the hilltop, in the woods
and rocky ravines, the peasants saw him butting his head
against the trees, looking for the nannies. He's gone wild,
and the reason why is this: if you don't make an animal work,
if you keep him only for stud, he likes to hurt, he kills.

Paesaggio II

La collina biancheggia alle stelle, di terra scoperta;
si vedrebbero i ladri, lassú. Tra le ripe del fondo
i filari son tutti nell'ombra. Lassú che ce n'è
e che è terra di chi non patisce, non sale nessuno:
qui nell'umidità, con la scusa di andare a tartufi,
entran dentro alla vigna e saccheggiano le uve.

Il mio vecchio ha trovato due graspi buttati
tra le piante e stanotte borbotta. La vigna è già scarsa:
giorno e notte nell'umidità, non ci viene che foglie.
Tra le piante si vedono al cielo le terre scoperte
che di giorno gli rubano il sole. Lassú brucia il sole
tutto il giorno e la terra è calcina: si vede anche al buio.
Là non vengono foglie, la forza va tutta nell'uva.

Il mio vecchio appoggiato a un bastone nell'erba bagnata,
ha la mano convulsa: se vengono i ladri stanotte,
salta in mezzo ai filari e gli fiacca la schiena.
Sono gente da farle un servizio da bestie,
ché non vanno a contarla. Ogni tanto alza il capo
annusando nell'aria: gli pare che arrivi nel buio
una punta d'odore terroso, tartufi scavati.

Sulle coste lassú, che si stendono al cielo,
non c'è l'uggia degli alberi: l'uva strascina per terra,
tanto pesa. Nessuno può starci nascosto:
si distinguono in cima le macchie degli alberi
neri e radi. Se avesse la vigna lassú,
il mio vecchio farebbe la guardia da casa, nel letto,
col fucile puntato. Qui, al fondo, nemmeno il fucile
non gli serve, perché dentro il buio non c'è che fogliami.

Landscape II

Starlight on the hill: the fields shine white and clear.
Up there, you couldn't miss the thieves. Down here, in these ravines,
the vineyard is all darkness. Up there, the grapes are lush, really lush,
easy pickings and no sweat, but the thieves won't make the long climb
      up.
Down here, where it's wet, they pretend to be hunting for truffles,
then they sneak off into the vines and strip the vineyards bare.

The old man found a pair of grape-hooks thrown away somewhere
among the vines. Tonight he's grumbling. The pickings are poor
      enough as it is,
what with this wetness day and night, and everything running to
      leaves.
Come dawn, he peers through the leaves, and those fields up there on
      the hill
are stealing his sun, soaking it up. There the vines get sunlight
all day long, and the land's all lime: a man can see in the dark.
Things don't go to leaves up there, all the strength goes into the grape.

The old man stands in the soaking grass, holding his stick,
his hands waving wildly. If those damned thieves try it tonight,
he'll jump them! By God, he'll drub their backs with his stick,
treat 'em like animals. That's all they deserve—lazy,
good-for-nothing bastards! Now and then he lifts his head,
sniffing the air: he can smell it now, he thinks, drifting
out of the darkness—yes—a smell of earth and fresh-dug truffles!

There, higher up the hill, the slopes lie open to the sky—
it's not all leaves and shadow. The vines are so loaded up there,
the grapes trail on the ground. No room for thieves to hide, not there:
up at the top of the hill there's nothing but a few scattered trees—
you can see the splotches. Now, if my old man had his vineyard there,
he could stay at home and watch his vines, lie in bed with his rifle
loaded and already aimed. But down here, even the gun's no good
down here, what with these damned leaves and the darkness.

Può accadere ogni cosa nella bruna osteria,
può accadere che fuori sia un cielo di stelle,
al di là della nebbia autunnale e del mosto.
Può accadere che cantino dalla collina
le arrochite canzoni sulle aie deserte
e che torni improvvisa sotto il cielo d'allora
la donnetta seduta in attesa del giorno.

Tornerebbero intorno alla donna i villani
dalle scarne parole, in attesa del sole
e del pallido cenno di lei, rimboccati
fino al gomito, chini a fissare la terra.
Alla voce del grillo si unirebbe il frastuono
della cote sul ferro e un più rauco sospiro.
Tacerebbero il vento e i brusii della notte.
La donnetta seduta parlerebbe con ira.

Lavorando i villani ricurvi lontano,
la donnetta è rimasta sull'aia e li segue
con lo sguardo, poggiata allo stipite, affranta
dal gran ventre maturo. Sul volto consunto
ha un amaro sorriso impaziente, e una voce
che non giunge ai villani le solleva la gola.
Batte il sole sull'aia e sugli occhi arrossati
ammiccanti. Una nube purpurea vela la stoppia
seminata di gialli covoni. La donna
vacillando, la mano sul grembo, entra in casa.

Donne corrono con impazienza le stanze deserte
comandate dal cenno e dall'occhio che, soli,
di sul letto le seguono. La grande finestra
che contiene colline e filari e il gran cielo,
manda un fioco ronzio che è il lavoro di tutti.
La donnetta dal pallido viso ha serrate le labbra
alle fitte del ventre e si tende in ascolto
impaziente. Le donne la servono, pronte.

Anything can happen in the murk of the tavern.
Beyond the haze of new wine and the autumn fog,
the night outside could be starry and clear.
There might be voices singing on the harvested
hill, and the husky songs of the threshers drifting out
over the empty yard. The past could suddenly
come back: weather, hour, season,
and the small woman sitting there waiting for day.

The peasants would all return, hardly speaking, huddled
around the woman, waiting for day, waiting for orders, her
pale nod of command, their sleeves rolled back to the elbow,
heads down, staring at the ground.
And the cry of the cricket would fuse with the scraping
of steel on stone, and a huskier, rasping sigh.
The wind would fall, the sounds of night would stop.
And the woman sitting there would speak, angry.

Off in the fields the peasants bend to their scythes.
The woman watches, her eyes following the work
from the threshing-yard where she stands leaning against the door,
        sad,
with her great swollen belly. Her face is worn,
her smile is anxious and bitter, and a cry,
unheard by the peasants, heaves in her throat.
The sun beats down on the threshing-yard, on blinking
reddened eyes. A crimson cloud blurs the stubble
sown with yellow sheaves. Hesitant, slowly,
her hand on her belly, she goes back to the house.

Fretting women scurry through the empty rooms,
obeying a nod and the eyes that follow them, all eyes
watching from the bed. Through the big window,
framing hills and hedgerows and the giant sky,
a muffled drone comes in—everybody working.
Haggard, pale, the woman grits her teeth
against the pains in her belly, straining anxiously
to hear. The midwives come running, fast.

Luna d'agosto

Al di là delle gialle colline c'è il mare,
al di là delle nubi. Ma giornate tremende
di colline ondeggianti e crepitanti nel cielo
si frammettono prima del mare. Quassú c'è l'ulivo
con la pozza dell'acqua che non basta a specchiarsi,
e le stoppie, le stoppie, che non cessano mai.

E si leva la luna. Il marito è disteso
in un campo, col cranio spaccato dal sole
—una sposa non può trascinare un cadavere
come un sacco—. Si leva la luna, che getta un po' d'ombra
sotto i rami contorti. La donna nell'ombra
leva un ghigno atterrito al faccione di sangue
che coagula e inonda ogni piega dei colli.
Non si muove il cadavere disteso nei campi
né la donna nell'ombra. Pure l'occhio di sangue
pare ammicchi a qualcuno e gli segni una strada.

Vengon brividi lunghi per le nude colline
di lontano, e la donna se li sente alle spalle,
come quando correvano il mare del grano.
Anche invadono i rami dell'ulivo sperduto
in quel mare di luna, e già l'ombra dell'albero
pare stia per contrarsi e inghiottire anche lei.

Si precipita fuori, nell'orrore lunare,
e la segue il fruscío della brezza sui sassi
e una sagoma tenue che le morde le piante,
e la doglia nel grembo. Rientra curva nell'ombra
e si butta sui sassi e si morde la bocca.
Sotto, scura la terra si bagna di sangue.

August Moon

There's the sea, far beyond the yellow hills,
far beyond the clouds. But between the sea and here
are long terrible days, hills rippling and cresting
in the sky. Here on the hill is the olive tree,
and the pond of water so small a man can't see his face,
and the stubble: mile after mile of stubble.

And the moon, rising. Her husband lies stretched out
in a field, his skull cracked open by the sun.
A woman can't drag a corpse around as if it were
a sack. The moon rises, casting a little shadow
under the gnarled branches. The woman in shadow looks up,
grinning in terror at that huge face, all blood,
clotting and soaking every crease in the hills.
The corpse stretched out in the fields doesn't move,
or the woman in the shadow. Only the eye of blood
seems to be winking at someone, pointing the way.

Slow shudders crawl across the naked hills
in the distance, and the woman feels them at her back,
like when they were running through that sea of wheat.
And the branches of the olive, lost in that sea
of moonlight, move in—even the tree's shadow
starts to darken and thicken and swallow her up.

She runs out into the moonlight and its horror,
and the breeze comes after her rustling over the rocks
and a thin fine shape gnawing at her bare feet,
and the pain in her womb. Doubled over, she hides in the shadow,
crumpling on the rocks and gnawing at her lips.
The ground beneath her dark, drenched with blood.

Luna tenera e brina sui campi nell'alba
assassinano il grano.

        Sul piano deserto,
qua e là putrefatto (ci vuole del tempo
perché il sole e la pioggia sotterrino i morti),
era ancora un piacere svegliarsi e guardare
se la brina copriva anche quelli. La luna
inondava, e qualcuno pensava al mattino
quando l'erba sarebbe spuntata piú verde.

Ai villani che guardano piangono gli occhi.
Per quest'anno al ritorno del sole, se torna,
foglioline bruciate saran tutto il grano.
Trista luna—non sa che mangiare le nebbie,
e le brine al sereno hanno un morso di serpe,
che del verde fa tanto letame. Ne han dato letame
alla terra; ora torna in letame anche il grano,
e non serve guardare, e sarà tutto arso,
putrefatto. È un mattino che toglie ogni forza
solamente svegliarsi e girare da vivi
lungo i campi.

        Vedranno piú tardi spuntare
qualche timido verde sul piano deserto,
sulla tomba del grano, e dovranno lottare
a ridurre anche quello in letame, bruciando.
Perché il sole e la pioggia proteggono solo le erbacce
e la brina, toccato che ha il grano, non torna.

A new moon, and dawn frost in the fields—
they murder the wheat.

                There were patches of rot
in the empty fields (it takes time
for sun and rain to bury the dead),
but it was still a pleasure waking and going out to see
if even the dead had been touched by frost. The moonlight
came like a flood, somebody there must have been thinking
of that day when the grass would all be green again.

The peasants look, their eyes fill with tears.
This year, when the sun starts shining again—if it does—
the only thing left of all that wheat will be black
and shriveled leaves. Damned, miserable moon—
it's only good for swallowing the fog. And frost,
when the air's still, is fanged like a snake,
it makes manure of all that green. The peasants fed
their fields manure, and now their crops are nothing
but manure. No use looking. Everything will be black
with rot. Mornings like this it takes all the strength you have
to wake up and go wandering around the fields,
like one of the survivors.

                Later on, they'll see the timid
shoots of fresh green sprouting in the empty
fields, there on the grave of the wheat, and they'll have to sweat
making manure of that too. They'll have to burn it off.
Sun and rain are only kind to weeds, nothing else. And now, of course,
now that the wheat's all dead, the frost is over.

Paesaggio III

Tra la barba e il gran sole la faccia va ancora,
ma è la pelle del corpo, che biancheggia tremante
tra le toppe. Non basta lo sporco a confonderla
nella pioggia e nel sole. Villani anneriti
l'han guardato una volta, ma l'occhiata perdura
su quel corpo, cammini o si accasci al riposo.

Nella notte le grandi campagne si fondono
in un'ombra pesante, che sprofonda i filari
e le piante: soltanto le mani conoscono i frutti.
L'uomo lacero pare un villano, nell'ombra,
ma rapisce ogni cosa e i cagnacci non sentono.
Nella notte la terra non ha piú padroni,
se non voci inumane. Il sudore non conta.
Ogni pianta ha un suo freddo sudore nell'ombra
e non c'è piú che un campo, per nessuno e per tutti.

Al mattino quest'uomo stracciato e tremante
sogna, steso ad un muro non suo, che i villani
lo rincorrono e vogliono morderlo, sotto il gran sole.
Ha una barba stillante di fredda rugiada
e tra i buchi la pelle. Compare un villano
con la zappa sul collo, e s'asciuga la bocca.
Non si scosta nemmeno, ma scavalca quell'altro:
un suo campo quest'oggi ha bisogno di forza.

Landscape III

Thanks to the beard and the summer sun, the face will pass.
The problem's the body, all that flabby white skin showing
through the rags. He's dirty, he just isn't dirty enough
to blend with sun and weather. Sunburned peasants
gave him a passing glance, but the glance lingers
over that body, whether it's walking or sprawled in the sun.

At night the countryside dissolves, the fields fuse
in a thick darkness, blurring the rows in the vineyards,
blurring the plants. Only a hand could tell the fruit.
At night the man in rags could pass for a peasant,
but he pilfers everything, even the dogs can't hear him.
At night the earth has no owners, no masters,
only inhuman voices. Sweat doesn't count.
In the darkness, every plant has its own cold sweat,
there's nothing but one huge field, every man's and none's.

At dawn, this man in rags lies shivering, slumped
against a wall that isn't his, dreaming the sun is high,
the peasants are chasing him, they'd like to eat him alive.
His beard glistens with cold dew, the white skin shows
through the rags. A peasant appears, hoe on shoulder,
and wipes his hand across his face. He doesn't turn or stop,
he walks right over the man, he tramples him into the dirt, hard.
That field of his wasn't bearing, the earth could use a push.

La notte

Ma la notte ventosa, la limpida notte
che il ricordo sfiorava soltanto, è remota,
è un ricordo. Perduta una calma stupita
fatta anch'essa di foglie e di nulla. Non resta,
di quel tempo di là dai ricordi, che un vago
ricordare.

       Talvolta ritorna nel giorno
nell'immobile luce del giorno d'estate,
quel remoto stupore.

         Per la vuota finestra
il bambino guardava la notte sui colli
freschi e neri, e stupiva di trovarli ammassati:
vaga e limpida immobilità. Fra le foglie
che stormivano al buio, apparivano i colli
dove tutte le cose del giorno, le coste
e le piante e le vigne, eran nitide e morte
e la vita era un'altra, di vento, di cielo,
e di foglie e di nulla.

        Talvolta ritorna
nell'immobile calma del giorno il ricordo
di quel vivere assorto, nella luce stupita.

The Night

But the windy night, the transparent night,
barely grazed by memory, has faded now,
is a memory. A still, stunned awe lingers on,
like the night, made of leaves and nothing. Nothing is left
of that time beyond memories, only a faint
remembering.

At times it returns,
in the motionless light of the summer day—
that faded awe.

Through the open window,
the boy gazed out in awe at night on the hills—
the fresh, dark hills—stunned to find them massed together,
vague, transparent, still. Between the leaves
that rustled in the dark, the hills loomed up
where all the daylight things, the slopes
and the plants and the vines, stood defined and dead,
and life was a different thing, a thing of wind and sky
and leaves and nothing.

At times it returns,
in the motionless calm of the day, that memory
of living immersed, absorbed, in the stunned light.

Dopo • Afterwards

Incontro

Queste dure colline che han fatto il mio corpo
e lo scuotono a tanti ricordi, mi han schiuso il prodigio
di costei, che non sa che la vivo e non riesco a comprenderla.

L'ho incontrata, una sera: una macchia piú chiara
sotto le stelle ambigue, nella foschía d'estate.
Era intorno il sentore di queste colline
piú profondo dell'ombra, e d'un tratto suonò
come uscisse da queste colline, una voce piú netta
e aspra insieme, una voce di tempi perduti.

Qualche volta la vedo, a mi vive dinanzi
definita, immutabile, come un ricordo.
Io non ho mai potuto afferrarla: la sua realtà
ogni volta mi sfugge e mi porta lontano.
Se sia bella, non so. Tra le donne è ben giovane:
mi sorprende, a pensarla, un ricordo remoto
dell'infanzia vissuta tra queste colline,
tanto è giovane. È come il mattino. Mi accenna negli occhi
tutti i cieli lontani di quei mattini remoti.
E ha negli occhi un proposito fermo: la luce piú netta
che abbia avuto mai l'alba su queste colline.

L'ho creata dal fondo di tutte le cose
che mi sono piú care, e non riesco a comprenderla.

Encounter

These hard hills which made my body
and whose many memories still shake it so, have revealed the
       miracle—
this *she* who does not know I live her and cannot understand her.

I encountered her one evening: a brighter patch of scrub
under the flickering starlight, in the summer haze.
The smell of these hills was all around me, everywhere,
a smell deeper than shadow, and suddenly I heard a sound,
as though it came from these hills, a voice at once purer
and harsher, the voice of things past.

Sometimes I see her. She stands there before me, looking at me,
distinct and defined, unchanging, like a memory.
I have never succeeded in holding her fast: always her reality
slips through my fingers and carries me far away.
She may be beautiful, I do not know. Compared to women, she is
       very young:
so young that when I think of her, I am surprised
by a faint memory of a childhood spent among these hills.
She is like morning. Her eyes hint to me
of all the faraway skies of those long-ago mornings.
And her eyes shine with a firm purpose: the purest light
dawn has ever thrown upon these hills.

I created her from the ground of everything
I love the most, and I cannot understand her.

Mania di solitudine

Mangio un poco di cena alla chiara finestra.
Nella stanza è già buio e si vede nel cielo.
A uscir fuori, le vie tranquille conducono
dopo un poco, in aperta campagna.
Mangio e guardo nel cielo—chi sa quante donne
stan mangiando a quest'ora—il mio corpo è tranquillo;
il lavoro stordisce il mio corpo e ogni donna.

Fuori, dopo la cena, verranno le stelle a toccare
sulla larga pianura la terra. Le stelle son vive,
ma non valgono queste ciliege, che mangio da solo.
Vedo il cielo, ma so che tra i tetti di ruggine
qualche lume già brilla e che, sotto, si fanno rumori.
Un gran sorso e il mio corpo assapora la vita
delle piante e dei fiumi, e si sente staccato da tutto.
Basta un po' di silenzio e ogni cosa si ferma
nel suo luogo reale, cosí come'è fermo il mio corpo.

Ogni cosa è isolata davanti ai miei sensi,
che l'accettano senza scomporsi: un brusío di silenzio.
Ogni cosa nel buio la posso sapere
come so che il mio sangue trascorre le vene.
La pianura è un gran scorrere d'acqua tra l'erbe,
una cena di tutte le cose. Ogni pianta e ogni sasso
vive immobile. Ascolto i miei cibi nutrirmi le vene
di ogni cosa che vive su questa pianura.

Non importa la notte. Il quadrato di cielo
mi susurra di tutti i fragori, e una stella minuta
si dibatte nel vuoto, lontana dai cibi,
dalle case, diversa. Non basta a se stessa,
e ha bisogno di troppe compagne. Qui al buio, da solo,
il mio corpo è tranquillo e si sente padrone.

Passion for Solitude

I eat a bite of supper beside the bright window.
By now it's dark inside the room, you look into the sky.
Step outside the house, and the quiet lanes will lead you,
after a short walk, into the open country.
I eat and look into the sky—think of all the women
who are eating supper now—and my body is still.
Drudgery deadens my body, it deadens women too.

Outside, after supper, the stars will come
to touch the earth on the great plain. The stars are alive,
but they're no match for these cherries which I eat alone.
I see the sky, but I know the lights are shining
among the reddish roofs, and there are sounds below.
A healthy gulp, and my body tastes the life
of trees and brooks, and feels cut off from everything.
Then a little silence, and everything stops, arrested
in its real place, the way my body rests.

Everything stands isolated before my senses,
which accept it calmly: a rustling of silence.
Everything in this darkness—I can know it all,
the way I know my blood is flowing through my veins.
The plain is a great flowing of water through the grass,
a supper of all things. Every plant, every stone
lives and rests. I hear my food nourishing my veins
with all the things that live on this plain.

Night makes no difference. The square of sky
whispers to me of all the sounds, and a tiny star
is struggling in the sky, far from food and home:
a different thing from me. It isn't self-sufficient,
it needs too many companions. Here, in the dark, alone,
my body rests and feels it is the one master of itself.

Rivelazione

L'uomo solo rivede il ragazzo dal magro
cuore assorto a scrutare la donna ridente.
Il ragazzo levava lo sguardo a quegli occhi,
dove i rapidi sguardi trasalivano nudi
e diversi. Il ragazzo raccoglieva un segreto
in quegli occhi, un segreto come il grembo nascosto.

L'uomo solo si preme nel cuore il ricordo.
Gli occhi ignoti bruciavano come brucia la carne,
vivi d' umida vita. La dolcezza del grembo
palpitante di calda ansietà traspariva
in quegli occhi. Sbocciava angoscioso il segreto
come un sangue. Ogni cosa era fatta tremenda
nella luce tranquilla delle piante e del cielo.

Il ragazzo piangeva nella sera sommessa
rade lacrime mute, come fosse già uomo.
L'uomo solo ritrova sotto il cielo remoto
quello sguardo raccolto che la donna depone
sul ragazzo. E rivede quegli occhi e quel volto
ricomporsi sommessi al sorriso consueto.

The man alone sees the boy again. Faint-hearted boy, all
eyes, watching the woman laughing. Slowly,
the boy lifted his gaze, looking deep into those eyes
where the bright glances were flashing and darting—naked,
other. The boy was probing for a secret deep
in those eyes, a dark secret, guarded like the womb.

The man alone remembers—and tries to forget.
Those unknown eyes were strange, moist with sudden life,
they burned like flesh on fire. All the womb's
sweetness, throbbing with desire, blazed
from those eyes. The secret blossomed out like pain,
like blood. Everything went huge and scary, terror seized
the boy. Sky and trees were shining, a quiet light.

On soft summer nights, the boy sometimes cried
a little, sobbing to himself, like a man, inside.
Now, the man's alone. Another time, another sky.
Remembering, it all comes back now, all the terror
of that deep, probing look the woman's gaze imposes
on the boy. And he sees those eyes again, he sees the face
softly composing itself in its usual smile.

Mattino

La finestra socchiusa contiene un volto
sopra il campo del mare. I capelli vaghi
accompagnano il tenero ritmo del mare.

Non ci sono ricordi su questo viso.
Solo un'ombra fuggevole, come di nube.
L'ombra è umida e dolce come la sabbia
di una cavità intatta, sotto il crepuscolo.
Non ci sono ricordi. Solo un sussurro
che è la voce del mare fatta ricordo.

Nel crepuscolo l'acqua molle dell'alba
che s'imbeve di luce, rischiara il viso.
Ogni giorno è un miracolo senza tempo,
sotto il sole: una luce salsa l'impregna
e un sapore di frutto marino vivo.

Non esiste ricordo su questo viso.
Non esiste parola che lo contenga
o accomuni alle cose passate. Ieri,
dalla breve finestra è svanito come
svanirà tra un istante, senza tristezza
né parole umane, sul campo del mare.

Morning

The window, half open, holds a face
over the meadow of the sea. The hair sways
with the gentle rhythm of the sea, moving.

There are no memories on this face.
Only a passing shadow, like the shadow of a cloud.
In the half-light the shadow is moist and sweet
like the sand of a hollow cove, untouched.
There are no memories. Only a murmur
which is the sound of the sea made memory.

In the half-light the soft water of dawn
is saturated with light and illumines the face.
When the sun is high, each day is a miracle.
It has no time. A salt light suffuses it,
and a smell of living things from the salt sea.

No memory lives on this face.
No word could hold it, no word
connect it to vanished things. Yesterday
it vanished from the little window as it will
always vanish, instantly, no sadness,
no human words, over the field of the sea.

C'è un giardino chiaro, fra mura basse,
di erba secca e di luce, che cuoce adagio
la sua terra. È una luce che sa di mare.
Tu respiri quell'erba. Tocchi i capelli
e ne scuoti il ricordo.

                    Ho veduto cadere
molti frutti, dolci, su un'erba che so,
con un tonfo. Cosí trasalisci tu pure
al sussulto del sangue. Tu muovi il capo
come intorno accadesse un prodigio d'aria
e il prodigio sei tu. C'è un sapore uguale
nei tuoi occhi e nel caldo ricordo.

                         Ascolti.
Le parole che ascolti ti toccano appena.
Hai nel viso calmo un pensiero chiaro
che ti finge alle spalle la luce del mare.
Hai nel viso un silenzio che preme il cuore
con un tonfo, e ne stilla una pena antica
come il succo dei frutti caduti allora.

Summer

A garden between low walls, bright,
made of dry grass and a light that slowly bakes
the ground below. The light smells of sea.
You breathe that grass. You touch your hair
and shake out the memory of grass.

                              I have seen ripe
fruit droping thickly on remembered grass with a soft
thudding. So too the pulsing of the blood
surprises even you. You move your head
as though a miracle of air had happened around you,
and the miracle is you. Your eyes have a savor
like the heat of memory.

                    You listen.
You listen to the words, but they barely graze you.
Your face has a radiance of thought that shines
around your shoulders, like light from the sea. The silence
in your face touches the heart with a soft
thud, exuding drop by drop,
like fruit that fell here years ago,
an old pain, still.

Notturno

La collina è notturna, nel cielo chiaro.
Vi s'inquadra il tuo capo, che muove appena
e accompagna quel cielo. Sei come una nube
intravista fra i rami. Ti ride negli occhi
la stranezza di un cielo che non è il tuo.

La collina di terra e di foglie chiude
con la massa nera il tuo vivo guardare,
la tua bocca ha la piega di un dolce incavo
tra le coste lontane. Sembri giocare
alla grande collina e al chiarore del cielo:
per piacermi ripeti lo sfondo antico
e lo rendi piú puro.

        Ma vivi altrove.
Il tuo tenero sangue si è fatto altrove.
Le parole che dici non hanno riscontro
con la scabra tristezza di questo cielo.
Tu non sei che una nube dolcissima, bianca
impigliata una notte fra i rami antichi.

Nocturne

The hill is part of night, the sky is clear.
They frame your head, which scarcely moves,
moving with that sky. You are like a cloud
glimpsed between the branches. In your eyes there shines
the strangeness of a sky which isn't yours.

The hill with its earth and leaves contains
in its black mass your living look.
The curve of your mouth is like a gentle dip
between the distant slopes. You seem to play at being
the great hill and the clarity of the sky:
to please me you repeat the ancient setting,
you make it purer.

           But you live somewhere else.
Your tender blood was made in some other place.
The words you speak have no echo here
in the harsh desolation of this sky.
You are just a wandering cloud, white and very sweet,
tangled one night among these ancient branches.

Agonia

Girerò per le strade finché non sarò stanca morta
saprò vivere sola e fissare negli occhi
ogni volto che passa e restare la stessa.
Questo fresco che sale a cercarmi le vene
è un risveglio che mai nel mattino ho provato
cosí vero: soltanto, mi sento piú forte
che il mio corpo, e un tremore piú freddo accompagna il mattino.

Son lontani i mattini che avevo vent'anni.
E domani, ventuno: domani uscirò per le strade,
ne ricordo ogni sasso e le striscie di cielo.
Da domani la gente riprende a vedermi
e sarò ritta in piedi e potrò soffermarmi
e specchiarmi in vetrine. I mattini di un tempo,
ero giovane e non lo sapevo, e nemmeno sapevo
di esser io che passavo—una donna, padrona
di se stessa. La magra bambina che fui
si è svegliata da un pianto durato per anni:
ora è come quel pianto non fosse mai stato.

E desidero solo colori. I colori non piangono,
sono come un risveglio: domani i colori
torneranno. Ciascuna uscirà per la strada,
ogni corpo un colore—perfino i bambini.
Questo corpo vestito di rosso leggero
dopo tanto pallore riavrà la sua vita.
Sentirò intorno a me scivolare gli sguardi
e saprò d'esser io: gettando un'occhiata,
mi vedrò tra la gente. Ogni nuovo mattino,
uscirò per le strade cercando i colori.

Death Agony

I'll wander around the streets until I'm dead tired
I'll learn to live alone and look every passing face
square in the eye and still stay what I am.
This coolness rising in me and reaching for my veins
is a morning waking I've never felt before,
never so real. Except I feel stronger
than my body, and this morning's shiver is colder than ever.

The mornings I had when I was twenty seem long ago.
And tomorrow, twenty-one: tomorrow I'll walk down the streets
I remember every cobble and the shafts of sunlight.
Starting tomorrow people will begin to see me
and I'll walk straight and stop for a while
and inspect myself in the windows. There were mornings once
when I was young and didn't know it. I didn't even know
the person passing was me—a woman, her own
mistress. The skinny little girl I used to be
was wakened by a wail of grief that lasted for years:
now it's as though that grief had never been.

And all I want is colors. Colors don't cry,
they're like a waking up. Tomorrow the colors
will all come back. Every woman will walk down the street,
every body will be a color—even the children.
This body of mine will wear light red
will live again after all those colorless years.
I'll feel the glances of men go gliding around me
and I'll know I'm me: just a look and I'll see
I'm there, like other people. In the cool of the mornings
I'll step out in the streets, I'll go looking for colors.

Paesaggio VII

Basta un poco di giorno negli occhi chiari
come il fondo di un'acqua, e la invade l'ira,
la scabrezza del fondo che il sole riga.
Il mattino che torna e la trova viva,
non è dolce né buono: la guarda immoto
tra le case di pietra, che chiude il cielo.

Esce il piccolo corpo tra l'ombra e il sole
come un lento animale, guardandosi intorno,
non vedendo null'altro se non colori.
Le ombre vaghe che vestono la strada e il corpo
le incupiscono gli occhi, socchiusi appena
come un'acqua, e nell'acqua traspare un'ombra.

I colori riflettono il cielo calmo.
Anche il passo che calca i ciottoli lento
sembra calchi le cose, pari al sorriso
che le ignora e le scorre come acqua chiara.
Dentro l'acqua trascorrono minacce vaghe.
Ogni cosa nel giorno s'increspa al pensiero
che la strada sia vuota, se non per lei.

Landscape VII

A little light is all it takes, and anger invades
those eyes, clear as the depths of a pool,
the harshness of depths streaked by sun.
The dawning day that finds this anger still alive
is neither sweet nor good; unmoving, between
stone houses shutting out the sky, it watches her.

The small body emerges, between sun and shadow,
like a slow animal, looking everywhere
but seeing nothing, only colors.
Vague shadows wrap street and body,
darkening those eyes, almost closed,
like a pond, a darkness shivers in the water.

The colors mirror the quiet sky.
Even her step moving slowly over the cobbles
seems to walk on things, ignoring them,
like her smile, gliding over them like water.
Down below, vague menaces begin to move.
Everything under the sun ripples at the thought
that the street is empty, but for her.

Donne appassionate

Le ragazze al crepuscolo scendono in acqua,
quando il mare svanisce, disteso. Nel bosco
ogni foglia trasale, mentre emergono caute
sulla sabbia e si siedono a riva. La schiuma
fa i suoi giochi inquieti, lungo l'acqua remota.

Le ragazze han paura delle alghe sepolte
sotto le onde, che afferrano le gambe e le spalle:
quant'è nudo, del corpo. Rimontano rapide a riva
e si chiamano a nome, guardandosi intorno.
Anche le ombre sul fondo del mare, nel buio,
sono enormi e si vedono muovere incerte,
come attratte dai corpi che passano. Il bosco
è un rifugio tranquillo, nel sole calante,
piú che il greto, ma piace alle scure ragazze
star sedute all'aperto, nel lenzuolo raccolto.

Stanno tutte accosciate, serrando il lenzuolo
alle gambe, e contemplano il mare disteso
come un prato al crepuscolo. Oserebbe qualcuna
ora stendersi nuda in un prato? Dal mare
balzerebbero le alghe, che sfiorano i piedi,
a ghermire e ravvolgere il corpo tremante.
Ci son occhi nel mare, che traspaiono a volte.

Quell'ignota straniera, che nuotava di notte
sola e nuda, nel buio quando muta la luna,
è scomparsa una notte e non torna mai piú.
Era grande e doveva esser bianca abbagliante
perché gli occhi, dal fondo del mare, giungessero a lei.

Women in Love

The girls come down to the water at twilight
when the sea stretches away and disappears in the distance.
The leaves in the woods shiver as the girls step
cautiously out and sit on the shore. Far away,
at the water's edge, the foam plays restlessly.

The girls are scared of the seaweed which hides
beneath the water and sticks to their legs and shoulders—
wherever the body is bare. They scurry back, calling
each other by name and nervously peering around.
Even the shadows at the bottom of the sea grow huge
at twilight, and begin to stir, uneasily,
as though attracted by the bodies passing overhead.
At sunset the woods are a haven of peace,
more restful than the gravel beach, but the dark girls
like sitting among their piles of laundry, out in the open.

They squat, huddling together, holding the sheets
between their knees, and watching the sea stretch away
like a meadow at twilight. Suppose some girl dared
stretch out naked in a meadow now? The seaweed,
brushed by her feet, would suddenly lunge up
from the water to seize and surround her shuddering body.
There are eyes in the sea. And sometimes they stare.

That foreign girl, the girl who went swimming at night
alone, naked, in the dark of the changing moon,
disappeared one night and was never seen again.
She was big, and her body must have been dazzling white
for those eyes to reach her from the bottom of the sea.

Terre bruciate

Parla il giovane smilzo che è stato a Torino.
Il gran mare si stende, nascosto da rocce,
e dà in cielo un azzurro slavato. Rilucono gli occhi
di ciascuno che ascolta.

A Torino si arriva di sera
e si vedono subito per la strada le donne
maliziose, vestite per gli occhi, che camminano sole.
Là, ciascuna lavora per la veste che indossa,
ma l'adatta a ogni luce. Ci sono colori
da mattino, colori per uscire nei viali,
per piacere di notte. Le donne, che aspettano
e si sentono sole, conoscono a fondo la vita.
Sono libere. A loro non rifiutano nulla.

Sento il mare che batte e ribatte spossato alla riva.
Vedo gli occhi profondi di questi ragazzi
lampeggiare. A due passi il filare di fichi
disperato s'annoia sulla roccia rossastra.

Ce ne sono di libere che fumano sole.
Ci si trova la sera e abbandona il mattino
al caffè, come amici. Sono giovani sempre.
Voglion occhi e prontezza nell'uomo e che scherzi
e che sia sempre fine. Basta uscire in collina
e che piova: si piegano come bambine,
ma si sanno godere l'amore. Piú esperte di un uomo.
Sono vive e slanciate e, anche nude, discorrono
con quel brio che hanno sempre.

Lo ascolto.
Ho fissato le occhiaie del giovane smilzo
tutte intente. Han veduto anche loro una volta quel verde.
Fumerò a notte buia, ignorando anche il mare.

Sultry Lands

The skinny young man from Torino is speaking.
Hidden by the rocks, the huge sea stretches away
pale blue in the sunlight. A light shines in the eyes
of everyone listening.

You arrive in Torino one night,
and the first thing you see is the women in the streets, sly
flirtatious women, dressed to be seen, walking alone.
Every woman works for the dress she wears,
but she suits it to every light. There are colors
for morning, colors for strolling along the avenues,
and having fun at night. These women waiting
feel their loneliness. They know life to its depths.
They're free. Nothing is ever refused them.

I feel the sea pounding and throbbing on the shore.
Deep in the eyes of these listening boys a light
gleams. Nearby, the desperate row of figs
is dying of boredom on the reddish rocks.

Those women are so free they even smoke alone.
You pick them up at night and leave them in the morning,
like friends, at the café. They're always young.
They want a man with eyes, ready, who likes to laugh and joke,
a man of taste. Walk up the hill with them,
and they crumple like little girls if it starts to rain.
But they know how to love. They know more than the men.
They have liveliness and grace. Even when they're naked, they talk
as vivaciously as ever.

I listen to him speaking.
My eyes are riveted on this skinny young stranger.
I saw that green country once. I saw it with my own eyes.
I'll stay up late and smoke, I won't notice the sea.

Tolleranza

Piove senza rumore sul prato del mare.
Per le luride strade non passa nessuno.
È discesa dal treno una femmina sola:
tra il cappotto si è vista la chiara sottana
e le gambe sparire nella porta annerita.

Si direbbe un paese sommerso. La sera
stilla fredda su tutte le soglie, e le case
spandon fumo azzurrino nell'ombra. Rossastre
le finestre s'accendono. S'accende una luce
tra le imposte accostate nella casa annerita.

L'indomani fa freddo e c'è il sole sul mare.
Una donna in sottana si strofina la bocca
alla fonte, e la schiuma è rosata. Ha capelli
biondo-ruvido, simili alle bucce d'arancia
sparse in terra. Protesa alla fonte, sogguarda
un monello nerastro che la fissa incantato.
Donne fosche spalancano imposte alla piazza
—i mariti sonnecchiano ancora, nel buio.

Quando torna la sera, riprende la pioggia
scoppiettante sui molti bracieri. Le spose,
ventilando i carboni, dànno occhiate alla casa
annerita e alla fonte deserta. La casa
ha le imposte accecate, ma dentro c'è un letto,
e sul letto una bionda si guadagna la vita.
Tutto quanto il paese riposa la notte,
tutto, tranne la bionda, che si lava al mattino.

Tolerance

It rains without sound on the green stretch
of the sea. In the dirty streets nobody moves.
A woman got off the train, a woman alone.
Through her raincoat you can see her bright skirt,
and her legs disappearing through the dark doorway.

The town is like a place under water. Night
drips cold at every doorway, and the houses
spread a bluish haze in the darkness. Red
windows are kindled. Between the shuttered blinds
of the blackened house, a light goes on.

Morning is cold, with sunlight on the sea.
A woman in a skirt stands rinsing her mouth
at the fountain, and the water is reddish. Her hair
is dirty blond, like the orange peels scattered
on the ground. Bending to the spout, she peers up
at a blackish urchin staring at her, fascinated.
Women in black are opening shutters on the piazza—
their husbands still lie dozing in the dark.

At night the rain begins again, spattering
the braziers hissing at the doorways. Wives
stand fanning the coals and glancing at the black
house and the deserted fountain. The windows
are shuttered tight, but inside there's a bed,
and on the bed a blonde is earning her living.
At night the whole town goes to sleep,
all but the blonde, who washes in the morning.

La puttana contadina

La muraglia di fronte che accieca il cortile
ha sovente un riflesso di sole bambino
che ricorda la stalla. E la camera sfatta
e deserta al mattino quando il corpo si sveglia,
sa l'odore del primo profumo inesperto.
Fino il corpo, intrecciato al lenzuolo, è lo stesso
dei primi anni, che il cuore balzava scoprendo.

Ci si sveglia deserte al richiamo inoltrato
del mattino e riemerge nella greve penombra
l'abbandono di un altro risveglio: la stalla
dell'infanzia e la greve stanchezza del sole
caloroso sugli usci indolenti. Un profumo
impregnava leggero il sudore consueto
dei capelli, e le bestie annusavano. Il corpo
si godeva furtivo la carezza del sole
insinuante e pacata come fosse un contatto.

L'abbandono del letto attutisce le membra
stese giovani e tozze, come ancora bambine.
La bambina inesperta annusava il sentore
del tabacco e del fieno e tremava al contatto
fuggitivo dell'uomo: le piaceva giocare.
Qualche volta giocava distesa con l'uomo
dentro il fieno, ma l'uomo non fiutava i capelli:
le cercava nel fieno le membra contratte,
le fiaccava, schiacciandole come fosse suo padre.
Il profumo eran fiori pestati sui sassi.

Molte volte ritorna nel lento risveglio
quel disfatto sapore di fiori lontani
e di stalla e di sole. Non c'è uomo che sappia
la sottile carezza di quell'acre ricordo.
Non c'è uomo che veda oltre il corpo disteso
quell'infanzia trascorsa nell'ansia inesperta.

The Country Whore

The high wall around the courtyard catches the first
groping fingers of boyish sun, the way the barn once
caught the morning light. Except for the body slowly
waking out of sleep, the room is deserted, untidy,
filled with the first fumbling smell of adolescence.
Even the body tangled in the sheets is the same body
it once was, in the first wild abandon of discovery.

Now she wakes alone, deserted, to the call
of morning in its prime. Forming in the heavy shadow of the room
is another waking, another abandon: the cowbarn
of childhood, and the warm stupor of sunlight shining
at the listless doorway. Fragrance of barn and light
mixed with the smell of sweat that's always
in her hair, and the animals nuzzling it. Secretly,
her body took its pleasure from the sun's sweet
insinuating light, softly probing.

Now, in the abandon of the empty bed, her legs go weak
and faint. Short, stocky legs, the legs of a young girl.
The awkward adolescent girl liked to sniff the fragrance
of tobacco mixed with hay, shivering at the man's
fleeting touch; she liked playing games.
Sometimes she used to play games in the hay, lying there
beside the man. But the man wasn't nuzzling her hair,
he was groping in the hay, forcing her clenched legs apart,
squeezing the way her father did, but he wouldn't stop.
The fragrance was flowers. Flowers crushed on rock.

Now, as she slowly wakes from sleep, it keeps returning,
out of the past, that overpowering fragrance of flowers,
of cowbarn and sun. The memory is pungent, sharp,
caresses like a touch. No man can touch like that.
No man can see, beyond the body lying there,
the need, the anguish, of those fumbling adolescent years.

Pensieri di Deola

Deola passa il mattino seduta al caffè
e nessuno la guarda. A quest'ora in città corron tutti
sotto il sole ancor fresco dell'alba. Non cerca nessuno
neanche Deola, ma fuma pacata e respira il mattino.
Fin che è stata in pensione, ha dovuto dormire a quest'ora
per rifarsi le forze: la stuoia sul letto
la sporcavano con le scarpacce soldati e operai,
i clienti che fiaccan la schiena. Ma, sole, è diverso:
si può fare un lavoro più fine, con poca fatica.
Il signore di ieri, svegliandola presto,
l'ha baciata e condotta (*mi fermerei, cara,*
a Torino con te, se potessi) con sé alla stazione
a augurargli buon viaggio.

È intontita ma fresca stavolta,
e le piace esser libera, Deola, e bere il suo latte
e mangiare brioches. Stamattina è una mezza signora
e, se guarda i passanti, fa solo per non annoiarsi.
A quest'ora in pensione si dorme e c'è puzzo di chiuso
—la padrona va a spasso—è da stupide stare là dentro.
Per girare la sera i locali, ci vuole presenza
e in pensione, a trent'anni, quel po' che ne resta, si è perso.

Deola siede mostrando il profilo a uno specchio
e si guarda nel fresco del vetro. Un po' pallida in faccia:
non è il fumo che stagni. Corruga le ciglia.
Ci vorrebbe la voglia che aveva Marí, per durare
in pensione (*perché, cara donna, gli uomini*
vengon qui per cavarsi capricci che non glieli toglie
né la moglie né l'innamorata) e Marí lavorava
instancabile, piena di brio e godeva salute.
I passanti davanti al caffè non distraggono Deola
che lavora soltanto la sera, con lente conquiste
nella musica del suo locale. Gettando le occhiate

Deola Thinking

Deola spends her mornings sitting in the café,
and nobody looks at her. In the city this is the time
when people are rushing around in the cool of the morning.
Nobody's even looking for Deola. Undisturbed, she smokes
      and breathes
the morning. At the house, this was when she had to sleep
to recover her strength: the coverlet on her bed
was always black with the boot-marks of workers and soldiers.
They're the johns who break your back. But it's different
when you're on your own: you get a better sort of trick,
and you don't work so hard. Like that businessman yesterday:
he woke her up early, kissed her ("I'd stay with you, baby,
here in Torino, if I could"), and took her with him
to the station to see him off.

                    She was amazed, but now
she feels fresh, and she loves having the morning to herself,
drinking milk and eating her brioches. This morning
she's almost a lady. She sits and watches people going by,
but it's just a way of killing time. Back at the house now
the girls are still sleeping, and the air's so foul—
the madam goes for a walk—it makes you sick to breathe it.
Hustling in the bars at night, you have to look your best.
But back at the house what little is left of your looks
is gone by thirty.

                    Deola sits sideways, profiled in the mirror,
inspecting herself in the cool of the glass. A little
pale in the face maybe: it's not smoking that makes you pale.
And she frowns. If you want to last back there at the house,
you have to have a will like Marí's ("Because, honey, the guys
we hustle are looking for things their wives and lovers
won't give them"). And Marí always worked like a dog,
in good spirits all the time, and nothing wrong with her health.
The people passing her café don't distract Deola now:
now she only works nights, making leisurely conquests
in the music of her usual bar. While giving some john the eye

a un cliente o cercandogli il piede, le piaccion le orchestre
che la fanno parere un'attrice alla scena d'amore
con un giovane ricco. Le basta un cliente
ogni sera e ha da vivere. (*Forse il signore di ieri*
mi portava davvero con sé). Stare sola, se vuole,
al mattino, e sedere al caffè. Non cercare nessuno.

or nudging him with her foot, she likes to listen to the orchestra:
it makes her feel like a movie star in the big love scene
with the young millionaire. One trick a night is all it takes
to make a living. ("Maybe that businessman yesterday will really
take me with him.") Now, in the morning, she can be alone
if she wants, just sitting in the café. No need of anyone.

Due sigarette

Ogni notte è la liberazione. Si guarda i reflessi
dell'asfalto sui corsi che si aprono lucidi al vento.
Ogni rado passante ha una faccia e una storia.
Ma a quest'ora non c'è piú stanchezza: i lampioni a migliaia
sono tutti per chi si sofferma a sfregare un cerino.

La fiammella si spegne sul volto alla donna
che mi ha chiesto un cerino. Si spegne nel vento
e la donna delusa ne chiede un secondo
che si spegne: la donna ora ride sommessa.
Qui possiamo parlare a voce alta e gridare,
ché nessuno ci sente. Leviamo gli sguardi
alle tante finestre—occhi spenti che dormono—
e attendiamo. La donna si stringe le spalle
e si lagna che ha perso la sciarpa a colori
che la notte faceva da stufa. Ma basta appoggiarci
contro l'angolo e il vento non è piú che un soffio.
Sull'asfalto consunto c'è già un mozzicone.
Questa sciarpa veniva da Rio, ma dice la donna
che è contenta d'averla perduta, perché mi ha incontrato.
Se la sciarpa veniva da Rio, è passata di notte
sull'oceano inondato di luce dal gran transatlantico.
Certo, notti di vento. È il regalo di un suo marinaio.
Non c'è piú il marinaio. La donna bisbiglia
che, se salgo con lei, me ne mostra il ritratto
ricciolino e abbronzato. Viaggiava su sporchi vapori
e puliva le macchine: io sono piú bello.

Sull'asfalto c'è due mozziconi. Guardiamo nel cielo:
la finestra là in alto—mi addita la donna—è la nostra.
Ma lassú non c'è stufa. La notte, i vapori sperduti
hanno pochi fanali o soltanto le stelle.
Traversiamo l'asfalto a braccetto, giocando a scaldarci.

Two Cigarettes

Every night is freedom: reflections on the pavement
in the streets which open wide, gleaming in the wind.
Hardly anyone around. Now everybody has a history, a face.
This late no one is tired: streetlights by the thousands shine
only for those who stop and rummage for a match.

The spurt of light vanishes from the face of the woman
who asked me for a match. The wind snuffs the flame.
Disappointed, the woman asks me for another,
which also goes out. The woman chuckles softly.
Nights like this you can talk out loud, even shout,
no one will hear you. We raise our eyes and look up
at all the windows above us—eyes snuffed in sleep—
and we wait. The woman shivers, hugging herself
and complaining she's lost the scarf she used to wear
to keep warm at night. All we have to do is lean
against the corner, and the wind dies down to nothing.
One butt is already lying there on the worn pavement.
This scarf of hers, the woman is saying, came from Rio,
but she doesn't mind losing it because now she's met me.
If the scarf came from Rio, it must have come at night
across the ocean—windy nights like this—drenched
with light by the great liner. It was a gift from a sailor.
No, she doesn't see him now. If I come up to her room,
the woman whispers to me, she'll show me a snapshot of him—
tanned and curly-headed. He shipped on dirty tramps
and kept the engines clean. But I'm better-looking.

Two butts on the pavement now. We look up at the sky.
That window at the top—the woman points—is ours. But
it isn't heated. At night, in the wake of the passing liners,
a few lights shine or only the stars. Playfully,
arm in arm, we cross the pavement, each warming the other.

Dopo

La collina è distesa e la pioggia l'impregna in silenzio.

Piove sopra le case: la breve finestra
s'è riempita di un verde piú fresco e piú nudo.
La compagna era stesa con me: la finestra
era vuota, nessuno guardava, eravamo ben nudi.
Il suo corpo segreto cammina a quest'ora per strada
col suo passo, ma il ritmo è piú molle; la pioggia
scende come quel passo, leggera e spossata.
La compagna non vede la nuda collina
assopita nell'umidità: passa in strada
e la gente che l'urta non sa.

                    Verso sera
la collina è percorsa da brani di nebbia,
la finestra ne accoglie anche il fiato. La strada
a quest'ora è deserta; la sola collina
ha una vita remota nel corpo piú cupo.
Giacevamo spossati nell'umidità
dei due corpi, ciascuno assopito sull'altro.

Una sera piú dolce, di tiepido sole
e di freschi colori, la strada sarebbe una gioia.
È una gioia passare per strada, godendo
un ricordo del corpo, ma tutto diffuso d'intorno.

Nelle foglie dei viali, nel passo indolente di donne,
nelle voci di tutti, c'è un po' della vita
che i due corpi han scordato ma è pure un miracolo,
E scoprire giú in fondo a una via la collina
tra le case, e guardarla e pensare che insieme
la compagna la guardi, dalla breve finestra.

Dentro il buio è affondata la nuda collina
e la pioggia bisbiglia. Non c'è la compagna
che ha portato con sé il corpo dolce e il sorriso.
Ma domani nel cielo lavato dall'alba
la compagna uscirà per le strade, leggera
del suo passo. Potremo incontrarci, volendo.

Afterwards

The rain falls silently, fertilizing the sprawling hill.

It rains on the houses: the little window is filled
with a greenness more naked, a fresher green.
My girl lay sprawled beside me: the window
was empty, no one was watching, and we were naked.
Now her body's hidden, walking down the street
as she usually walks, but more gently. The rain
falls like her footsteps, languidly, softly.
My girl isn't looking at the naked hillside
drowsing in the dampness: she walks through the street
jostled by people she doesn't know.

                          Toward night
the hill is streaked by little patches of fog,
and a breath of fog comes in the window. Now
the street is deserted: in its darkest body
the solitary hill lives a hidden life.
We lay languidly together in the dampness
of two bodies, each one drowsing on the other.

On a brighter afternoon, a day of warm sun
and fresh colors, the street would be a joy.
It's a joy just walking down the street, savoring
the body's memory, and feeling it diffused around you.

In the leaves along the avenues, in the lazy walk of the women,
in everybody's voice, there's a little part of life
which the two bodies have forgotten, but which is still a miracle.
And it's a joy to see the hill loom up at the end of the street
between the houses, to look at it, and think that she's there
looking at it too, from the little window.

The naked hill has slumped down in the darkness,
and the rain is a whisper. My girl's not at my side,
she's gone away with her sweet body and her smile.
But tomorrow in a light scrubbed clean by dawn,
my girl will come strolling down the street, stepping
lightly as she goes. And we can meet, if we desire.

Città in campagna • City in Country

Il tempo passa

Quel vecchione, una volta, seduto sull'erba,
aspettava che il figlio tornasse col pollo
mal strozzato, e gli dava due schiaffi. Per strada
—camminavano all'alba su quelle colline—
gli spiegava che il pollo si strozza con l'unghia
—tra le dita—del pollice, senza rumore.
Nel crepuscolo fresco marciavano sotto le piante
imbottiti di frutta e il ragazzo portava
sulle spalle una zucca giallastra. Il vecchione diceva
che la roba nei campi è di chi ne ha bisogno
tant'è vero che al chiuso non viene. Guardarsi d'attorno
bene prima, e poi scegliere calmi la vite piú nera
e sedersele all'ombra e non muovere fin che si è pieni.

C'è chi mangia dei polli in città. Per le vie
non si trovano i polli. Si trova il vecchiotto
—tutto ciò ch'è rimasto dell'altro vecchione—
che, seduto su un angolo, guarda i passanti
e, chi vuole, gli getta due soldi. Non apre la bocca
il vecchiotto: a dir sempre una cosa, vien sete,
e in città non si trova le botti che versano,
né in ottobre né mai. C'è la griglia dell'oste
che sa puzzo di mosto, specialmente la notte.
Nell'autunno, di notte, il vecchiotto cammina,
ma non ha piú la zucca, e le porte fumose
delle tampe dàn fuori ubriachi che cianciano soli.
È una gente che beve soltanto di notte
(dal mattino ci pensa) e cosí si ubriaca.
Il vecchiotto, ragazzo, beveva tranquillo;
ora, solo annusando, gli balla la barba:
fin che ficca il bastone tra i piedi a uno sbronzo
che va in terra. Lo aiuta a rialzarsi, gli vuota le tasche
(qualche volta allo sbronzo è avanzato qualcosa),
e alle due lo buttano fuori anche lui
dalla tampa fumosa, che canta, che sgrida
e che vuole la zucca e distendersi sotto la vite.

The old gent's seen better days. Once, he was sitting
in clover. His boy had brought him a chicken, badly strangled, still
squawking, and he knocked the kid around. Later, on the road—
they were strolling along the hills at dawn—he explained:
you press against the throat, hard, with the nail of your thumb
between the fingers, so. That way, there's no squawking.
They were tramping along in the first cool light, the vines
overhead purple with grapes, and the boy had a yellow gourd
on his shoulder. The fruits of the field are yours for the taking—
that's what the old man used to say—so long as you need to eat,
and the gate isn't locked. First, make certain nobody's
looking. Take your time, pick yourself the lushest grapes,
then settle down in the shade of the vine. Stay put, eat. Eat
your fill.

      City folk eat chicken. But you won't find
chickens scratching in the streets. You find a little old man—
all that's left of the old gent who was sitting pretty—
squatting at the corner, looking at people passing. Looking,
not asking. People can give or not, as they please. The old man
doesn't open his mouth, no need to say it, he's thirsty,
and barrels of wine in the city don't flow for free,
not in October, not ever. The tavern has a huge iron
grate, and a musty smell of new wine, especially at night.
Nights in October, the old gent still goes for a stroll,
but he doesn't have his gourd, and the door of the murky tavern
only opens to heave out drunks, maundering and mumbling
to themselves. They're a sad lot, bums who only drink at night
(all day long they dream of wine): that's why they're drunks.
In younger days when the old man drank, he felt relaxed, easy;
now, at the first whiff of wine, his beard chatters so badly
he can't stop, he pokes his stick in front of a drunk,
who falls flat. The old man picks his pockets, helping him up
(sometimes even a drunk has a little change left over),
and at 2 a.m. when the murky tavern throws out the drunks,
he's there with the other bums, he's singing and shouting:
all he wants is his gourd, he wants to sleep, under the vine.

Gente che non capisce

Sotto gli alberi della stazione si accendono i lumi.
Gella sa che a quest'ora sua madre ritorna dai prati
col grembiale rigonfio. In attesa del treno,
Gella guarda tra il verde e sorride al pensiero
di fermarsi anche lei, tra i fanali, a raccogliere l'erba.

Gella sa che sua madre da giovane è stata in città
una volta: lei tutte le sere col buio ne parte
e sul treno ricorda vetrine specchianti
e persone che passano e non guardano in faccia.
La città di sua madre è un cortile rinchiuso
tra muraglie, e la gente s'affaccia ai balconi.
Gella torna ogni sera con gli occhi distratti
di colori e di voglie, e spaziando dal treno
pensa, al ritmo monotono, netti profili di vie
tra le luci, a colline percorse di viali e di vita
e gaiezze di giovani, schietti nel passo e nel riso padrone.

Gella è stufa di andare e venire, e tornare la sera
e non vivere né tra le case né in mezzo alle vigne.
La città la vorrebbe su quelle colline,
luminosa, segreta, e non muoversi piú.
Cosí, è troppo diversa. Alla sera ritrova
i fratelli, che tornano scalzi da qualche fatica,
e la madre abbronzata, e si parla di terre
e lei siede in silenzio. Ma ancora ricorda
che, bambina, tornava anche lei col suo fascio dell'erba:
solamente, quelli erano giochi. E la madre che suda
a raccogliere l'erba, perché da trent'anni
l'ha raccolta ogni sera, potrebbe una volta
ben restarsene in casa. Nessuno la cerca.

Anche Gella vorrebbe restarsene, sola, nei prati,
ma raggiungere i piú solitari, e magari nei boschi.
E aspettare la sera e sporcarsi nell'erba

People Who Don't Understand

Under the trees by the station the lights flick on. Dusk.
And Gella thinks of her mother coming back from the fields now,
her apron full of wild greens. While she waits for the train,
Gella glances down at the stretch of green, amused at the thought
of stooping there herself, under the lights, and picking wild greens.

Gella's mother went to the city as a girl, she only went
once. Gella leaves the city every night. Sitting there
on the train, she remembers: windows shining with reflections,
and streets, and people passing by who never look you
in the face. Her mother's city is a courtyard with high walls
around it, all balconies filled with people, and faces
appearing. Every night, going home, her eyes are a daze
of colors and desires, and she sits there in the monotonous clack
of the moving train, dreaming of avenues running straight and clean
between their borders of lights, of hills crisscrossed with streets,
and life in the city, so gay and good, and all the charming young men
with their honest way of walking and their poise when they laugh.

Gella's fed up with always coming and going, of going back
at night, of always living somewhere in between, neither apartments,
nor vineyards. She'd like a city, she'd set it on those hills
and let it shine, her own private city. And she'd stay there, always.
Now, it's like two different lives. She gets back home at night
to find her brothers coming back from their chores, barefoot,
and her mother all brown with sun, and they talk about the fields
while she sits there, silent. She remembers when she was a girl,
coming back home at dusk with her little bundle of grass.
That was make-believe. It's hard work picking greens, harder still
when you've picked them every night for thirty years. But suppose.
Suppose her mother didn't always have to go and pick greens,
what if she just stayed home? Suppose she isn't needed? Everyone
leaves her alone.

That's what Gella wants. She wants to be alone
in the fields, in the loneliest, wildest places, even the woods.
She'd wait until night, then wallow around in the grass,

e magari nel fango e mai piú ritornare in città.
Non far nulla, perché non c'è nulla che serva a nessuno.
Come fanno le capre strappare soltanto le foglie piú verdi
e impregnarsi i capelli, sudati e bruciati,
di rugiada notturna. Indurirsi le carni
e annerirle e strapparsi le vesti, cosí che in città
non la vogliano piú. Gella è stufa di andare e venire
e sorride al pensiero di entrare in città
sfigurata e scomposta. Finché le colline e le vigne
non saranno scomparse, e potrà passeggiare
per i viali, dov'erano i prati, le sere, ridendo,
Gella avrà queste voglie, guardando dal treno.

even the mud. She'll never go back to the city. What she'd like
is doing nothing. What's the use of doing anything, for anyone?
She'll live like a goat, she'll only eat the greenest shoots,
she won't wash, her hair will be all sweat, bleached with sun,
dripping with dew. She'll let her body harden, her skin
turn brown, she'll strip herself stark naked, so nobody in the city
will ever want her again. Gella's fed up with coming and going,
she likes the thought of someday showing up in the city
all dirty and disheveled. So long as those hills and vineyards
last, so long as she can still go strolling down those avenues
where the fields used to be, at late afternoon, laughing,
that will be what she wants, as she stares from the window.

Casa in costruzione

Coi canneti è scomparsa anche l'ombra. Già il sole, di sghembo
attraversa le arcate e si sfoga per vuoti
che saranno finestre. Lavorano un po' i muratori,
fin che dura il mattino. Ogni tanto rimpiangono
quando qui ci frusciavano ancora le canne,
e un passante accaldato poteva gettarsi sull'erba.

I ragazzi cominciano a giungere a sole piú alto.
Non lo temono il caldo. I pilastri isolati nel cielo
sono un campo di gioco migliore che gli alberi
o la solita strada. I mattoni scoperti
si riempion d'azzurro, per quando le volte
saran chiuse, e ai ragazzi è una gioia vedersi dal fondo
sopra il capo i riquadri di cielo. Peccato il sereno,
ché un rovescio di pioggia lassú da quei vuoti
piacerebbe ai ragazzi. Sarebbe un lavare la casa.

Certamente stanotte—poterci venire—era meglio:
la rugiada bagnava i mattoni e, distesi tra i muri,
si vedevan le stelle. Magari potevano accendere
un bel fuoco e qualcuno assalirli e pigliarsi a sassate.
Una pietra di notte può uccidere senza rumore.
Poi ci sono le biscie che scendono i muri
e che cadono come una pietra, soltanto piú molli.

Cosa accada di notte là dentro, lo sa solo il vecchio
che al mattino si vede discendere per le colline.
Lascia braci di fuoco là dentro e ha la barba strinata
dalla vampa e ha già preso tant'acqua, che, come il terreno,
non potrebbe cambiare colore. Fa ridere tutti

House under Construction

When they cleared the cane-brake, the shade went too. Now, the
    early light
slants in across the passageways, spilling out the blank holes
they've left for windows. The masons don't work long,
only the morning hours. You can hear them grumbling. Remember
how it used to be? When the whole grove rustled with shade,
and a man could stretch out in the grass? Away from that fierce
    sun?

The sun is higher when the boys start trooping in.
Kids aren't afraid of the heat. The piers standing there naked
against the sky make a better playground than trees
or the same old street. You can see the bare red bricks,
with blue sky between. It won't be long before they're hidden
by the roof. And the kids like standing there looking up
at the squares of sky overhead. It's too bad the weather's
good. The boys would love to see the rain sloshing down
between those holes. Rain would be like washing the house, making it
    clean.

One thing's sure, if they could have come last night,
night's the time to come. The bricks are wet with dew, they could
    have stretched out
flat on their backs, between the walls, looking up at the stars
overhead. Maybe they could have built a big bonfire even,
right there in the house, maybe somebody would have gotten fighting
    mad
and showered them with stones. A stone at night can kill—
and not a sound. There are snakes too, tree snakes
that climb the walls, and drop like a stone, but softer.

What really happens there at night, only the old man knows.
Mornings, you see him slowly walking back down along the hills.
You find the ashes of his fire inside, and his beard's all singed
from the flame. Rain and dew have weathered him, he's like the
    earth, so dark
he couldn't change color even if he wanted. The kids all laugh

perché dice che gli altri si fanno la casa
col sudore e lui senza sudare ci dorme. Ma un vecchio
non dovrebbe durare alla notte scoperta.
Si capisce una coppia in un prato: c'è l'uomo e la donna
che si tengono stretti, e poi tornano a casa.
Ma quel vecchio non ha piú una casa e si muove a fatica.
Certamente qualcosa gli accade là dentro,
perché ancora al mattino borbotta tra sé.

Dopo un po' i muratori si buttano all'ombra.
È il momento che il sole ha investito ogni cosa
e un mattone a toccarlo ci scotta le mani.
S'è già visto una biscia piombare fuggendo
nella pozza di calce: è il momento che il caldo
fa impazzire perfino le bestie. Si beve una volta
e si vedono le altre colline ogn'intorno, bruciate,
tremolare nel sole. Soltanto uno scemo
resterebbe al lavoro e difatti quel vecchio
a quest'ora traversa le vigne, rubando le zucche.
Poi ci sono i ragazzi sui ponti, che salgono e scendono.
Una volta una pietra è finita sul cranio
del padrone e hanno tutti interrotto il lavoro
per portarlo al torrente e lavargli la faccia.

when he tells them other men have to sweat to build a house,
and he sleeps in the house and never sweats. But he's getting on,
he can't last forever, not lying there all night out in the open.
It's not like it is with lovers. A man and woman, they lie there
in the grass, all wrapped around each other, and then they go home.
But the old man doesn't have a house, not now, and it hurts him
to walk. Something happens to him in there at night.
Something *must* happen, or he wouldn't still be mumbling to himself
come morning.

      Soon the masons are sprawled in whatever shade
they can find. The sun's everywhere now, it's beating down
like crazy. The bricks are so hot they burn your hand.
Somebody startled a snake, which slithered off and fell
with a soft plop into the lime-pit below. This is the hour
when the heat drives animals mad. You take a gulp of wine
and look at the hills around you everywhere, all scorched
and trembling in the sun. Only a damned fool
would keep on working. As a matter of fact, the old man's trudging
through the vineyards this very minute, stealing the pumpkins.
And the boys are still at it, there on the scaffolding, climbing
up and down. At one point a stone dropped and hit the boss
on the head, and they all knocked off work for a spell.
They took him down to the river and washed away the blood.

Papà beve al tavolo avvolto da pergole verdi
e il ragazzo s'annoia seduto. Il cavallo s'annoia
posseduto da mosche: il ragazzo vorrebbe acchiapparne,
ma Papà l'ha sott'occhio. Le pergole dànno nel vuoto
sulla valle. Il ragazzo non guarda piú al fondo,
perché ha voglia di fare un gran salto. Alza gli occhi:
non c'è piú belle nuvole: gli ammassi splendenti
si son chiusi a nascondere il fresco del cielo.

Si lamenta, Papà, che ci sia da patire piú caldo
nella gita per vendere l'uva, che a mietere il grano.
Chi ha mai visto in settembre quel sole rovente
e doversi fermare al ritorno, dall'oste,
altrimenti gli crepa il cavallo. Ma l'uva è venduta;
qualcun altro ci pensa, di qui alla vendemmia:
se anche grandina, il prezzo è già fatto. Il ragazzo s'annoia,
il suo sorso Papà gliel'ha già fatto bere.
Non c'è piú che guardare quel bianco maligno,
sotto il nero dell'afa, e sperare nell'acqua.

Le vie fresche di mezza mattina eran piene di portici
e di gente. Gridavano in piazza. Girava il gelato
bianco e rosa: pareva le nuvole sode nel cielo.
Se faceva sto caldo in città, si fermavano a pranzo
nell'albergo. La polvere e il caldo non sporcano i muri
in città: lungo i viali le case son bianche.
Il ragazzo alza gli occhi alle nuvole orribili.
In città stanno al fresco a far niente, ma comprano l'uva,
la lavorano in grandi cantine e diventano ricchi.
Se restavano ancora, vedevano in mezzo alle piante,
nella sera, ogni viale una fila di luci.

Tra le pergole nasce un gran vento. Il cavallo si scuote
e Papà guarda in aria. Laggiú nella valle
c'è la casa nel prato e la vigna matura.

Father's drinking at a table, wrapped in the green of the arbor.
The boy's bored, just sitting around. The horse is bothered
with flies, and the boy's so bored he'd like to catch them,
but he can't, Father's looking. The arbor hangs in empty air,
the valley is miles below. The boy can't look down
any more, he knows he'd feel like jumping. So he looks up,
and the wonderful clouds are gone, all those glorious billowing masses
have come together, solid, shutting out the blue of the sky.

Father's grumbling to himself. This damn heat's worse
when you're out selling grapes than getting in the wheat.
Never knew a September like this, sun's so scorching hot
you have to stop at a country tavern on your way home
so you don't drive the nag to death. But the grapes are sold;
from now till harvest, the grapes are somebody else's worry.
So what if it hails; he's got his price. The boy's bored,
the little drink his father bought him is long since gone.
There's nothing to do, nothing but sit there looking at that ugly
white sky, and the black haze overhead, hoping for rain.

This morning the streets were cool, full of porticoes
and people. Peddlers shouting in the square. And carts of ice cream:
great scoops of pink and white, piled up like clouds in the sky.
In the city, in weather like this, they would have had lunch
at the hotel. And the walls in the city aren't all grimy
with dust and heat. The houses on the avenues are white.
The boy looks at the clouds, they're really getting scary.
Rain or shine, city people just stand around, not doing anything,
buying up the grapes, putting them in bottles, and getting rich.
If they stayed overnight, he would have seen, row after row,
through the leaves, at night, every avenue a blaze of lights.

A stiff wind stirs in the trellis. The horse shivers,
and Father inspects the sky. Way down below in the valley,
he can see their house, with the vineyards ripening and the meadow.

Tutt'a un tratto fa freddo e le foglie si staccano
e la polvere vola. Papà beve sempre.
Il ragazzo alza gli occhi alle nuvole orribili.
Sulla valle c'è ancora una chiazza di sole.
Se si fermano qui, mangeranno dall'oste.

All of a sudden, it's cold, the leaves start flying,
and clouds of dust swirl in the air. Father's still drinking.
The boy looks at the clouds, they're really getting scary.
Far below, the valley is still flecked with patches of light.
If they stay on now, they'll get to eat at the tavern.

Atavismo

Il ragazzo respira piú fresco, nascosto
dalle imposte, fissando la strada. Si vedono i ciottoli
per la chiara fessura, nel sole. Nessuno cammina
per la strada. Il ragazzo vorrebbe uscir fuori
cosí nudo—la strada è di tutti—e affogare nel sole.

In città non si può. Si potrebbe in campagna,
se non fosse, sul capo, il profondo del cielo
che atterrisce e avvilisce. C'è l'erba che fredda
fa il solletico ai piedi, ma le piante che guardano
ferme, e i tronchi e i cespugli son occhi severi
per un debole corpo slavato, che trema.
Fino l'erba è diversa e ripugna al contatto.

Ma la strada è deserta. Passasse qualcuno
il ragazzo dal buio oserebbe fissarlo
e pensare che tutti nascondono un corpo.
Passa invece un cavallo dai muscoli grossi
e rintronano i ciottoli. Da tempo il cavallo
se ne va, nudo e senza ritegno, nel sole:
tantoché marcia in mezzo alla strada. Il ragazzo
che vorrebbe esser forte a quel modo a annerito
e magari tirare a quel carro, oserebbe mostrarsi.

Se si ha un corpo, bisogna vederlo. Il ragazzo non sa
se ciascuno abbia un corpo. Il vecchiotto rugoso
che passava al mattino, non può avere un corpo
cosí pallido e triste, non può avere nulla
che atterrisca a quel modo. E nemmeno gli adulti
o le spose che dànno la poppa al bambino
sono nudi. Hanno un corpo soltanto i ragazzi.
Il ragazzo non osa guardarsi nel buio,
ma sa bene che deve affogare nel sole
e abituarsi agli sguardi del cielo, per crescere uomo.

Atavism

Hidden behind the shutters, watching the street,
the boy breathes more easily. Through the bright
chink, he can see the cobbles in the sun. Nobody
in the street. The boy would like to go outside stark
naked—who owns the street?—and soak up the sun.

In the city you can't. You could in the country,
if it weren't for the huge sky overhead, which is scary
and makes you feel small. The grass is cold
and tickles your feet, but the plants just
stare, and the trees and shrubs look so sternly
at your white, skinny body that it makes you shiver.
Even the grass feels funny and shrinks from your touch.

But the street's empty. If someone went by,
the boy would stare boldly out of the darkness
and think to himself that everyone has a body.
But a horse with rippling muscles goes plodding by,
making the cobbles clatter. It seemed forever—
the horse moving naked and shameless in the sun
right down the middle of the street. A boy
who wanted to be brown and strong as a horse
and even pull a wagon, wouldn't be afraid of being seen.

People with bodies shouldn't hide them. But the boy
isn't sure everyone has a body. The grizzled
old man who went by that morning is too pale and pitiful
to have a body, to have anything as scary
as a body. And not even grown-ups are naked;
not even mothers who give their breasts to their babies
are really bare. Only boys have bodies.
The boy's afraid to look at himself in the dark,
but he knows for a fact his body must soak up the sun
and get used to the sky, before he can be a man.

Sulla nera collina c'è l'alba e sui tetti
s'assopiscono i gatti. Un ragazzo è piombato
giú dal tetto stanotte, spezzandosi il dorso.
Vibra un vento tra gli alberi freschi: le nubi
rosse, in alto, son tiepide e viaggiano lente.
Giú nel vicolo spunta un cagnaccio, che fiuta
il ragazzo sui ciottoli, ma un rauco gnaulío
sale su tra i comignoli: qualcuno è scontento.

Nella notte cantavano i grilli, e le stelle
si spegnevano al vento. Al chiarore dell'alba
si son spenti anche gli occhi dei gatti in amore
che il ragazzo spiava. La gatta, che piange,
è perché non ha gatto. Non c'è nulla che valga
—né le vette degli alberi né le nuvole rosse—:
piange al cielo scoperto, come fosse ancor notte.

Il ragazzo spiava gli amori dei gatti.
Il cagnaccio, che fiuta il suo corpo ringhiando,
è arrivato e non era ancor l'alba: fuggiva
il chiarore dell'altro versante. Nuotando
dentro il fiume che infradicia come nei prati
la rugiada, l'ha colto la luce. Le cagne
ululavano ancora.

        Scorre il fiume tranquillo
e lo schiumano uccelli. Tra le nuvole rosse
piomban giú dalla gioia di trovarlo deserto.

Love Affairs

It's dawn on the black hills, and the cats
drowse on the tiles. A boy fell from the roof
last night and broke his back. The wind
quivers in the cool of the leaves. The red clouds,
high in the sky, are warm and move slowly.
Down in the alley a stray dog's sniffing
the dead boy on the cobbles. But a shrill wail
rises among the tiles: someone's unhappy.

The crickets were chirping all night, and the stars
went out in the breeze. The brightness of dawn
quenches even the eyes of cats in heat—
the cats the boy was watching. The female
was wailing for her tom. Nothing's any use—
not the treetops or the red clouds—she wails
to the bright sky, as if it were still night.

The boy was spying on the cats making love.
The snarling dog nosing the boy's body
was there before dawn. He was running from the light
on the back of the hill when the light caught him
swimming in the river, drenched with water
like a meadow in the morning dew. The bitches
were still howling.

The stream runs smoothly, skimmed
by swallows. Down from the red clouds they dip
in joy at finding the river deserted.

Certo il giorno non trema, a guardarlo. E le case
sono ferme, piantate ai selciati. Il martello
di quell'uomo seduto scalpiccia su un ciottolo
dentro il molle terriccio. Il ragazzo che scappa
al mattino, non sa che quell'uomo lavora,
e si ferma a guardarlo. Nessuno lavora per strada.

L'uomo siede nell'ombra, che cade dall'alto
di una casa, piú fresca che un'ombra di nube,
e non guarda ma tocca i suoi ciottoli assorto.
Il rumore dei ciottoli echeggia lontano
sul selciato velato dal sole. Ragazzi
non ce n'è per le strade. Il ragazzo è ben solo
e s'accorge che tutti sono uomini o donne
che non vedono quel che lui vede e trascorrono svelti.

Ma quell'uomo lavora. Il ragazzo lo guarda,
esitando al pensiero che un uomo lavori
sulla strada, seduto come fanno i pezzenti.
E anche gli altri che passano, paiono assorti
a finire qualcosa e nessuno si guarda
alle spalle o dinanzi, lungo tutta la strada.
Se la strada è di tutti, bisogna goderla
senza fare nient'altro, guardandosi intorno,
ora all'ombra ora al sole, nel fresco leggero.

Ogni via si spalanca che pare una porta,
ma nessuno l'infila. Quell'uomo seduto
non s'accorge nemmeno, come fosse un pezzente,
della gente che viene e che va, nel mattino.

Of course the day doesn't tremble, not so you can see it. And
      the houses
are still, rooted in the pavement. The hammer in the hand
of the man sitting there tamps a cobble down
into the soft dirt below. The kid cutting school
that morning doesn't know the man is working
and stops to look. People don't work in the street.

The man is sitting in the shade that falls from the top
of a house, cooler than a cloud's shadow,
tapping his cobbles, concentrating, not looking.
The pounding of the cobbles echoes in the distance
where the street, in sunlight, shimmers away. There are no
children on the street. The boy's all alone,
he knows nobody else is around but men and women,
who don't see what he sees and rush busily by.

But that man there is working. The boy stops and looks,
struggling with the idea that a man is working
in the street, sitting there like a beggar.
Even the people passing seem to be concentrating
on getting something done. The whole length of the street,
nobody's looking behind him, nobody's looking ahead.
But if the street belongs to everyone, it ought to be enjoyed,
not doing anything else, just looking,
now in sunlight, now in shade, in the crisp air of the morning.

Every street opens out wide like a doorway,
which nobody enters. The man sitting on the street
looks like a beggar, looks like he doesn't see
the people going and coming, in the cool of the morning.

Ulisse

Questo è un vecchio deluso, perché ha fatto suo figlio
troppo tardi. Si guardano in faccia ogni tanto,
ma una volta bastava uno schiaffo. (Esce il vecchio
e ritorna col figlio che si stringe una guancia
e non leva piú gli occhi). Ora il vecchio è seduto
fino a notte, davanti a una grande finestra,
ma non viene nessuno e la strada è deserta.

Stamattina, è scappato il ragazzo, e ritorna
questa notte. Starà sogghignando. A nessuno
vorrà dire se a pranzo ha mangiato. Magari
avrà gli occhi pesanti e andrà letto in silenzio:
due scarponi infangati. Il mattino era azzurro
sulle piogge di un mese.

                    Per la fresca finestra
scorre amaro un sentore di foglie. Ma il vecchio
non si muove dal buio, non ha sonno la notte,
e vorrebbe aver sonno e scordare ogni cosa
come un tempo al ritorno dopo un lungo cammino.
Per scaldarsi, una volta gridava e picchiava.

Il ragazzo, che torna fra poco, non prende piú schiaffi.
Il ragazzo comincia a esser giovane e scopre
ogni giorno qualcosa e non parla a nessuno.

Non c'è nulla per strada che non possa sapersi
stando a questa finestra. Ma il ragazzo cammina
tutto il giorno per strada. Non cerca ancor donne
e non gioca piú in terra. Ogni volta ritorna.
Il ragazzo ha un suo modo di uscire di casa
che, chi resta, s'accorge di non farci piú nulla.

This old man feels cheated and bitter. His son was born
too late. Now and then they look each other in the eyes,
but a slap in the face stops all that. (The old man goes outside,
comes back with the boy holding his cheek in his hand,
his eyes lowered). Now the old man
sits waiting until it's dark in front of the big window,
but the road is empty, nobody's coming.

This morning the boy took off, he'll be back home
tonight. A smile of contempt on his face. And he won't tell
anyone whether he's had his supper or not. No,
his eyes will look tired, he'll go to bed without a word:
a pair of boots spattered with mud. After a month of rain
the morning was blue.

A sharp smell of leaves
flows through the cool of the window. But the old man doesn't
budge in the darkness, he isn't sleepy at night.
And he would love to sleep and forget it all,
the way he used to once, coming home after a long walk.
Once, he kept warm by shouting and slapping himself.

The boy comes home before long. Too big to be beaten,
the boy is turning into a young man, every day
discovering something, and not talking, not to anyone.

There's nothing on that road that can't be seen
by standing at the window. But the boy is walking the road
all day long. Not out looking for women, not yet,
he's done with playing in the mud. He always comes back.
The boy has a way of leaving the house that tells
the man inside he's finished with home, and him, it's over.

Disciplina

I lavori cominciano all'alba. Ma noi cominciamo
un po' prima dell'alba a incontrare noi stessi
nella gente che va per la strada. Ciascuno ricorda
di esser solo e aver sonno, scoprendo i passanti
radi—ognuno trasogna fra sé,
tanto sa che nell'alba spalancherà gli occhi.
Quando viene il mattino ci trova stupiti
a fissare il lavoro che adesso comincia.
Ma non siamo piú soli e nessuno piú ha sonno
e pensiamo con calma i pensieri del giorno
fino a dare in sorrisi. Nel sole che torna
siamo tutti convinti. Ma a volte un pensiero
meno chiaro—un sogghigno—ci coglie improvviso
e torniamo a guardare come prima del sole.
La città chiara assiste ai lavori e ai sogghigni.
Nulla può disturbare il mattino. Ogni cosa
può accadere e ci basta di alzare la testa
dal lavoro e guardare. Ragazzi scappati
che non fanno ancor nulla camminano in strada
e qualcuno anche corre. Le foglie dei viali
gettan ombre per strada e non manca che l'erba,
tra le case che assistono immobili. Tanti
sulla riva del fiume si spogliano al sole.
La città ci permette di alzare la testa
a pensarci, e sa bene che poi la chiniamo.

Discipline

Jobs begin at dawn. But we begin
just before dawn to encounter ourselves
in people walking down the street. Each one remembers
he's alone and sleepy, discovering himself in the few
passersby—each man daydreams to himself, knowing
the dawn light will force his eyes open.
When morning comes, it finds us numbly
staring at the job of work, which now begins.
But now nobody's alone, nobody's sleepy any more,
and we think our daylight thoughts so serenely
we start to smile. That returning sunlight
has us all convinced. But sometimes a thought less bright
and clear—a mocking grin—suddenly surprises us,
and we go back to looking the way we did, before the light.
The bright city watches our working, it sees us grinning.
Nothing can upset the morning. Anything
can happen, all we have to do is raise our heads
from work and watch. Boys skipping school,
who do no work at all, are roaming in the streets,
some of them are running. Along the avenues the leaves
throw shadows on the streets, only grass is missing from
between the houses which watch, not moving. In the sunlight
along the river by the swimming-place, kids are undressing.
The city lets us lift our heads and think
about these things, knowing we'll lower them later.

Le colline insensibili che riempiono il cielo
sono vive nell'alba, poi restano immobili
come fossero secoli, e il sole le guarda.
Ricoprirle di verde sarebbe una gioia
e nel verde, disperse, le frutta e le case.
Ogni pianta nell'alba sarebbe una vita
prodigiosa e le nuvole avrebbero un senso.

Non ci manca che un mare a risplendere forte
e inondare la spiaggia in un ritmo monotono.
Su dal mare non sporgono piante, non muovono foglie:
quando piove sul mare, ogni goccia è perduta,
come il vento su queste colline, che cerca le foglie
e non trova che pietre. Nell'alba, è un istante:
si disegnano in terra le sagome nere
e le chiazze vermiglie. Poi torna il silenzio.

Hanno un senso le coste buttate nel cielo
come case di grande città? Sono nude.
Passa a volte un villano stagliato nel vuoto,
cosí assurdo che pare passeggi su un tetto
di città. Viene in mente la sterile mole
delle case ammucchiate, che prende la pioggia
e si asciuga nel sole e non dà un filo d'erba.

Per coprire le case e le pietre di verde
—sí che il cielo abbia un senso—bisogna affondare
dentro il buio radici ben nere. Al tornare dell'alba
scorrerebbe la luce fin dentro la terra
come un urto. Ogni sangue sarebbe piú vivo:
anche i corpi son fatti di vene nerastre.
E i villani che passano avrebbero un senso.

Landscape V

These hard, unfeeling hills that fill the sky
come alive at dawn, but then are still
for centuries, it seems, while the sun watches them.
What a joy to cover them with green again,
to scatter houses and fruit trees among the green.
At dawn each tree would be a miracle
of life, the clouds would have a meaning.

The only thing missing would be a sea to shine
flooding the shore with its insistent moving.
Trees don't sprout from the sea, leaves don't move.
When it rains at sea, the drops disappear
like the wind on these hills: it looks for leaves
but all it finds is stones. Briefly, at dawn,
the black silhouettes and the ruddy stains
make shapes on the ground. Then silence again.

These slopes thrusting into the sky like buildings
in big cities—do they have a meaning? They're naked.
Now and then a peasant passes, profiled so absurdly
in the void he seems to be walking on a city
roof. And he brings to mind that barren pile
of huddled buildings, which the rain drenches
and the sun dries, but which never grow a blade of grass.

To cover the buildings and stones with green—
so the sky would have a meaning—black black roots
would have to thrust down in the darkness. At dawn
the light would run deep down into the earth,
like a blow. All blood would come alive:
bodies too are made of blackish veins.
And the peasants passing would have a meaning.

Indisciplina

L'ubriaco si lascia alle spalle le case stupite.
Mica tutti alla luce del sole si azzardano
a passare ubriachi. Traversa tranquillo la strada,
e potrebbe infilarsi nei muri, ché i muri ci stanno.
Solo un cane trascorre a quel modo, ma un cane si ferma
ogni volta che sente la cagna e la fiuta con cura.
L'ubriaco non guarda nessuno, nemmeno le donne.

Per la strada la gente, stravolta a guardarlo, non ride
e non vuole che sia l'ubriaco, ma i molti che inciampano
per seguirlo con gli occhi, riguardano innanzi
imprecando. Passato che c'è l'ubriaco,
tutta quanta la strada si muove piú lenta
nella luce del sole. Qualcuno che corre
come prima, è qualcuno che non sarà mai l'ubriaco.
Gli altri fissano, senza distinguere, il cielo e le case
che continuano a esserci, se anche nessuno li vede.

L'ubriaco non vede né case né cielo,
ma li sa, perché a passo malfermo percorre uno spazio
netto come le striscie di cielo. La gente impacciata
non comprende piú a cosa ci stiano le case,
e le donne non guardano gli uomini. Tutti
hanno come paura che a un tratto la voce
rauca scoppi a cantare e li segua nell'aria.

Ogni casa ha una porta, ma è inutile entrarci.
L'ubriaco non canta, ma tiene una strada
dove l'unico ostacolo è l'aria. Fortuna
che di là non c'è il mare, perché l'ubriaco
camminando tranquillo entrerebbe anche in mare
e, scomparso, terrebbe sul fondo lo stesso cammino.
Fuori, sempre, la luce sarebbe la stessa.

Lack of Discipline

The drunk leaves stunned houses behind him.
It's risky passing a drunk in broad daylight,
not everyone dares. He quietly crosses the street, he could slide
right into the walls—that's what the wall is for.
Dogs sidle along like that, but a dog stops
when he smells a bitch, stops and smells her all over.
The drunk isn't looking at anybody, not even women.

On the street heads turn and stare. Nobody laughs,
nobody wants to be the drunk. Everyone's following him,
all eyes, that's why so many are stumbling and cursing,
then looking straight ahead. Once the drunk is gone,
the whole street moves along in the bright sunlight,
but slowly, more slowly than before. A man who rushes along
the way he was rushing before—he'll never be the drunk.
The others stare, they don't see houses or sky,
which go right on being, whether anyone's looking or not.

The drunk doesn't see sky or houses, but he knows
they're there. He weaves and staggers, but the space he walks
is straight as the band of blue overhead. Everyone's
embarrassed, people no longer know what houses are for,
the women won't look at the men. They're all somehow
afraid. A husky voice might suddenly start singing,
they're afraid the voice might follow them, in the air.

Every house has a door, but there's no point going in.
The drunk isn't singing, he's headed down a road
where the only obstacle's air. A good thing for him
the sea isn't in his way. The drunk would keep on going,
he'd walk into the water, calm as you please, he'd sink
and keep right on, lurching his way along the bottom.
Outside, the light would be what it was, always.

Ritratto d'autore

a Leone

La finestra che guarda il selciato sprofonda
sempre vuoto. L'azzurro d'estate, sul capo,
pare invece piú fermo e vi spunta una nuvola.
Qui non spunta nessuno. E noi siamo seduti per terra.

Il collega—che puzza—seduto con me
sulla pubblica strada, senza muovere il corpo
s'è levato i calzoni. Io mi levo la maglia.
Sulla pietra fa un gelo e il collega lo gode
piú di me che lo guardo, ma non passa nessuno.
La finestra di botto contiene una donna
color chiaro. Magari ha sentito quel puzzo
e ci guarda. Il collega è già in piedi che fissa.
Ha una barba, il collega, dalle gambe alla faccia,
che gli scusa i calzoni e germoglia tra i buchi
della maglia. È una barba che basta da sola.
Il collega è saltato per quella finestra,
dentro il buio, e la donna è scomparsa. Mi scappano gli occhi
alla striscia del cielo bel solido, nudo anche lui.

Io non puzzo perché non ho barba. Mi gela, la pietra,
questa mia schiena nuda che piace alle donne
perché è liscia: che cosa non piace alle donne?
Ma non passano donne. Passa invece la cagna
inseguita da un cane che ha preso la pioggia
tanto puzza. La nuvola liscia, nel cielo,
guarda immobile: pare un ammasso di foglie.
Il collega ha trovato la cena stavolta.
Trattan bene, le donne, chi è nudo. Compare
finalmente alla svolta un gorbetta che fuma.
Ha le gambe d'anguilla anche lui, testa riccia,
pelle dura: le donne vorranno spogliarlo
un bel giorno e annusare se puzza di buono.
Quando è qui, stendo un piede. Va subito in terra
e gli chiedo una cicca. Fumiamo in silenzio.

Portrait of the Author

for Leone Ginzburg

The window looking down at the pavement
is always empty. The blue of summer overhead
seems more solid somehow, there's a cloud passing through.
Nobody passes here. And we're sitting in the street.

My friend—who smells—is sitting beside me
on the public street. Somehow, without moving his body,
he's taken off his pants. I take off my sweater.
The cobbles under us are freezing cold, and my friend likes it
more than me. I'm watching him, but nobody's watching us.
Suddenly the window has a woman in it:
bright color. Maybe she got a whiff of that smell
and came to see. My chum is on his feet, staring back.
He's shaggy, my friend, hair from his legs to his face.
He doesn't need pants, what with all that hair
sticking through the holes in his sweater.
My chum jumped in through the hole of the window,
into the darkness, and the woman vanished. My eyes move up
to the beautiful band of solid sky. It's naked too.

I don't smell, I'm not hairy. The cobbles make me cold,
and women like the feel of my naked back
because it's so smooth: is there anything women don't like?
But there aren't any women. There's only a bitch in heat
followed by a male dog soaked to the skin, so wet
he stinks. The smooth cloud up in the sky
looks down, not moving: it looks like a pile of leaves.
My chum has gotten himself a good meal tonight.
Women are good to a man when he's naked. At last,
a kid comes walking around the corner, he's smoking.
He has legs like me, legs like an eel, curly hair,
and rough skin. Someday the women will want to undress him,
they'll sniff him to see if he has a serious smell.
He walks by, and I stick out my foot. He trips and falls,
and I ask for a butt. We sit there smoking, not a word.

Grappa a settembre

I mattini trascorrono chiari e deserti
sulle rive del fiume, che all'alba s'annebbia
e incupisce il suo verde, in attesa del sole.
Il tabacco, che vendono nell'ultima casa
ancor umida, all'orlo dei prati, ha un colore
quasi nero e un sapore sugoso: vapora azzurrino.
Tengon anche la grappa, colore dell'acqua.

È venuto un momento che tutto si ferma
e matura. Le piante lontano stan chete:
sono fatte piú scure. Nascondono frutti
che a una scossa cadrebbero. Le nuvole sparse
hanno polpe mature. Lontano, sui corsi,
ogni casa matura al tepore del cielo.

Non si vede a quest'ora che donne. Le donne non fumano
e non bevono, sanno soltanto fermarsi nel sole
e riceverlo tiepido addosso, come fossero frutta.
L'aria, cruda di nebbia, si beve a sorsate
come grappa, ogni cosa vi esala un sapore.
Anche l'acqua del fiume ha bevuto le rive
e le macera al fondo, nel cielo. Le strade
sono come le donne, maturano ferme.

A quest'ora ciascuno dovrebbe fermarsi
per la strada e guardare come tutto maturi.
C'è persino una brezza, che non smuove le nubi,
ma che basta a dirigere il fumo azzurrino
senza romperlo: è un nuovo sapore che passa.
E il tabacco va intinto di grappa. È cosí che le donne
non saranno le sole a godere il mattino.

Grappa in September

The mornings run their course, bright and deserted
along the river's banks, which at dawn turn foggy,
darkening their green, while they wait for the sun.
In the last house, still damp, at the field's edge,
they sell tobacco, which is blackish in color
and tastes of sugar: it gives off a bluish haze.
They have grappa there too, the color of water.

There comes a moment when everything stands still
and ripens. The trees in the distance are quiet,
their darkness deepens, concealing fruit so ripe
it would drop at a touch. The scattered clouds
are swollen and ripe. Far away, in city streets,
every house is mellowing in the mild air.

This early, you see only women. The women don't smoke,
or drink. All they can do is stand in the sunlight,
letting it warm their bodies, as if they were fruit.
The air, raw with fog, has to be swallowed in sips,
like grappa. Everything here distills its own fragrance.
Even the water in the river has absorbed the banks,
steeping them to their depths in the soft air. The streets
are like women. They ripen standing still.

This is the time when every man should stand
still in the street and see how everything ripens.
There's even a breeze, which doesn't move the clouds
but somehow succeeds in maneuvering the bluish haze
without scattering it. The smell drifting by is a new smell,
the tobacco is tinged with grappa. So it seems
the women aren't the only ones to enjoy the morning.

Balletto

È un gigante che passa volgendosi appena,
quando attende una donna, e non sembra che attenda.
Ma non fa mica apposta: lui fuma e la gente lo guarda.

Ogni donna che va con quest'uomo è una bimba
che si addossa a quel corpo ridendo, stupita
della gente che guarda. Il gigante s'avvia
e la donna è una parte di tutto il suo corpo,
solamente piú viva. La donna non conta,
ogni sera è diversa, ma sempre una piccola
che ridendo contiene il culetto che danza.

Il gigante non vuole un culetto che danzi
per la strada, e pacato lo porta a sedersi
ogni sera alla sfida e la donna è contenta.
Alla sfida, la donna è stordita dagli urli
e, guardando il gigante, ritorna bambina.
Dai due pugilatori si sentono i tonfi
dei saltelli e dei pugni, ma pare che danzino
cosí nudi allacciati, e la donna li fissa
con gli occhietti e si morde le labbra contenta.
Si abbandona al gigante e ritorna bambina:
è un piacere appoggiarsi a una rupe che accoglie.

Se la donna e il gigante si spogliano insieme
—lo faranno piú tardi—il gigante somiglia
alla placidità di una rupe, una rupe bruciante,
e la bimba, a scaldarsi, si stringe a quel masso.

Ballet

A giant going by, he hardly turns around
when he's waiting for a woman. And he doesn't seem to be waiting.
But he doesn't do it on purpose. He smokes, and people stare.

Every woman who goes with this man is a little girl.
She snuggles up to that body of his, laughing with surprise
at all the people staring. The giant moves away,
and the woman might be part of his body—she's just
more frisky. The woman doesn't matter,
she's different every night, but she's always small,
she likes to laugh, and her little bottom dances when she walks.

The giant doesn't want a bottom dancing down
the street, so every night he takes it quietly off
to a seat at the fights. The woman doesn't mind.
All that yelling at the fights startles the woman,
she looks at the giant, becomes a girl again.
She can hear the thudding fists, the boxers skipping
and bobbing, but it looks to her like they're dancing, dancing naked,
cheek to cheek, and the woman just stares
with her big little eyes, biting her lips. She's happy.
She surrenders to the giant, becomes a girl again.
It's good to snuggle against a rock, a cliff that cradles.

If the woman and the giant take off their clothes together—
later on they'll get undressed—the giant looks like
a huge cliff of comfortable rock, ruddy with light.
The woman's hugging the cliff, she wants to be warm.

Paternità

Fantasia della donna che balla, e del vecchio
che è suo padre e una volta l'aveva nel sangue
e l'ha fatta una notte, godendo in un letto, bel nudo.
Lei s'affretta per giungere in tempo a svestirsi,
e ci sono altri vecchi che attendono. Tutti
le divorano, quando lei salta a ballare, la forza
delle gambe con gli oochi, ma i vecchi ci tremano.
Quasi nuda è la giovane. E i giovani guardano
con sorrisi, e qualcuno vorrebbe esser nudo.

Sembran tutti suo padre i vecchiotti entusiasti
e son tutti, malfermi, un avanzo di corpo
che ha goduto altri corpi. Anche i giovani un giorno
saran padri, e la donna è per tutti una sola.
È accaduto in silenzio. Una gioia profonda˙
prende il buio davanti alla giovane viva.
Tutti i corpi non sono che un corpo, uno solo
che si muove inchiodando gli sguardi di tutti.

Questo sangue, che scorre le membra diritte
della giovane, è il sangue che gela nei vecchi;
e suo padre che fuma in silenzio, a scaldarsi,
lui non salta, ma ha fatto la figlia che balla.
C'è un sentore e uno scatto nel corpo di lei
che è lo stesso nel vecchio, e nei vecchi. In silenzio
fuma il padre e l'attende che ritorni, vestita.
Tutti attendono, giovani e vecchi, e la fissano;
e ciascuno, bevendo da solo, ripenserà a lei.

Fatherhood

Fantasy of the dancing woman and the old man
who made her, who once had her in his blood, who fathered her
one night in bed, stark naked, with pleasure and joy.
She hurries, she wants to be there in time to change,
her father and the other old men are waiting. She leaps,
dancing, and the men are all eyes, all devouring
her strong young legs, but the old men shiver, watching.
The girl is almost naked. And the young men smile
as they stare. More than one would like to be naked.

They could be her father, all those old men admiring.
All of them, old and feeble, are the remnant of a body
that enjoyed other bodies. Someday the young men
will be fathers too. Women, for them all, is one woman.
It happened in silence. A deep joy
seized the darkness in front of the living girl,
all the bodies fuse into one, a single moving
body, everybody's gaze is riveted on her.

The blood that runs in the girl's springing legs
is the blood that freezes in the old men's veins.
Her father is smoking in silence, he's warm:
he doesn't dance, he made the daughter who's dancing.
There's a feeling that throbs and beats in her body,
that beats in him, in all the old men. Her father smokes
in silence, waiting for her to change and return.
Young and old, they wait, staring where she was. Every man,
alone with a drink, will see her again. She'll always be there.

Il meccanico sbronzo è felice buttato in un fosso.
Dalla piola, di notte, con cinque minuti di prato,
uno è a casa; ma prima c'è il fresco dell'erba
da godere, e il meccanico dorme che viene già l'alba.
A due passi, nel prato, è rizzato il cartello
rosso e nero: chi troppo s'accosti, non riesce piú a leggerlo,
tanto è largo. A quest'ora è ancor umido
di rugiada. La strada, di giorno, lo copre di polvere,
come copre i cespugli. Il meccanico, sotto, si stira nel sonno.

È l'estremo silenzio. Tra poco, al tepore del sole,
passeranno le macchine senza riposo, svegliando la polvere.
Improvvise alla cima del colle, rallentano un poco,
poi si buttano giú dalla curva. Qualcuna si ferma
nella polvere, avanti al garage, che la imbeve di litri.
I meccanici, un poco intontiti, saranno al mattino
sui bidoni, seduti, aspettando un lavoro.
Fa piacere passare il mattino seduto nell'ombra.
Qui la puzza degli olii si mesce all'odore di verde,
di tabacco e di vino, e il lavoro li viene a trovare
sulla porta di casa. Ogni tanto, c'è fino da ridere:
contadine che passano e dànno la colpa, di bestie e di spose
spaventate, al garage che mantiene il passaggio;
contadini che guardano bieco. Ciascuno, ogni tanto,
fa una svelto discesa a Torino e ritorna piú sgombro.

Poi, tra il ridere e il vendere litri, qualcuno si ferma:
questi campi, a guardarli, son pieni di polvere
della strada e, a sedersi sull'erba, si viene scacciati.
Tra le coste, c'è sempre una vigna che piace sulle altre:
finirà che il meccanico sposa la vigna che piace
con la cara ragazza, e uscirà dentro il sole,
ma a zappare, e verrà tutto nero sul collo
e berrà del suo vino, torchiato le sere d'autunno in cantina.

Atlantic Oil

The mechanic's lying in the ditch, dead drunk. He's happy.
Home at night is a five-minute walk across the fields
from the pump. But first there's that stretch of cool green grass,
it smells so good and fresh—and the mechanic's dead to the world
till dawn. A few feet away is the big black and red
sign. If you get too close, you can't make out the letters,
the sign's so big. Now, dawn, it's all dew, still dripping.
Days, it's completely covered over with dust from the cars,
like the shrubs along the road. Under the sign, the mechanic stirs
in his sleep.

       Dead silence. Before long car after car will go
roaring by in the blazing sun, swirling up dust. The traffic's
endless. At the pass they suddenly hit the brakes, slowing
for the curve, then plunge downhill. Now and then a car stops
in a cloud of dust in front of the station and they fill her up.
This early, the mechanics still look tired and groggy,
you see them sitting around on the oil drums, waiting for work.
It's not bad, sitting there in the shade, in the cool of the morning,
killing time. The smell of oil is all mixed with fresh hay,
with tobacco and wine. When a job shows up, they're practically
at their own front door. They even get a laugh now and then—
peasant girls, grumbling about the station (Look at the traffic
it's brought, scaring the devil out of women and chickens);
and peasants looking sullen. Every so often a peasant
makes a quick trip down to Torino, he always comes home with less.

They're laughing, selling gas, when suddenly one of them stops:
you know, those fields are nothing to look at, nothing but dust,
every time you sit on the grass, a cloud of dust flies up.
Now, higher up the hill, *there's* a vineyard, a vineyard he loves.
And the story ends with the mechanic marrying the vineyard of
       his choice,
and the girl that goes with it. He'll work outdoors in the sun,
a hoe instead of a wrench. His neck will turn brown, and he'll drink
his own wine, pressed himself, in his own vats, September nights.

Anche a notte ci passano macchine, ma silenziose,
tantoché l'ubriaco, nel fosso, non l'hanno svegliato.
Nello notte non levano polvere e il fascio dei fari
svela in pieno il cartello sul prato, alla curva.
Sotto l'alba trascorrono caute e non s'ode rumore,
se non brezza che passa, e toccata la cima
si dileguano nella pianura, affondando nell'ombra.

At night the traffic doesn't stop, but the cars move quietly,
so quietly the mechanic sleeping in the ditch doesn't even stir.
At night the traffic doesn't raise the dust. In the glare
of headlights, you can even make out the words on the big sign
by the curve. Come dawn, the cars move cautiously, not a sound,
only the breeze blowing. And once they make it over the pass,
they disappear, plunging into the valley below, down in the darkness.

Crepuscolo di sabbiatori

I barconi risalgono adagio, sospinti e pesanti:
quasi immobili, fanno schiumare la viva corrente.
È già quasi la notte. Isolati, si fermano:
si dibatte e sussulta la vanga sott'acqua.
Di ora in ora, altre barche son state fin qui.
Tanti corpi di donna han varcato nel sole
su quest'acqua. Son scese nell'acqua o saltate alla riva
a dibattersi in coppia, qualcuna, sull'erba.
Nel crepuscolo, il fiume è deserto. I due o tre sabbiatori
sono scesi con l'acqua alla cintola e scavano il fondo.
Il gran gelo dell'inguine fiacca e intontisce le schiene.

Quelle donne non sono che un bianco ricordo.
I barconi nel buio discendono grevi di sabbia,
senza dare una scossa, radenti: ogni uomo è seduto
a una punta e un granello di fuoco gli brucia alla bocca.
Ogni paio di braccia strascina il suo remo,
un tepore discende alle gambe fiaccate
e lontano s'accendono i lumi. Ogni donna è scomparsa,
che al mattino le barche portavano stesa
e che un giovane, dritto alla punta, spingeva sudando.
Quelle donne eran belle: qualcuna scendeva
seminuda e spariva ridendo con qualche compagno.
Quando un qualche inesperto veniva a cozzare,
sabbiatori levavano il capo e l'ingiuria moriva
sulla donna distesa come fosse già nuda.
Ora tornano tutti i sussulti, intravisti nell'erba,
a occupare il silenzio e ogni cosa s'accentra
sulla punta di fuoco, che vive. Ora l'occhio
si smarrisce nel fumo invisibile ch'esce di bocca
e le membra ritrovano l'urto del sangue.

In distanza, sul fiume, scintillano i lumi
di Torino. Due o tre sabbiatori hanno acceso
sulla prua il fanale, ma il fiume è deserto.

Sand-Diggers' Twilight

Slowly, poling hard, the little barges push their way
upstream, barely moving. The current churns against the bows, white
foam. It's getting dark. The boats put in and stop; each rower's
on his own. Underwater, the shovels struggle and heave.
Other boats have put in here before. So many women's bodies
have crossed this stretch of water, back and forth, flashing
in the sun. They dived from the boats or leapt on shore,
then paired off, girl and man. Couples tumbling, struggling
in the grass. Twilight. The river's deserted. A few diggers
stand waist-deep in the water, working the bottom.
The water's like ice in the groin, their tired backs are chilled
and numb.

Now those girls are just a memory of white.
Loaded with sand, the boats move downstream in the darkness,
scraping softly along the bottom. Each man sits
on the stern of the boat, a spark of fire burning at his mouth.
From every pair of arms an oar trails in the water,
a warmness slowly inches down to tired legs.
Far off the lights go on. This morning's girls have disappeared.
Each boat had its girl—she lay there lolling in the sun,
while a young man stood on the stern, sweating, poling hard
with his oar. Beautiful girls: they dived into the water
half-naked, then disappeared, laughing, girl and boy together.
Not every man can steer, two boats sometimes collide.
The diggers all look up from work but anger dies when they see
the girl's body lying in the sun, as if she were naked
already. Now they think of morning, of tumbling in the grass.
The memory fills the silence, everything converges
on that dot of fire, still alive. Eyes blur, blinded
by the haze of smoke drifting from the mouth, and suddenly it all
        comes back,
their bodies feel it now, again, the shock of blood on blood,
colliding.

Far off down the river the lights of Torino
glow. Some of the boats have lit the lanterns hanging
at the prows, but the river's deserted: no boats but theirs.

La fatica del giorno vorrebbe assopirli
e le gambe son quasi spezzate. Qualcuno non pensa
che a attraccare il barcone e cadere sul letto
e mangiare nel sonno, magari sognando.
Ma qualcuno rivede quei corpi nel sole
e avrà ancora la forza di andare in città, sotto i lumi,
a cercare ridendo tra la folla che passa.

The long day's work has left them dead, they can't keep their
            eyes open,
their legs are killing them. Some can only think
of hitching up their boats, and bed, and sleep. Sleep's
the only supper they want, maybe they'll dream of food.
But some remember. They can't forget those white bodies lying
in the sun. Somehow, they'll find the strength to head for town
and have a look. They'll be standing there beneath the lights, watching
the girls go by, laughing and joking, looking them over.

Il carrettiere

Lo stridore del carro scuote la strada.
Non c'è letto piú solo per chi, sotto l'alba,
dorme ancora disteso, sognando il buio.
Sotto il carro s'è spenta—lo dice il cielo—
la lanterna che dondola notte e giorno.

Va col carro un tepore che sa d'osteria,
di mammelle premute e di notte chiara,
di fatica contenta senza risveglio.
Va col carro nel sonno un ricordo già desto
di parole arrochite, taciute all'alba.
Il calore del vivo camino acceso
si riaccende nel corpo che sente il giorno.

Lo stridore piú roco, del carro che va,
ha dischiuso nel cielo che pesa in alto
una riga lontana di luce fredda.
È laggiú che s'accende il ricordo di ieri.
È laggiú che quest'oggi sarà il calore
l'osteria la veglia le voci roche
la fatica. Sarà sulla piazza aperta.
Ci saranno quegli occhi che scuotono il sangue.

Anche i sacchi, nell'alba che indugia, scuotono
chi è disteso e li preme, con gli occhi al cielo
che si schiude—il ricordo si stringe ai sacchi.
Il ricordo s'affonda nell'ombra di ieri
dove balza il camino e la fiamma viva.

The Teamster

The creaking wagon shakes the street. Dawn.
Somebody's lying there on the sacks of grain, sleeping,
dreaming of night. No lonelier bed than this.
Under the wagon a lantern dangles, night and day.
The light's out, you can tell from the sky.

The wagon moves, a tavern warmth moves with it:
clear night, warm; the woman's breasts under his hand, squeezing;
hot, hard work; good work; sleeping heavy.
A memory moves with the wagon, it quickens in sleep:
whispered words, hoarse and sweet, dying at dawn.
The heat of the flame that leaps in the chimney
kindles afresh: the body smells the day.

The wagon creaks, a hoarse rasp, louder now,
disclosing in the dull gray cover overhead, way off there
in the distance, a streak of light: clear, cold.
It's there that yesterday's memory starts to kindle.
It's there today will be: warmth, tavern,
chimney, fire, drinking late, whispered words,
exhaustion. It will be there in the square, in the open market.
Those eyes will be there, eyes that shake the blood.

Dawn comes slow. The warm sacks beneath his body shake
and jounce, the roused body presses back, the eyes don't see
the dawning light. Memory digs down, hugging the sacks.
Memory dozes, sinking down in yesterday's dark,
the chimney leaps with a sudden flame.

Traversare una strada per scappare di casa
lo fa solo un ragazzo, ma quest'uomo che gira
tutto il giorno le strade, non è piú un ragazzo
e non scappa di casa.

          Ci sono d'estate
pomeriggi che fino le piazze son vuote, distese
sotto il sole che sta per calare, e quest'uomo, che giunge
per un viale d'inutili piante, si ferma.
Val la pena esser solo, per essere sempre piú solo?
Solamente girarle, le piazze e le strade
sono vuote. Bisogna fermare una donna
e parlarle e deciderla a vivere insieme.
Altrimenti, uno parla da solo. È per questo che a volte
c'è lo sbronzo notturno che attacca discorsi
e racconta i progetti di tutta la vita.

Non è certo attendendo nella piazza deserta
che s'incontra qualcuno, ma chi gira le strade
si sofferma ogni tanto. Se fossero in due,
anche andando per strada, la casa sarebbe
dove c'è quella donna e varrebbe la pena.
Nella notte la piazza ritorna deserta
e quest'uomo, che passa, non vede le case
tra le inutili luci, non leva piú gli occhi:
sente solo il selciato, che han fatto altri uomini
dalle mani indurite, come sono le sue.
Non è giusto restare sulla piazza deserta.
Ci sarà certamente quella donna per strada
che, pregata, vorrebbe dar mano alla casa.

Hard Labor, Getting Tired

Walking across a street to run away from home
is something only children do. But this man roaming
the streets all day long isn't a child any more,
and he isn't running away from home.

                                There are summer
afternoons when even the piazzas are empty
under the sinking sun, and this man, walking down
some avenue of useless trees, suddenly stops.
What's the point of being alone, of being always more alone?
If all you do is wander through the streets and squares,
they're always empty. You've got to stop a woman,
you have to start talking to her, persuade her to live with you.
Otherwise you're just talking to yourself. This is why
sometimes at night a drunk starts talking to people,
telling them his plans, the whole story of his life.

Just hanging around the square, you can't be sure
of meeting someone. But the man who wanders along the streets
keeps stopping. If there were two instead of one,
they could walk down a street, there would be a house
where the woman was, there would be some point to it all.
At night the square is as empty as always,
and this man walking by doesn't see the houses
among the useless lights, he no longer even looks up.
All he feels is the pavement, which other men have made—
men with calloused hands, hands like his.
It's no good just standing in the empty square.
That woman must be there, somewhere down the street—
The woman who'd give him her hand, if he asked, and take him home.

Maternità • Motherhood

Una stagione

Questa donna una volta era fatta di carne
fresca e solida: quando portava un bambino,
si teneva nascosta e intristiva da sola.
Non amava mostrarsi sformata per strada.
Le altre volte (era giovane e senza volerlo
fece molti bambini) passava per strada
con un passo sicuro e sapeva godersi gli istanti.
I vestiti diventano vento le sere di marzo
e si stringono e tremano intorno alle donne che passano.
Il suo corpo di donna muoveva sicuro nel vento
che svaniva lasciandolo saldo. Non ebbe altro bene
che quel corpo, che adesso è consunto dai troppi figliuoli.

Nelle sere di vento si spande un sentore di linfe,
il sentore che aveva da giovane il corpo
tra le vesti superflue. Un sapore di terra bagnata,
che ogni marzo ritorna. Anche dove in città non c'è viali
e non giunge col sole il respiro del vento,
il suo corpo viveva, esalando di succhi
in fermento, tra i muri di pietra. Col tempo, anche lei,
che ha nutrito altri corpi, si è rotta e piegata.
Non è bello guardarla, ha perduto ogni forza;
ma, dei molti, una figlia ritorna a passare
per le strade, la sera, e ostentare nel vento
sotto gli alberi, solido e fresco, il suo corpo che vive.

E c'è un figlio che gira e sa stare da solo
e si sa divertire da solo. Ma guarda nei vetri,
compiaciuto del modo che tiene a braccetto
la compagna. Gli piace, d'un gioco di muscoli,
accostarsela mentre rilutta e baciarla sul collo.
Soprattutto gli piace, poi che ha generato
su quel corpo, lasciarlo intristire e tornare a se stesso.
Un amplesso lo fa solamente sorridere e un figlio
lo farebbe indignare. Lo sa la ragazza, che attende,
e prepara se stessa a nascondere il ventre sformato
e si gode con lui, compiacente, e gli ammira la forza
di quel corpo che serve per compiere tante altre cose.

A Season

Once this woman's body was all firm, young
flesh. When she was carrying a child,
she saddened into herself, grew lonely and depressed.
She hated to be seen on the street with her body all
bulging. The rest of the time (she was young, she had
more children than she wanted), she walked down the street,
poised and confident, making the most of every passing minute.
There are evenings in March when dresses turn into wind,
rippling and clinging around the bodies of women going by.
Her woman's body moved in the wind, secure and poised,
even when the wind died. Her one and only blessing
was that body, worn out now from having too many children.

On windy evenings there's a smell of moisture in the air,
the smell her body had when it was young
under all those clothes. A wet smell of soggy earth,
which every March brings back. There are places in the city
where there are no streets, only alleys where the sun doesn't reach
and the wind never blows. Even there, with walls of stone
around her, her body managed to live, giving off its moisture
like fermenting sap. What with time and feeding all those
other bodies with her own, even she was broken.
She's nothing to look at now, all her strength gone.
But a girl, one of her many children, still comes home
and walks down the street at evening, under the trees, in the gusting wind,
flaunting that body of hers, so firm and fresh and alive.

She also has a son. He knocks around, keeping to himself,
a loner who enjoys a good time. He likes looking at reflections
in windows, likes seeing himself with his arm around a girl,
watching the muscles ripple when he pulls the girl close
and she struggles back, as he bends to kiss her on the neck.
What he likes best is making love to that body, and afterwards,
just letting it sadden, while he retreats into himself.
A kiss, a hug, would only make him smile; a baby
would make him angry. The girl knows this, she's pregnant,
ready to hide her belly when it swells, but for now she does what he likes,
just enjoying being with him, admiring that man's body
of his. There are so many things, other things, it can do.

Piaceri notturni

Anche noi ci fermiamo a sentire la notte
nell'istante che il vento è piú nudo: le vie
sono fredde di vento, ogni odore è caduto;
le narici si levano verso le luci oscillanti.

Abbiam tutti una casa che attende nel buio
che torniamo: una donna ci attende nel buio
stesa al sonno: la camera è caldi di odori.
Non sa nulla del vento la donna che dorme
e respira; il tepore del corpo di lei
è lo stesso del sangue che mormora in noi.

Questo vento ci lava, che giunge dal fondo
delle vie spalancate nel buio; le luci
oscillanti e le nostre narici contratte
si dibattono nude. Ogni odore è un ricordo.
Da lontano nel buio sbucò questo vento
che s'abbatte in città: giú per prati e colline,
dove pure c'è un'erba che il sole ha scaldato
e una terra annerita di umori. Il ricordo
nostro è un aspro sentore, la poca dolcezza
della terra sventrata che esala all'inverno
il respiro del fondo. Si è spento ogni odore
lungo il buio, e in città non ci giunge che il vento.

Torneremo stanotte alla donna che dorme,
con le dita gelate a cercare il suo corpo,
e un calore ci scuoterà il sangue, un calore di terra
annerita di umori: un respiro di vita.
Anche lei si è scaldata nel sole e ora scopre
nella sua nudità la sua vita piú dolce,
che nel giorno scompare, e ha sapore di terra.

Night Pleasures

We too stop to smell the night.
The wind is nothing but air. Naked. The streets
are cold with wind, every smell has faded.
Nostrils lift to the flickering lights.

We all have a home, a house is waiting for us
in the dark, a woman lies there sleeping, waiting for us all
in the darkness. The room is warm with smells.
The woman knows nothing of the wind. She sleeps,
she breathes. The warmth of the woman's body
is the same as the blood that murmurs in us.

This wind washes us clean, blowing from way down there at the
                end of the streets
where they swing wide, opening out in the darkness. Flickering
lights struggle with straining nostrils, tensed in air—
they grapple, naked. Every smell is a memory.
This wind sweeping down on the city blew from way out there
in the darkness, beating down through hills and fields
thick with grass, real grass, waving warm in the sunlight
and the dark, wet earth. The memory we smell
has nothing sweet about it, the strong, sour
smell of the gashed earth in winter, a breath rising
from below. All along the darkness, every smell has been
blown out. Nothing reaches the city. Only wind.

Tonight we'll all go home to a sleeping woman,
with frozen fingers feeling for her body,
and a warmth will rouse our blood, a warmth
of dark wet earth: a breath of life.
She too was warmed by sunlight, this body of hers which now reveals,
in all its nakedness, the sweetest life she has.
In daytime it disappears, it tastes of earth.

La cena triste

Proprio sotto la pergola, mangiata la cena.
C'è lí sotto dell'acqua che scorre sommessa.
Stiamo zitti, ascoltando e guardando il rumore
che fa l'acqua a passare nel solco di luna.
Quest'indugio è il piú dolce.

                        La compagna, che indugia,
pare ancora che morda quel grappolo d'uva
tanto ha viva la bocca; e il sapore perdura,
come il giallo lunare, nell'aria. Le occhiate, nell' ombra,
hanno il dolce dell'uva, ma le solide spalle
e le guance abbrunite rinserrano tutta l'estate.

Son rimasti uva e pane sul tavolo bianco.
Le due sedie si guardano in faccia deserte.
Chissà il solco di luna che cosa schiarisce,
con quel suo lume dolce, nei boschi remoti.
Può accadere, anzi l'alba, che un soffio piú freddo
spenga luna e vapori, e qualcuno compaia.
Una debole luce ne mostri la gola
sussultante e le mani febbrili serrarsi
vanamente sui cibi. Continua il sussulto dell'acqua,
ma nel buio. Né l'uva né il pane son mossi.
I sapori tormentano l'ombra affamata,
che non riesce nemmeno a leccare sul grappolo
la rugiada che già si condensa. E, ogni cosa stillando
sotto l'alba, le sedie si guardano, sole.
Qualche volta alla riva dell'acqua un sentore,
come d'uva, di donna ristagna sull'erba,
e la luna fluisce in silenzio. Compare qualcuno,
ma traversa le piante incorporeo, e si lagna
con quel gemito rauco di chi non ha voce,
e si stende sull'erba e non trova la terra:
solamente, gli treman le nari. Fa freddo, nell'alba,
e la stretta di un corpo sarebbe la vita.
Piú diffusa del giallo lunare, che ha orrore
di filtrare nei boschi, è quest'ansia inesausta
di contatti e sapori che macera i morti.
Altre volte, nel suolo li tormenta la pioggia.

Sad Supper

Under the trellised arbor, supper over.
Below, the water slides softly by.
We sit, not speaking, watching and listening to the sound
of the water and the moon's wake passing through it.
This lingering is very sweet.

My companion lingers.
Even now she seems to be eating that bunch of grapes,
her mouth is so alive; and the smell persists,
like the yellow moonlight, in the air. In shadow, her glances
are as sweet as grapes, but her strong shoulders
and sunburned cheeks contain the whole of summer.

Bread and grapes still sit on the white table.
The two chairs look at each other, empty now.
Who can say what the moon's wake, with its sweet
light, reveals in the distant woods?
At dawn, maybe the wind turns chilly, snuffing out
moon and mist together, and someone appears.
A pale light shows the mouth and the rippling
throat, and the feverish hands groping, closing in vain
on the food. The water ripples by,
in darkness now. Bread and grapes lie where they were,
their smell tormenting that famished ghost,
helpless even to lick away the dew starting to gather
on the grapes. At dawn, everything is dripping
wet, and the two chairs look at each other, alone.

At times on the bank of the river, a smell,
like the smell of grapes or a woman, gathers on the grass,
and the moon flows quietly by. Someone without a body
appears, passing through the plants, grieving
with that hoarse cry of someone who can't speak;
stretches out on the grass, but cannot find the ground:
only the nostrils quiver. It's dawn, and cold,
and life wants to be warm, wants a body to embrace.
Subtler, stronger than the moon's yellow light,
afraid of sifting through the woods, is this unappeasable
longing for touch and smell, which afflicts the dead.
Other times, in the ground, the rain torments them.

Paesaggio IV

a Tina

I due uomini fumano a riva. La donna che nuota
senza rompere l'acqua, non vede che il verde
del suo breve orizzonte. Tra il cielo e le piante
si distende quest'acqua e la donna vi scorre
senza corpo. Nel cielo si posano nuvole
come immobili. Il fumo si ferma a mezz'aria.

Sotto il gelo dell'acqua c'è l'erba. La donna
vi trascorre sospesa; ma noi la schiacciamo,
l'erba verde, col corpo. Non c'è lungo le acque
altro peso. Noi soli sentiamo la terra.
Forse il corpo allungato di lei, che è sommerso,
sente l'avido gelo assorbirle il torpore
delle membra assolate e discioglierla viva
nell'immobile verde. Il suo capo non muove.

Era stesa anche lei, dove l'erba è piegata.
Il suo volto socchiuso posava sul braccio
e guardava nell'erba. Nessuno fiatava.
Stagna ancora nell'aria quel primo sciacquío
che l'ha accolto nell'acqua. Su noi stagna il fumo.
Ora è giunta alla riva e ci parla, stillante
nel suo corpo annerito che sorge fra i tronchi.
La sua voce è ben l'unico suono che si ode sull'acqua
—rauca e fresca, è la voce di prima.

                              Pensiamo, distesi
sulla riva, a quel verde piú cupo e piú fresco
che ha sommerso il suo corpo. Poi, uno di noi
piomba in acqua e traversa, scoprendo le spalle
in bracciate schiumose, l'immobile verde.

Landscape IV

for Tina

The two men smoke on the bank. The girl in swimming
doesn't break the water, all she sees is the short green
arc of her horizon. Sky and trees. Between them
nothing but water and the woman moving, gliding
without a body. Clouds hold, hanging in the sky,
still. The smoke holds, hovering in air.

Cold water, and the grass growing below. Floating,
the woman glides across the green. But we have bodies,
we crush the grass. We feel the earth. Apart from us,
no other weight exists the whole length of the water.
Maybe her body where it lengthens out under water,
touches the cold, feels it greedily absorb the heat
of sun-warmed arms and legs, dissolving her alive
in that motionless green. Her head doesn't move.

She too was lying where the grass is flattened down,
her face half hidden, resting on her arm,
staring into the grass. None of us breathed.
The water took her body with a splash; the sound
still holds in the air. Overhead, the smoke hovers.
Now she reaches the shore, her brown body dripping
wet as she rises up between the trees, and speaks.
Over the water the only sound is that voice of hers—
husky and fresh, as it was before, as it was
in the beginning.

                    Lying there on the green grass,
we think of that other green, darker and colder,
where her body disappeared. Then one of us dives
heavily into the water. Shoulders out, flailing and churning
the water white, he cuts across the motionless green.

Un ricordo

Non c'è uomo che giunga a lasciare una traccia
su costei. Quant'è stato dilegua in un sogno
come via in un mattino, e non resta che lei.
Se non fosse la fronte sfiorata da un attimo,
sembrerebbe stupita. Sorridon le guance
ogni volta.

          Nemmeno s'ammassano i giorni
sul suo viso, a mutare il sorriso leggero
che s'irradia alle cose. Con dura fermezza
fa ogni cosa, ma sembra ogni volta la prima;
pure vive fin l'ultimo istante. Si schiude
il suo solido corpo, il suo sguardo raccolto,
a una voce sommessa e un po' rauca: una voce
d'uomo stanco. E nessuna stanchezza la tocca.

A fissarle la bocca, socchiude lo sguardo
in attesa: nessuno può osare uno scatto.
Molti uomini sanno il suo ambiguo sorriso
o la ruga improvvisa. Se quell'uomo c'è stato
che la sa mugolante, umiliata d'amore,
paga giorno per giorno, ignorando di lei
per chi viva quest'oggi.

          Sorride da sola
il sorriso piú ambiguo camminando per strada.

A Memory

No man yet has left a mark on her.
Every trace of him disappears, dissolving like a dream,
like a dream in the light. Nothing else is left. Only she.
Now, except for the instant that grazes her brow,
her face would seem surprised. Her cheeks smile.
Always, that smile.

        The days pile up but leave no mark,
nothing. Nothing changes the smile that hovers on her face,
shining in things. Decisive, poised, in everything she does;
but each time seems the first, fresh always, alive,
in all of every moment. Dense, absorbed,
body and gaze seem to open out, unfolding in a voice,
soft and a little husky, as if a tired man
were talking. No tiredness touches her. None, ever.

The lips close, and the eyes open, parting,
smiling, waiting: no one dares to breathe.
Many men have seen her smile that ambiguous smile,
that sudden wrinkling of her brow. If any man exists
who sees her in the throes of love, moaning, humbled by passion,
that man pays. Day after day he pays, ignorant of this *she*
for whom the day exists.

        Walking down the street
she smiles to herself. Her most ambiguous smile.

La voce

Ogni giorno il silenzio della camera sola
si richiude sul lieve sciacquío d'ogni gesto
come l'aria. Ogni giorno la breve finestra
s'apre immobile all'aria che tace. La voce
rauca e dolce non torna nel fresco silenzio.

S'apre come il respiro di chi sia per parlare
l'aria immobile, e tace. Ogni giorno è la stessa.
E la voce è la stessa, che non rompe il silenzio,
rauca e uguale per sempre nell'immobilità
del ricordo. La chiara finestra accompagna
col suo palpito breve la calma d'allora.

Ogni gesto percuote la calma d'allora.
Se suonasse la voce, tornerebbe il dolore.
Tornerebbero i gesti nell'aria stupita
e parole parole alla voce sommessa.
Se suonasse la voce anche il palpito breve
del silenzio che dura, si farebbe dolore.

Tornerebbero i gesti del vano dolore,
percuotendo le cose nel rombo del tempo.
Ma la voce non torna, e il susurro remoto
non increspa il ricordo. L'immobile luce
dà il suo palpito fresco. Per sempre il silenzio
tace rauco e sommesso nel ricordo d'allora.

The Voice

Every day the silence of the lonely room
closes on the rustle of movement, of every gesture,
like air. Every day the little window,
unmoving, opens on the quiet air. In the fresh silence
the voice, husky and sweet, does not return.

Opens like the breathing of a voice just beginning
to speak. Then silence. Every day is the same.
And the voice is the same as always, the silence unbroken.
Only that huskiness, gathering always, in memory
stilled. The window swims. Quivering
light. With the light, the stillness of before.

Every gesture jars it, this stillness of before.
If the voice spoke, the pain would return,
gestures would break in the startled air,
and the voice would speak. Softly. Words, words.
If the voice spoke, if anything jarred this barely
quivering silence of always, the sound would be pain.

The gestures would all return, the pain would come back,
pointless, jarring. The jangle of time would begin.
But no voice returns, the faraway whisper stirs
no ripple. Memory is still. Quivering freshness
comes with the motionless light. The silence is always
stilled, husky and gentle, in the memory of before.

Maternità

Questo è un uomo che ha fatto tre figli: un gran corpo
poderoso, che basta a se stesso; a vederlo passare
uno pensa che i figli han la stessa statura.
Dalle membra del padre (la donna non conta)
debbon esser usciti, già fatti, tre giovani
come lui. Ma comunque sia il corpo dei tre,
alle membra del padre non manca una briciola
né uno scatto: si sono staccati da lui
camminandogli accanto.

                La donna c'è stata,
una donna di solido corpo, che ha sparso
su ogni figlio del sangue e sul terzo c'è morta.
Pare strano ai tre giovani vivere senza la donna
che nessuno conosce e li ha fatti, ciascuno, a fatica
annientandosi in loro. La donna era giovane
e rideva e parlava, ma è un gioco rischioso
prender parte alla vita. È cosí che la donna
c'è restata in silenzio, fissando stravolta il suo uomo.

I tre figli hanno un modo di alzare le spalle
che quell'uomo conosce. Nessuno di loro
sa di avere negli occhi e nel corpo una vita
che a suo tempo era piena e saziava quell'uomo.
Ma, a vedere piegarsi un suo giovane all'orlo del fiume
e tuffarsi, quell'uomo non ritrova piú il guizzo
delle membra di lei dentro l'acqua, e la gioia
dei due corpi sommersi. Non ritrova piú i figli
se li guarda per strada e confronta con sé.
Quanto tempo è che ha fatto dei figli? I tre giovani
vanno invece spavaldi e qualcuno per sbaglio
s'è già fatto un figliolo, senza farsi la donna.

Motherhood

This man has made three sons: a big, heavy
body, his own man, self-sufficient. Watching him go by,
you think, that man's sons are built like him.
They must have issued straight from their father's limbs
(the woman doesn't count), already formed, three young sons
just like him. No matter how their three bodies were made,
nothing is missing of their father's body, not a gesture,
not one square inch: they detached themselves from him
walking at his side.

There was a woman of course,
a strong, healthy body of a woman, who spilled her own blood
on each of those three boys and died, bleeding, on the third.
The youngsters think it's strange, living without the woman
none of them knows, who made them, every one, in pain,
destroying herself in them. The woman was young,
she liked to talk and laugh, but taking part in life
is a risky game. Too risky. The woman lay there,
silent, twisted in surprise, staring at her man.

The three sons have a way of shrugging their shoulders,
a way the man remembers. None of them seems to know
that in his body, in his eyes, there's a life
which in its time was rich and full and satisfied the man.
Now, watching one of his sons bend down to dive
at the river' edge, the man no longer recognizes
the flash of her body moving in the stream, or the joy
of two bodies swimming underwater. He doesn't recognize his sons
when he sees them on the street and compares them with himself.
How long has it been since he made his sons? The three young men
have grown up arrogant and vain, and one of them, by accident,
has fathered a boy of his own, who only has a mother.

La moglie del barcaiolo

Qualche volta nel tiepido sonno dell'alba,
sola in sogno, le accade che ha sposato una donna.

Si distacca dal corpo materno una donna
magra e bianca che abbassa la piccola testa
nella stanza. Nel freddo barlume la donna
non attende il mattino; lavora. Trascorre
silenziosa: fra donne occorre parola.

Mentre dorme, la moglie sa la barca sul fiume
e la pioggia che fuma sulla schiena dell'uomo.
Ma la piccola moglie chiude svelta la porta
e s'appoggia, e solleva gli sguardi nei suoi.
La finestra tintinna alla pioggia che scroscia
e la donna distesa, che mastica adagio,
tende un piatto. La piccola moglie lo riempie
e si siede sul letto e comincia a mangiare.

Mangia in fretta la piccola moglie furtiva
sotto gli occhi materni, come fosse una bimba
e resiste alla mano che le cerca la nuca.
Corre a un tratto alla porta e la schiude: le barche
sono tutte attraccate alla trave. Ritorna
piedi scalzi nel letto e s'abbracciano svelte.

Sono gelide e magre le labbra accostate,
ma nel corpo si fonde un profondo calore
tormentoso. La piccola moglie ora dorme
stesa accanto al suo corpo materno. È sottile
aspra come un ragazzo, ma dorme da donna.
Non saprebbe portare una barca, alla pioggia.

Fuori scroscia la pioggia nella luce sommessa
della porta socchiusa. Entra un poco di vento
nella stanza deserta. Se si aprisse la porta,
entrerebbe anche l'uomo, che ha veduto ogni cosa.
Non direbbe parola: crollerebbe la testa
col suo viso di scherno, alla donna delusa.

The Boatman's Wife

Sometimes, in the warm sleep of dawn, alone
and dreaming, it seems as if she's married to a woman.

In the room, a pale, skinny woman detaches herself
from the big motherly body; her head is small,
her eyes lowered. In the cold half-light, the woman
is working, not waiting for morning. It all happens
in silence. Between women no words are needed.

The sleeping woman knows the boat is on the river
and the man's back steams in the rain.
But the little wife quickly runs and closes the door;
leaning against the door, she lifts her eyes to the other.
The rain pelts down, drumming against the window,
and the woman lying on the bed chews slowly,
holding out a plate. The little wife fills her plate,
then sits down on the bed and starts to eat.

The little wife eats hurriedly, furtively,
as if she were a girl, watched by those motherly eyes,
and stiffening as the hand reaches out to touch her neck.
Suddenly she rushes to the door and peers out: the boats
are all there, berthed at the dock. Barefoot,
she rushes back to bed, and they embrace, hurriedly.

The lips pressing hers are thin and cold,
but the body melts inside with a deep, tormenting
heat. Now the little wife lies sleeping
alongside the motherly body. She's lean
and wiry like a boy, but she sleeps like a woman.
She couldn't handle a boat, not in this rain.

Outside the rain comes pelting down in the soft light
of the half-open door. Into the empty room
pokes a finger of wind. If the door blew open,
the man would come in, the man would have seen it all.
He wouldn't say a word, he'd be shaking his head,
snorting at the woman's crazy, disappointed dreams.

La vecchia ubriaca

Piace pure alla vecchia distendersi al sole
e allargare le braccia. La vampa pesante
schiaccia il piccolo volto come schiaccia la terra.

Delle cose che bruciano non rimane che il sole.
L'uomo e il vino han tradito e consunto quelle ossa
stese brune nell'abito, ma la terra spaccata
ronza come una fiamma. Non occore parola
non occorre rimpianto. Torna il giorno vibrante
che anche il corpo era giovane, piú rovente del sole.

Nel ricordo compaiono le grandi colline
vive e giovani come quel corpo, e lo sguardo dell'uomo
e l'asprezza del vino ritornano ansioso
desiderio: una vampa guizzava nel sangue
come il verde nell'erba. Per vigne e sentieri
si fa carne il ricordo. La vecchia, occhi chiusi,
gode immobile il cielo col suo corpo d'allora.

Nella terra spaccata batte un cuore piú sano
come il petto robusto di un padre o di un uomo:
vi si stringe la guancia aggrinzita. Anche il padre,
anche l'uomo, son morti traditi. La carne
si è consunta anche in quelli. Né il calore dei fianchi
né l'asprezza del vino non li sveglia mai piú.

Per le vigne distese la voce del sole
aspra e dolce susurra nel diafano incendio,
come l'aria tremasse. Trema l'erba d'intorno.
L'erba è giovane come la vampa del sole.
Sono giovani i morti nel vivace ricordo.

The Old Drunk

Even the old woman likes stretching in the sun,
spreading out her arms. The heat is heavy,
pressing on her face as it presses on the ground.

Of things that warm, the only one left her is the sun.
Men and wine have betrayed, have consumed those brown
bones lying in the sun. But the cracked ground
hums like a flame. No words are needed,
no regrets. The quivering of a day returns
when her body too was young, hotter than the sun.

In her memories the huge hills swim into view,
young, alive, like that body of hers. And the man's look,
and the roughness of the wine, bring back the pain
of desire: a heat that quivered, humming in the blood
like greenness in the grass. Along paths and vineyards
her memory puts on flesh. Eyes shut, unmoving,
the old woman enjoys the sky with the body she used to have.

In the cracked earth beats a stronger heart
like the rugged chest of a husband or a father.
With her grizzled cheek she caresses it. In death
father and husband are both betrayed. Their flesh,
like hers, has been consumed. Neither warm thighs
nor rough wine will rouse them any more.

Far as the vineyards stretch, the sun's voice,
harsh and sweet, murmurs in the transparent blaze,
as if the air were quivering. The grass quivers around her.
The grass is as young as the heat of the sun.
The dead, in her green memories, grow young again.

Paesaggio VIII

I ricordi cominciano nella sera
sotto il fiato del vento a levare il volto
e ascoltare la voce del fiume. L'acqua
è la stessa, nel buio, degli anni morti.

Nel silenzio del buio sale uno sciacquo
dove passano voci e risa remote;
s'accompagna al brusío un colore vano
che è di sole, di rive e di sguardi chiari.
Un'estate di voci. Ogni viso contiene
come un frutto maturo un sapore andato.

Ogni occhiata che torna, conserva un gusto
di erba e cose impregnate di sole a sera
sulla spiaggia. Conserva un fiato di mare.
Come un mare notturno è quest'ombra vaga
di ansie e brividi antichi, che il cielo sfiora
e ogni sera ritorna. Le voci morte
assomigliano al frangersi di quel mare.

Landscape VIII

Memories begin at evening,
with a breath of wind, to lift their head
and listen to the river running. In the darkness
the water flows as it did in the dead years.

In the still darkness a rustling rises,
old voices, old laughter go flowing by,
and with them goes a flurry of empty color,
color of sunlight, and beaches, and bright looks.
A summer of sounds. Each face keeps,
like ripe fruit, a savor of something gone.

Each look, returning, keeps a taste
of grass and things suffused with late light
along a beach. It keeps a breath of the sea.
It's like the sea at night, this drifting blur
of old longings and tremblings, touched by the sky,
which every evening brings again. The dead
sounds are like that sea, breaking.

Legna verde • Green Wood

Esterno

Quel ragazzo scomparso al mattino, non torna.
Ha lasciato la pala, ancor fredda, all'uncino
—era l'alba—nessuno ha voluto seguirlo:
si è buttato su certe colline. Un ragazzo
dell'età che comincia a staccare bestemmie,
non sa fare discorsi. Nessuno
ha voluto seguirlo. Era un'alba bruciata
di febbraio, ogni tronco colore del sangue
aggrumato. Nessuno sentiva nell'aria
il tepore futuro.

Il mattino è trascorso
e la fabbrica libera donne e operai.
Nel bel sole, qualcuno—il lavoro riprende
tra mezz'ora—si stende a mangiare affamato.
Ma c'è un umido dolce che morde nel sangue
e alla terra dà brividi verdi. Si fuma
e si vede che il cielo è sereno, e lontano
le colline son viola. Varrebbe la pena
di restarsene lunghi per terra nel sole.
Ma a buon conto si mangia. Chi sa se ha mangiato
quel ragazzo testardo? Dice un secco operaio,
che, va bene, la schiena si rompe al lavoro,
ma mangiare si mangia. Si fuma persino.
L'uomo è come una bestia, che vorrebbe far niente.

Son le bestie che sentono il tempo, e il ragazzo
l'ha sentito dall'alba. E ci sono dei cani
che finiscono marci in un fosso: la terra
prende tutto. Chi sa se il ragazzo finisce
dentro un fosso, affamato? È scappato nell'alba
senza fare discorsi, con quattro bestemmie,
alto il naso nell'aria.

Ci pensano tutti
aspettando il lavoro, come un gregge svogliato.

Outside

The boy took off at dawn and isn't back yet. His shovel's
hanging on the hook where he left it, icy cold.
It was dawn, nobody wanted to go looking for the kid.
The hills, he must be headed there. He's a boy—
just the age when kids start cussing and swearing—
how could he explain? Nobody wanted
to go looking for the kid. February, a blazing
dawn, the tree trunks were the color of clotted
blood. In the cold air nobody could smell
the warm weather stirring.

                          The morning's over,
and the factory sets them free, women and workers.
Three or four are lying in the warm sun, eating
hungrily: half an hour till work begins again.
But the air is moist, sweet, it gnaws at the blood,
sending green shivers through the ground. They smoke,
gazing at the sky, how calm it is, and way over there,
the hills are purple. Say, wouldn't it be great
if they could just lie here loafing in the sun?
Still, they'd better eat. That stubborn kid,
he probably forgot to eat. That's right,
says a skinny worker. You break your back working,
but at least you get to eat. You can even smoke.
Men are like animals, they'd rather do nothing.

Some animals can smell the weather changing. At dawn
the boy had smelled it. Sure, and there are dogs
that end up rotting in a ditch: the earth takes it
all. Who can say, maybe that kid will end up
starving or lying in a ditch. He took off at dawn,
no explanations, nothing. Just cussed, and sniffed
the air.

        They're thinking it over, waiting for work,
a flock of sheep, no will of their own.

Fumatori di carta

Mi ha condotto a sentir la sua banda. Si siede in un angolo
e imbocca il clarino. Comincia un baccano d'inferno.
Fuori, un vento furioso e gli schiaffi, tra i lampi,
della pioggia fan sí che la luce vien tolta,
ogni cinque minuti. Nel buio, le facce
dànno dentro stravolte, a suonare a memoria
un ballabile. Energico, il povero amico
tiene tutti, dal fondo. E il clarino si torce,
rompe il chiasso sonoro, s'inoltra, si sfoga
come un'anima sola, in un secco silenzio.

Questi poveri ottoni son troppo sovente ammaccati:
contadine le mani che stringono i tasti,
e le fronti, caparbie, che guardano appena da terra.
Miserabile sangue fiaccato, estenuato
dalle troppe fatiche, si sente muggire
nelle note e l'amico li guida a fatica,
lui che ha mani indurite a picchiare una mazza,
a menare una pialla, a strapparsi la vita.

Li ebbe un tempo i compagni e non ha che trent'anni.
Fu di quelli di dopo la guerra, cresciuti alla fame.
Venne anch'egli a Torino, cercando una vita,
e trovò le ingiustizie. Imparò a lavorare
nelle fabbriche senza un sorriso. Imparò a misurare
sulla propria fatica la fame degli altri,
e trovò dappertutto ingiustizie. Tentò darsi pace
camminando, assonnato, le vie interminabili
nella notte, ma vide soltanto a migliaia i lampioni
lucidissimi, su iniquità: donne rauche, ubriachi,
traballanti fantocci sperduti. Era giunto a Torino
un inverno, tra lampi di fabbriche e scorie di fumo;
e sapeva cos'era lavoro. Accettava il lavoro
come un duro destino dell'uomo. Ma tutti gli uomini
lo accettassero e al mondo ci fosse giustizia.
Ma si fece i compagni. Soffriva le lunghe parole
e dovette ascoltarne, aspettando la fine.

He took me to hear his band. He sat in a corner
and put the trumpet to his lips. A noise like all hell broke loose.
Outside, a raging wind. Between flashes of lightning,
the rain gusted down so hard the lights kept failing
every five minutes. In the dark the faces
look twisted, turned inward, as if playing a number
by memory. In the back of the room my poor friend
is working briskly, trying to lead them all. His trumpet writhes,
breaks through the din, moves out beyond them all, then lets loose
like one of the damned, in a dry silence: solo.

These poor brass instruments are all banged and dented,
and the hands that press the stops are peasant hands,
with stubborn peasant brows and eyes that look at the ground
almost always. Poor, miserable blood, worn out
with hard work—you can hear it bellowing like an ox
in their notes. And my friend, as leader, has his work cut out,
with those calloused carpenter hands, stiff from hammering
and pushing a plane, barely squeezing out a living.

He had friends and comrades once, and he's almost thirty.
He's part of the postwar generation, they grew up hungry.
So he came to Torino with the rest, looking for life, a living,
and found injustice. He learned how to work in factories,
learned not to smile. He learned how to measure
the hunger of other men against his own fatigue, and found
injustice, it was everywhere. He tried resignation,
roaming around at night, half-dead, through the endless streets,
but all he saw was mile after mile of streetlights blazing on
injustice. Drunks, women with husky voices, puppets,
staggering, wandering, lost. He came to Torino
in winter, in the glare and slag and smoke of the factories.
And he learned what work was. Work was hard, work
was man's hard fate, and he accepted it. But what if all men
accepted work? Then there wouldn't be injustice in the world.

Se li fece i compagni. Ogni casa ne aveva famiglie.
La città ne era tutta accerchiata. E la faccia del mondo
ne era tutta coperta. Sentivano in sé
tanta disperazione da vincere il mondo.

Suona secco stasera, malgrado la banda
che ha istruito a uno a uno. Non bada al frastuono
della pioggia e alla luce. La faccia severa
fissa attenta un dolore, mordendo il clarino.
Gli ho veduto questi occhi una sera, che soli,
col fratello, piú triste di lui di dieci anni,
vegliavamo a una luce mancante. Il fratello studiava
su un inutile tornio costrutto da lui.
E il mio povero amico accusava il destino
che li tiene inchiodati alla pialla e alla mazza
a nutrire due vecchi, non chiesti.

                      D'un tratto gridò
che non era il destino se il mondo soffriva,
se la luce del sole strappava bestemmie:
era l'uomo, colpevole. *Almeno potercene andare,*
far la libera fame, rispondere no
a una vita che adopera amore e pietà,
la famiglia, il pezzetto di terra, a legarci le mani.

Men must be comrades then. He put up with long, boring
speeches, forced himself to listen, waiting for the end.
All men were comrades. There were families of comrades in
            every house.
The city was a circle of comrades. And the face of the world
was covered with comrades. They felt inside themselves
a desperation that could conquer the world.

The band sounds harsh tonight, though he's coached them all
in person, one by one. He doesn't seem to notice the sound
of the rain or the lights cutting out. His face is stern,
staring at a grief, while he lips his horn.
I've seen him with that look before. It was night, we were alone—
he and I and his brother, who was ten years sadder than he—
waiting, in a failing light. His brother was learning,
working at a useless lathe he'd put together on his own.
And my poor friend was cursing the fate that kept him nailed
down, chained to his hammer and plane
and feeding two old people nobody wanted.

                          Suddenly
he shouted that it wasn't fate that made the world suffer,
that made men curse the light and the day they were born.
The trouble was man, it was man's doing. *At least we could pull out,*
we could starve to death in freedom, and say No
to a life that makes use of love and family and pity
and a little plot of land to tie us together, and shackle our hands.

Una generazione

Un ragazzo veniva a giocare nei prati
dove adesso s'allungano i corsi. Trovava nei prati
ragazzoti anche scalzi e saltava di gioia.
Era bello scalzarsi nell'erba con loro.
Una sera di luci lontane echeggiavano spari,
in città, e sopra il vento giungeva pauroso
un clamore interrotto. Tacevano tutti.
Le colline sgranavano punti di luce
sulle coste, avvivati dal vento. La notte
che oscurava finiva per spegnere tutto
e nel sonno duravano solo freschezze di vento.

(Domattina i ragazzi ritornano in giro
e nessuno ricorda il clamore. In prigione
c'è operai silenziosi e qualcuno è già morto.
Nelle strade han coperto le macchie di sangue.
La città di lontano si sveglia nel sole
e la gente esce fuori. Si guardano in faccia).
I ragazzi pensavano al buio dei prati
e guardavano in faccia le donne. Perfino le donne
non dicevano nulla e lasciavano fare.
I ragazzi pensavano al buio dei prati
dove qualche bambina veniva. Era bello far piangere
le bambine nel buio. Eravamo i ragazzi.
La città ci piaceva di giorno: la sera, tacere
e guardare le luci in distanza e ascoltare i clamori.

Vanno ancora ragazzi a giocare nei prati
dove giungono i corsi. E la notte è la stessa.
A passarci si sente l'odore dell'erba.
In prigione ci sono gli stessi. E ci sono le donne
come allora, che fanno bambini e non dicono nulla.

A Generation

A boy used to come and play in these fields
where now there's nothing but streets. In the fields
there were other kids, barefoot like him, and he kicked up his heels
       for joy.
The whole gang running barefoot through the grass—it was great.
One night of faraway lights, they heard the noise of shooting
in the city: loud, broken bursts of sound carried up
on the wind, scary. The boys were still. Not a word.
Seeds of lights from the hills were sown all over
the slopes, sparked by the wind. Darkness
damped them down and finally put them out,
leaving nothing, only sleep and the cool wind blowing.

(Next morning the boys go back to their games,
and nobody remembers the shots. There are workers in prison,
silent, not talking, and a couple of men are dead.
They've covered the stains of blood in the streets.
The faraway city wakes in the sunlight, people
leave for work. They look each other in the face.)
The boys were thinking of the darkness in the fields
as they eyed the women passing. Even the women
were quiet, not a word, just letting them do it.
The boys were thinking of the darkness in the fields
where the girls used to come. It was fun making the girls
cry in the darkness. We were those boys.
Days, we preferred the city. Nights, we liked the silence,
watching the faraway lights and listening to the sounds.

Boys are still playing games in the fields
where the streets end. The night is the same as always.
You pass the fields, and you smell the smell of grass.
The men in prison are the same men. And the women
are still women, still making babies and saying nothing.

Rivolta

Quello morto è stravolto e non guarda le stelle:
ha i capelli incollati al selciato. La notte è piú fredda.
Quelli vivi ritornano a casa, tremandoci sopra.
È difficile andare con loro; si sbandano tutti
e chi sale una scala, chi scende in cantina.
C'è qualcuno che va fino all'alba e si butta in un prato
sotto il sole. Domani qualcuno sogghigna
disperato, al lavoro. Poi, passa anche questa.

Quando dormono, sembrano il morto: se c'è anche una donna,
è piú greve il sentore, ma paiono morti.
Ogni corpo si stringe stravolto al suo letto
come al rosso selciato: la lunga fatica
fin dall'alba, val bene una breve agonia.
Su ogni corpo coagula un sudicio buio.
Solamente, quel morto è disteso alle stelle.

Pare morto anche il mucchio di cenci, che il sole
scalda forte, appoggiato al muretto. Dormire
per la strada dimostra fiducia nel mondo.
C'è una barba tra i cenci e vi corrono mosche
che han da fare; i passanti si muovono in strada
come mosche; il pezzente è una parte di strada.
La miseria ricopre di barba i sogghigni
come un'erba, e dà un'aria pacata. Sto vecchio
che poteva morire stravolto, nel sangue,
pare invece una cosa ed è vivo. Cosí,
tranne il sangue, ogni cosa è una parte di strada.
Pure, in strada le stelle hanno visto del sangue.

Revolt

The dead man is sprawled face down and doesn't see the stars;
his hair is stuck to the pavement. The night is colder.
The living go back home, still shivering.
It's hard to follow them all, scattering as they do.
One goes up a staircase, another down to a basement.
Still others keep going till dawn, then pass out
in a sunny pasture. Tomorrow one of them smiles bitterly,
desperately, at work. Later, even this will pass.

Asleep, they look like the dead man. If they're with a woman,
the smell is stronger, but they all look dead.
Each body lies sprawled face down, flat on the bed,
as on the red pavement: the long hard work
since day began is as bad as a brief dying.
Over each body a sweaty darkness gathers.
Except for the dead man, who lies out under the stars.

Even that pile of rags, warmed by the sun and propped
against the wall, seems to be dead. Sleeping
on the street shows confidence in the world.
There's a beard among the rags, flies crawl busily
over it; the people passing in the street move
like flies; the beggar is part of the street.
Poverty's like grass, it buries the bitter smile on his face
with a beard, making it look like peace. This old man,
who might have died face down in his own blood,
seems instead to be something, seems to be alive. So,
except for the blood, everything's part of the street.
Still, the stars have seen blood, blood in the street.

Legna verde

a Massimo

L'uomo fermo ha davanti colline nel buio.
Fin che queste colline saranno di terra,
i villani dovranno zapparle. Le fissa e non vede,
come chi serri gli occhi in prigione ben sveglio.
L'uomo fermo—che è stato in prigione—domani riprende
il lavoro coi pochi compagni. Stanotte è lui solo.

Le colline gli sanno di pioggia: è l'odore remoto
che talvolta giungeva in prigione nel vento.
Qualche volta pioveva in città: spalancarsi
del respiro e del sangue alla libera strada.
La prigione pigliava la pioggia, in prigione la vita
non finiva, talvolta filtrava anche il sole:
i compagni attendevano e il futuro attendeva.

Ora è solo. L'odore inaudito di terra
gli par sorto dal suo stesso corpo, e ricordi remoti
—lui conosce la terra—costringerlo al suolo,
a quel suolo reale. Non serve pensare
che la zappa i villani la picchiano in terra
come sopra un nemico e che si odiano a morte
come tanti nemici. Hanno pure una gioia
i villani: quel pezzo di terra divelto.
Cosa importano gli altri? Domani nel sole
le colline saranno distese, ciascuno la sua.

I compagni non vivono nelle colline,
sono nati in città dove invece dell'erba
c'è rotaie. Talvolta lo scorda anche lui.
Ma l'odore di terra che giunge in città
non sa piú di villani. È una lunga carezza
che fa chiudere gli occhi e pensare ai compagni
in prigione, alla lunga prigione che attende.

Green Wood

for Massimo

Facing the hills in the dark, the man lies still, not moving.
As long as these hills are made of earth, peasants
will have to hoe them. He looks at the hills, not seeing,
like a man in prison, his eyes closed but wide-awake.
The man lying still—the ex-prisoner—starts work again
tomorrow, with the few comrades left. Tonight he's alone.

The hill gives off a smell of rain—that faraway smell
the wind some days would carry to the prison.
Sometimes it rained in the city too: breathing and blood
expanding, opening out to the street, to freedom.
The prison took the rain, life in prison
never stopped. Some days the sun filtered through:
his comrades were waiting, the future was waiting for them.

Now, he's alone. That unbelievable smell of earth seems
to be rising from his own body, and memories from way back—
his roots are there, in the land—bind him to the earth,
to that real earth. No point in thinking
that the peasants lift their hoes and hit the earth
as if they hated it, that they hate each other
with a deadly hatred. The peasants have one
joy: that piece of ground they till. So,
what do others matter? Tomorrow the sun will shine,
the hills will all be there, each man his hill.

His comrades, his friends, don't live in the hills.
They were born in cities, a place of streetcars,
not grass. There are days when even he forgets.
But that smell of earth drifting into the city now
has nothing of peasants in it. It's a long caress
that makes a man close his eyes and think of his comrades
in prison, of the long prison waiting them all.

Una breve finestra nel cielo tranquillo
calma il cuore; qualcuno c'è morto contento.
Fuori, sono le piante e le nubi, la terra
e anche il cielo. Ne giunge quassú il mormorío:
i clamori di tutta la vita.

                La vuota finestra
non rivela che, sotto le piante, ci sono colline
e che un fiume serpeggia lontano, scoperto.
L'acqua è limpida come il respiro del vento,
ma nessuno ci bada.

              Compare una nube
soda e bianca, che indugia, nel quadrato del cielo.
Scorge case stupite e colline, ogni cosa
che traspare nell'aria, vede uccelli smarriti
scivolare nell'aria. Viandanti tranquilli
vanno lungo quel fiume e nessuno s'accorge
della piccola nube.

             Ora è vuoto l'azzurro
nella breve finestra: vi piomba lo strido
di un uccello, che spezza il brusío. Quella nube
forse tocca le piante o discende nel fiume.
L'uomo steso nel prato dovrebbe sentirla
nel respiro dell'erba. Ma non muove lo sguardo,
l'erba sola si muove. Dev'essere morto.

A small window opening on a still sky,
it calms the heart: someone died happy.
Outside, trees and clouds and earth,
even sky. Up here, only the humming of that world:
the roar of all of life.

            The empty window
shows the trees, but not the hills beneath the trees,
or a river winding way off there in the distance.
The water's as clear as the breathing of the wind,
but nobody cares.

            A cloud appears,
a clump of white which lingers in the square of sky.
It sees astonished hills and houses, each thing
shining in the air, sees lost birds
soaring in the air. People move quietly
along that river, and nobody sees
the little cloud.

            Now, in the small window
the blue is blank: into it drops the cry
of a bird, breaking the hum. Maybe
that cloud is touching the trees or sinking into the river.
The man lying in the field ought to feel it
in the breathing of the grass. But he doesn't move his eyes,
only the grass moves. He must be dead.

Parole del politico

Si passava sul presto al mercato dei pesci
a lavarci lo sguardo: ce n'era d'argento,
di vermigli, di verdi, colore del mare.
Al confronto col mare tutto scaglie d'argento,
la vincevano i pesci. Si pensava al ritorno.

Belle fino le donne dall'anfora in capo,
ulivigna, foggiata sulla forma dei fianchi
mollemente: ciascuno pensava alle donne,
come parlano, ridono, camminano in strada.
Ridevamo, ciascuno. Pioveva sul mare.

Per le vigne nascoste negli anfratti di terra
l'acqua macera foglie e racimoli. Il cielo
si colora di nuvole scarse, arrossate
di piacere e di sole. Sulla terra sapori
e colori nel cielo. Nessuno con noi.

Si pensava ritorno, come dopo una notte
tutta quanta di veglia, si pensa al mattino.
Si godeva il colore dei pesci e l'umore
delle frutta, vivaci nel tanfo del mare.
Ubriachi eravamo, nel ritorno imminente.

Words from Confinement

Bright and early we went down to the fishmarket
to wash stale eyes alive. The fish were
scarlet, green, silver, color of the sea.
The sea was shining, all scales of silver,
but the fish were brighter. We thought of home.

Beautiful too the women, with jars on their heads,
olive green, and molded like their hips,
softly rounded. We thought of our women,
how they talk and laugh and walk down the street.
We all laughed. Out at sea, it was raining.

In vineyards, along ravines, grapes and leaves
glisten with rain. The sky is ruddy
with scattered clouds, colored with sun
and pleasure. On earth, smells; in the sky,
colors. We were on our own; unguarded.

We thought of home, the way a man thinks
of morning after a sleepless night. The sea
smelled musty, and we reveled in freshness,
in the moistness of the fruit and the colors of the fish.
We were drunk on the news: we were going home!

Paternità • Fatherhood

Parla poco l'amico e quel poco è diverso.
Val la pena incontrarlo un mattino di vento?
Di noi due uno, all'alba, ha lasciato una donna.
Si potrebbe discorrere del vento umidiccio,
della calma o di qualche passante, guardando la strada;
ma nessuno comincia. L'amico è lontano
e a fumare non pensa. Non guarda.

                    Fumava
anche il negro, un mattino, che insieme vedemmo
fisso, in piedi, nell'angolo a bere quel vino
—fuori il mare aspettava. Ma il rosso del vino
e la nuvola vaga non erano suoi:
non pensava ai sapori. Neanche il mattino
non pareva un mattino di quelli dell'alba;
era un giorno monotono fuori dei giorni
per il negro. L'idea di una terra lontana
gli faceva da sfondo. Ma lui non quadrava.

C'era donne per strada e una luce più fresca,
e il sentore del mare correva le vie.
Noi, nemmeno le donne o girare: bastava
star seduti e ascoltare la vita e pensare che il mare
era là, sotto il sole ancor fresco di sonno.
Donne bianche passavano, nostre, sul negro
che nemmeno abbassava lo sguardo alle mani
troppo fosche, e nemmeno muoveva il respiro.
Avevamo lasciato una donna, e ogni cosa
sotto l'alba sapeva di nostro possesso:
calma, strade, e quel vino.

                    Stavolta i passanti
mi distraggono e più non ricordo l'amico
che nel vento bagnato si è messo a fumare,
ma non pare che goda.

                Tra poco mi chiede:
Lo ricordi quel negro che fumava e beveva?

Mediterranean

My friend says little, and the little he says is different.
Will I take the trouble to meet with him some windy morning?
Two of us; one has left a woman at dawn.
We could talk of the wind, how humid it is, or the stillness,
or of someone passing by, while we look down the street.
But neither begins. My friend is so far away
he doesn't even think of smoking. Doesn't look.

                              The black man
was smoking that morning when we both saw him standing
in the corner of the bar, not moving, drinking that wine.
Outside, the sea was waiting. But the redness of the wine,
the cloud passing over, were ours, not his.
He wasn't thinking of the savor of things. Even the morning
was like a morning with no taste of dawn in it.
For the black, it was a monotonous day, a day set off
from other days. The idea of a distant country
gave him depth. But here he didn't fit in.

Now there were women around, the light was cooler,
and the smell of the sea went washing through the street.
We weren't out for women or walking: it was good
just sitting there, listening to life, and knowing that the sea
was there and the sun was up, shining and fresh.
White women, our women, were passing in front of the black,
who didn't even lower his eyes to those black
black hands of his; didn't even catch his breath.
We had left a woman behind, and everything
in the dawn air had the taste of our possessing:
stillness, streets, and that wine.

                           This time the people passing
distract me, and I forget about my friend,
who has lit a cigarette in the damp wind,
but doesn't seem to relish it.

                    Soon he says to me:
You remember that black man, the one who was smoking and
      drinking?

Paesaggio VI

Quest'è il giorno che salgono le nebbie dal fiume
nella bella città, in mezzo a prati e colline,
e la sfumano come un ricordo. I vapori confondono
ogni verde, ma ancora le donne dai vivi colori
vi camminano. Vanno nella bianca penombra
sorridenti: per strada può accadere ogni cosa.
Può accadere che l'aria ubriachi.

                 Il mattino
si sarà spalancato in un largo silenzio
attutendo ogni voce. Perfino il pezzente,
che non ha una città né una casa, l'avrà respirato,
come aspira il bicchiere di grappa a digiuno.
Val la pena aver fame o esser stato tradito
dalla bocca piú dolce, pur di uscire a quel cielo
ritrovando al respiro i ricordi piú lievi.

Ogni via, ogni spigolo schietto di casa
nella nebbia, conserva un antico tremore:
chi lo sente non può abbandonarsi. Non può abbandonare
la sua ebbrezza tranquilla, composta di cose
dalla vita pregnante, scoperte a riscontro
d'una casa o d'un albero, d'un pensiero improvviso.
Anche i grossi cavalli, che saranno passati
tra la nebbia nell'alba, parleranno d'allora.

O magari un ragazzo scappato di casa
torna proprio quest'oggi, che sale la nebbia
sopra il fiume, e dimentica tutta la vita,
le miserie, la fame e le fedi tradite,
per fermarsi su un angolo, bevendo il mattino.
Val la pena tornare, magari diverso.

Landscape VI

Today's the day when the fog lifts from the river
in the beautiful city among its fields and hills,
blurring it like a memory. The haze fuses
every green thing, but women in lively colors still
go strolling by. They pass in that white shadow,
smiling: anything can happen in the street.
At times the air intoxicates.

                              The morning
will suddenly swing wide on a spacious silence,
muffling every voice. Even the tramp,
who has no home, no city, gulps in that air, inhaling it
like a glass of grappa on an empty stomach.
Whether you're hungry or have been betrayed by the sweetest
mouth, it's worth it just to go out walking in that air
and feel your faintest memories quicken while you breathe.

In that fog every street, every simple corner of a house
retains a shiver from the past, an old tremor.
Once you feel it, you can't let it go. You can't give up
that quiet intoxication, composed of things that come
from your germinating life, discovered as you meet
a house, a tree, an unexpected thought.
Even the workhorses plodding down the street
in the dawn fog will tell you of those years.

Or maybe a boy who ran away from home comes
home today—today when the fog lifts
across the river, and he forgets his whole life—
the hard times, the hunger, the betrayal of trust—
as he stops at a corner and drinks in the morning air.
It's worth it, coming home, though you're not the same.

Mito

Verrà il giorno che il giovane dio sarà un uomo,
senza pena, col morto sorriso dell'uomo
che ha compreso. Anche il sole trascorre remoto
arrossando le spiagge. Verrà il giorno che il dio
non saprà piú dov'erano le spiagge d'un tempo.

Ci si sveglia un mattino che è morta l'estate,
e negli occhi tumultuano ancora splendori
come ieri, e all'orecchio i fragori del sole
fatto sangue. E mutato il colore del mondo.
La montagna non tocca piú il cielo; le nubi
non s'ammassano piú come frutti; nell'acqua
non traspare piú un ciottolo. Il corpo di un uomo
pensieroso si piega, dove un dio respirava.

Il gran sole è finito, e l'odore di terra,
e la libera strada, colorata di gente
che ignorava la morte. Non si muore d'estate.
Se qualcuno spariva, c'era il giovane dio
che viveva per tutti e ignorava la morte.
Su di lui la tristezza era un'ombra di nube.
Il suo passo stupiva la terra.

                    Ora pesa
la stanchezza su tutte le membra dell'uomo,
senza pena: la calma stanchezza dell'alba
che apre un giorno di pioggia. Le spiagge oscurate
non conoscono il giovane, che un tempo bastava
le guardasse. Né il mare dell'aria rivive
al respiro. Si piegano le labbra dell'uomo
rassegnate, a sorridere davanti alla terra.

Myth

There'll come a day when the young god becomes a man,
painlessly, with the dead smile of the grown man
who now understands. The sun moves off, distant now,
reddening the sand. There'll come a day when the young god
no longer knows the beaches where he once walked.

You wake one morning, and the summer's dead,
but your eyes are still dazed by the turbulent light
of yesterday, and in your ears you hear the roar of the sun
changed to blood. The world's color has changed.
The mountains no longer touch the sky; the clouds
are no longer piled up like ripe fruit. In the water now
you can no longer make out the small stones. A man's body
is bent in anxious thought where once a young god breathed.

The great sun is gone, and the smell of the earth,
and the open road, colored with people
who knew nothing of death. In summer nobody dies.
Maybe someone disappeared, but there was always the young god
who lived for everyone, who knew nothing of death.
Sadness touched him hardly at all, like a cloud's shadow.
His footstep astonished the earth.

                        Now a torpor
everywhere weighs on the man's arms and legs,
painlessly: the quiet torpor of a dawn
beginning a day of rain. The beach is dark
and no longer knows the god whose mere glance was once
the only thing that mattered. The sea of air no longer quickens
at his breathing. The man's lips are shut,
resigned to smiling in the presence of the earth.

Il paradiso sui tetti

Sarà un giorno tranquillo, di luce fredda
come il sole che nasce o che muore, e il vetro
chiuderà l'aria sudicia fuori del cielo.

Ci si sveglia un mattino, una volta per sempre,
nel tepore dell'ultimo sonno: l'ombra
sarà come il tepore. Empirà la stanza
per la grande finestra un cielo piú grande.
Dalla scala salita un giorno per sempre
non verranno piú voci, né visi morti.

Non sarà necessario lasciare il letto.
Solo l'alba entrerà nella stanza vuota.
Basterà la finestra a vestire ogni cosa
di un chiarore tranquillo, quasi una luce.
Poserà un'ombra scarna sul volto supino.
I ricordi saranno dei grumi d'ombra
appiattati cosí come vecchia brace
nel camino. Il ricordo sarà la vampa
che ancor ieri mordeva negli occhi spenti.

Paradise on the Roofs

The day will be still, the light cold
like the sun rising or setting, and the windowpane
will seal the stagnant air from the sky outside.

You wake one morning, once and for all,
in the warmth of the final sleep: the shadow will be
like the warmth. Through the big window
a vaster sky will fill the room.
Up the staircase one day forever
no more voices will come, no dead faces.

There'll be no need to get out of bed.
Only the dawn, spreading at the window,
will enter the empty room, dressing it all
in a quiet clarity, almost a light,
setting a thin shadow on the face looking up.
Memories will be lumps of shadow
flattened out like burnt embers sifting down
in the grate. Memory will be the blaze
that yesterday still smoldered in the spent eyes.

Semplicità

L'uomo solo—che è stato in prigione—ritorna in prigione
ogni volta che morde in un pezzo di pane.
In prigione sognava le lepri che fuggono
sul terriccio invernale. Nella nebbia d'inverno
l'uomo vive tra muri di strade, bevendo
acqua fredda e mordendo in un pezzo di pane.

Uno crede che dopo rinasca la vita,
che il respiro si calmi, che ritorni l'inverno
con l'odore del vino nella calda osteria,
e il buon fuoco, la stalla, e le cene. Uno crede,
fin che è dentro uno crede. Si esce fuori una sera,
e le lepri le han prese e le mangiano al caldo
gli altri, allegri. Bisogna guardarli dai vetri.

L'uomo solo osa entrare per bere un bicchiere
quando proprio si gela, a contempla il suo vino:
il colore fumoso, il sapore pesante.
Morde il pezzo di pane, che sapeva di lepre
in prigione, ma adesso non sa piú di pane
né di nulla. E anche il vino non sa che di nebbia.

L'uomo solo ripensa a quei campi, contento
di saperli già arati. Nella sala deserta
sottovoce si prova a cantare. Rivede
lungo l'argine il ciuffo di rovi spogliati
che in agosto fu verde. Dà un fischio alla cagna.
E compare la lepre e non hanno piú freddo.

Simplicity

The man alone—the ex-prisoner—goes back to prison
every time he bites into a piece of bread.
In prison he had dreams of the hares bounding across
plowed winter fields. In the winter fog
the man lives jailed between streets, drinking
his cold water, biting into his crust of bread.

Someday, you think, your life will start all over,
you'll breathe in peace, and the winter will return
with its smell of wine in the warm tavern—
a blazing fire, a booth, and supper. That's what you think
when you're still inside. Then one night you leave
and find that your hares have all been caught, that people are eating
        them,
steaming hot. You have to stand there watching through the window.

The man alone is freezing of cold, so cold he musters the strength
to go inside and buy a glass of wine. He contemplates his wine,
its cloudy color, its musty smell.
He bites into a piece of bread—in prison
it tasted of wild hares. But now it has no taste of bread,
no taste of anything at all. Even the wine tastes of fog.

The man alone thinks about those winter fields, glad
to know the plowing's done. In the empty room he tries
singing, softly, and it all comes back—he sees
along the river's edge, the clumps of brambles, naked now,
which were green in August. He whistles to his bitch.
The hare starts from the brambles, the chill is gone.

L'istinto

L'uomo vecchio, deluso di tutte le cose,
dalla soglia di casa nel tiepido sole
guarda il cane e la cagna sfogare l'istinto.

Sulla bocca sdentata si rincorrono mosche.
La sua donna gli è morta da tempo. Anche lei
come tutte le cagne non voleva saperne,
ma ci aveva l'istinto. L'uomo vecchio annusava
—non ancora sdentato—, la notte veniva,
si mettevano a letto. Era bello l'istinto.

Quel che piace nel cane è la gran libertà.
Dal mattino alla sera gironzola in strada;
e un po' mangia, un po' dorme, un po' monta le cagne:
non aspetta nemmeno la notte. Ragiona,
come fiuta, e gli odori che sente son suoi.

L'uomo vecchio ricorda una volta di giorno
che l'ha fatta da cane in un campo di grano.
Non sa piú con che cagna, ma ricorda il gran sole
e il sudore e la voglia di non smettere mai.
Era come in un letto. Se tornassero gli anni,
lo vorrebbe far sempre in un campo di grano.

Scende in strada una donna e si ferma a guardare;
passa il prete e si volta. Sulla pubblica piazza
si può fare di tutto. Persino la donna,
che ha ritegno a voltarsi per l'uomo, si ferma.
Solamente un ragazzo non tollera il gioco
e fa piovere sassi. L'uomo vecchio si sdegna.

Instinct

The old man, disappointed in everything,
stands in the doorway of a house in the warm sun,
watching dog and bitch satisfy their instinct.

The flies keep settling on his toothless gums.
His woman died some time ago. Like all bitches,
she didn't want to know anything about it,
but she had it, the instinct. The old man had a nose for it—
he still had his teeth then—and when night came,
they went to bed. It was fine, instinct.

What's good about dogs is their great freedom.
From morning till night they roam the street,
sometimes eating, sleeping sometimes, sometimes mounting the
        bitches.
A dog doesn't even wait for night. He thinks
the way he smells, and everything he smells is his.

The old man remembers how once, in full daylight,
he did it in a wheatfield, just like a dog.
Who the bitch was, he can't remember; he remembers the hot sun
and the sweat, and wanting to keep on going forever.
It was like in bed. If only he were young again,
he'd like to do it in a wheatfield, always.

A woman comes down the street and stops to watch;
the priest passes and turns away. On the public square
anything can happen. Even the woman,
modestly avoiding the gaze of the man, stops.
It's only a boy who can't bear the play of instinct,
who starts throwing stones. The old man is indignant.

Paternità

Uomo solo dinanzi all'inutile mare,
attendendo la sera, attendendo il mattino.
I bambini vi giocano, ma quest'uomo vorrebbe
lui averlo un bambino e guardarlo giocare.
Grandi nuvole fanno un palazzo sull'acqua
che ogni giorno rovina e risorge, e colora
i bambini nel viso. Ci sarà sempre il mare.

Il mattino ferisce. Su quest'umida spiaggia
striscia il sole, aggrappato alle reti e alle pietre.
Esce l'uomo nel torbido sole e cammina
lungo il mare. Non guarda le madide schiume
che trascorrono a riva e hanno piú pace.
A quest'ora i bambini sonnecchiano ancora
nel tepore del letto. A quest'ora sonnecchia
dentro il letto una donna, che farebbe l'amore
se non fosse lei sola. Lento, l'uomo si spoglia
nudo come la donna lontana, e discende nel mare.

Poi la notte, che il mare svanisce, si ascolta
il gran vuoto ch'è sotto le stelle. I bambini
nelle case arrossate van cadendo dal sonno
e qualcuno piangendo. L'uomo, stanco di attesa,
leva gli occhi alle stelle, che non odono nulla.
Ci son donne a quest'ora che spogliano un bimbo
e lo fanno dormire. C'è qualcuna in un letto
abbracciata ad un uomo. Dalla nera finestra
entra un ansito rauco, e nessuno l'ascolta
se non l'uomo che sa tutto il tedio del mare.

Fatherhood

A man alone facing the useless sea,
waiting for evening to come, waiting for morning.
There are kids out playing, but this man would like
to have a boy of his own, to watch him playing games.
Over the water huge clouds build a castle,
every day destroys it and builds it again, coloring
the children's faces. The sea will always be there.

The morning strikes. Over this soggy beach the sun
creeps, sticking to nets and stones.
The man steps out in the murky light and walks
along the sea. He doesn't look at the curving froth
always climbing up the shore, never at peace.
This is the hour when children are still dozing
in warm beds. This is the hour when a woman lies
dozing in her bed—she'd like to make love
if she weren't all alone. Slowly, the man strips
naked as the woman in her bed, he walks into the sea.

Then the night, when the sea disappears and there's only
the huge sound of emptiness under the stars. Children
in the reddened houses are falling asleep,
someone's crying. Tired of waiting, the man
lifts his eyes to the stars, they don't hear a thing.
This is the hour when a woman undresses a little boy
and puts him to bed. There's a woman in a bed,
embracing a man. From the black window
comes a hoarse gasping, and nobody hears but the man
who knows it all by heart, all the boredom of the sea.

Lo steddazzu

L'uomo solo si leva che il mare è ancor buio
e le stelle vacillano. Un tepore di fiato
sale su dalla riva, dov'è il letto del mare,
e addolcisce il respiro. Quest'è l'ora in cui nulla
può accadere. Perfino la pipa tra i denti
pende spenta. Notturno è il sommesso sciacquío.
L'uomo solo ha già acceso un gran fuoco di rami
e lo guarda arrossare il terreno. Anche il mare
tra non molto sarà come il fuoco, avvampante.

Non c'è cosa piú amara che l'alba di un giorno
in cui nulla accadrà. Non c'è cosa piú amara
che l'inutilità. Pende stanca nel cielo
una stella verdognola, sorpresa dall'alba.
Vede il mare ancor buio e la macchia di fuoco
a cui l'uomo, per fare qualcosa, si scalda;
vede, e cade dal sonno tra le fosche montagne
dov'è un letto di neve. La lentezza dell'ora
è spietata, per chi non aspetta piú nulla.

Val la pena che il sole si levi dal mare
e la lunga giornata cominci? Domani
tornerà l'alba tiepida con la diafana luce
e sarà come ieri e mai nulla accadrà.
L'uomo solo vorrebbe soltanto dormire.
Quando l'ultima stella si spegne nel cielo,
l'uomo adagio prepara la pipa e l'accende.

Morning Star

The man alone gets up while the sea's still dark
and the stars still flicker. A warmth like breathing
drifts from the shore where the sea has its bed,
sweetening the air he breathes. This is the hour when nothing
can happen. Even the pipe dangling from his teeth
is out. The sea at night makes a muffled plash.
By now the man alone has kindled a big fire of brush,
he watches it redden the ground. Before long
the sea will be like the fire, a blaze of heat.

Nothing's more bitter than the dawning of a day
when nothing will happen. Nothing's more bitter
than being useless. A greenish star, surprised
by the dawn, still droops feebly in the sky.
It looks down on the sea, still dark, and the brushwood fire
where the man, simply to do something, is warming himself.
It looks, then drops sleepily down among the dusky mountains
to its bed of snow. The hour drags by, cruelly
slow for a man who's waiting for nothing at all.

Why should the sun bother to rise from the sea
or the long day bother to begin? Tomorrow
the warm dawn with its transparent light will be back,
and everything will be like yesterday, and nothing will happen.
The man alone would like nothing more than to sleep.
When the last star in the sky is quenched and gone,
the man quietly tamps his tobacco and lights his pipe.

Appendice • Afterword

Unisco, in appendice all'edizione definitiva di questo mio libro (che integra e sostituisce la prima edizione licenziata nell'ottobre 1935), due studi con cui cercai successivamente di chiarirmene il significato e gli sbocchi. Il primo, *Il mestiere di poeta*, lo scrissi nel novembre 1934, e ha per me un interesse ormai solanto documentario. Quasi tutte le sue affermazioni e i suoi orgogli appaiono rientrati e superati nel secondo, *A proposito di certe poesie non ancora scritte*, composto nel febbraio 1940. Qualunque sia per essere il mio avvenire di scrittore, considero conclusa con questa prosa la ricerca di *Lavorare stanca*.

—C.P. (1943)

Il mestiere di poeta

a proposito di Lavorare stanca

La composizione della raccolta è durata tre anni.

Tre anni di giovinezza e di scoperte, durante i quali è naturale che la mia idea della poesia e insieme le mie capacità intuitive si sian venute approfondendo. E anche ora, benché questa profondità e quel vigore siano molto scaduti ai miei occhi, non credo che tutta, assolutamente tutta, la mia vita si sia appuntata per tre anni nel vuoto. Farò o non farò altri tentativi di poesia, mi occuperò d'altro o ridurrò ancora ogni esperienza a questo fine: tutto ciò, che già mi ha preoccupato, voglio per ora lasciare in disparte. Semplicemente, ho dinanzi un'opera che m'interessa, non tanto perché composta da me, quanto perché, almeno un tempo, l'ho creduta ciò che di meglio si stesse scrivendo in Italia e, ora come ora, sono l'uomo meglio preparato a comprenderla.

Invece di quella naturale evoluzione da poesia a poesia che ho accennato, qualcuno preferirà scoprire nella raccolta ciò che si chiama una costruzione, una gerarchia di momenti cioè, espressiva di un qualche concetto grande o piccolo, per sua natura astratto, esoterico magari, e cosí, in forme sensibili, rivelato. Ora, io non nego che nella mia raccolta di questi concetti se ne possano scoprire, e anche piú di due, nego soltanto di averceli messi.

Mi si intenda bene: io stesso mi sono fermato pensieroso davanti ai veri o presunti canzonieri costruiti (*Les Fleurs du Mal* o *Leaves of Grass*), dirò di piú, anch'io sono giunto a invidiarli per quella loro vantata qualità; ma al buono, al tentativo cioè di comprenderli e giustificarmeli, ho dovuto riconoscere che di poesia in poesia non c'è passaggio fantastico e nemmeno, in fondo, concettuale. Tutt'al piú, come nell'*Alcione*, si tratta di un legame temporale, fantasie da giugno a settembre. Un po' diverso naturalmente sarà il discorso a proposito di un racconto o poema, dove il passaggio fantastico e concettuale insieme è dato proprio dall'elemento narrativo, dalla consapevolezza cioè di un'unità ideale insieme e materiale che raccoglie i diversi momenti di un'esperienza. Ma allora bisogna rinuciare alla pretesa di costruire un poema semplicemente giustapponendo delle unità: si abbia il coraggio e la forza di concepire l'opera di maggior mole con un solo respiro. Come due poemi non formano un unico racconto (si fermano tutt'al piú a legami di parentela tra i rispettivi personaggi o consimili ripieghi), cosí due o piú poesie non formano un racconto o costruzione, se non a patto di riuscire ciascuna per sé non finita. Dovrebbe bastare alla nostra ambizione, e basta in questa raccolta alla mia, che nel suo giro breve ciascuna poesia riesca una costruzione a sé stante.

Tutto ciò pare quasi elementare, ma, non so se per ingenuità mia iniziale o per un gusto poetico che tuttora respiro nell'aria, è proprio in un lungo travaglio intorno a quest'identità—ogni poesia, un racconto—che tecnicamente si giustificano tutti i tentativi compresi in questo libro.

Il mio gusto voleva confusamente un'espressione essenziale di fatti essenziali, ma non la solita astrazione introspettiva, espressa in quel linguaggio, perché libresco, allusivo, che troppo gratuitamente posa a essenziale. Ora, il falso canzoniere-poema giunge appunto all'illusione construttiva attraverso gli addentellati che una pagina presta all'altra per mezzo dell'evanescenza delle sue voci e della concettosità dei suoi motivi.

Seguire il mio gusto e non cadere nel canzoniere-poema fu quindi una sola esigenza, tecnica per il rispetto sotto cui l'ho considerata sinora, ma, ben s'intende, impegnativa di tutte le mie facoltà.

Andava intanto prendendo in me consistenza una mia idea di poesia-racconto, che agli inizi mal riuscivo a distinguere dal genere poemetto. Naturalmente non è soltanto questione di mole. Le riserve del Poe, che ancora reggono, sul concetto di poema vanno integrate appunto di considerazioni contenutistiche, che saranno poi una cosa sola con quelle esteriori sulla mole di un componimento. È qui che, agli inizi, non vedevo chiaro ed anzi, con una certa baldanza, mi lusingavo bastasse un energico atto di fede nella poesia, che so io, chiara e distinta, muscolosa, oggettiva, essenziale, ed altri traslati. Parlavo in principio di evoluzione. E l'evoluzione è tutta qui. Nella crescente consapevolezza di questo problema, che ancor oggi mi pare, dal canto mio, tutt'altro che esaurito.

La prima realizzazione notevole di queste velleità è appunto la prima poesia della raccolta: *I mari del Sud*. Ma va da sé che, fin dal primo giorno che ho pensato a una poesia, ho lottato col presentimento di questa difficoltà. E innumerevoli tentativi hanno preceduto *I mari del Sud*, cui l'esperienza concomitante di una prosa narrativa, o soltanto discorsiva, toglieva ogni gioia di realizzazione e rivelava nella loro disperante banalità.

Come nettamente io sia passato da un lirismo tra di sfogo e di scavo (povero scavo che sovente dava nel gratuito e sfogo vizioso che sempre finí nell'urlo patologico) al pacato e chiaro racconto de *I mari del Sud*, ciò mi spiego soltanto ricordando che non d'un tratto è avvenuto, ma per quasi un anno prima de *I mari del Sud* non ho seriamente pensato a poetare e intanto, come già prima, ma con maggiore intensità, andavo da una parte occupandomi di studi e traduzioni dal nordamericano, dall'altra componendo certe novellette mezzo dialettali e, in collaborazione con un amico pittore, una dilettantesca pornoteca, di cui troppo piú che non sia lecito dovrei dire qui. Basti che questa pornoteca risultò un corpo di ballate, tragedie, canzoni, poemi in ottave, il tutto vigorosamente sotadico, e questo poco importa ora, ma anche, ciò che importa, vigorosamente immaginato, narrato, goduto nell'espressione, diretto a un pubblico di amici e da alcuno apprezzatissimo, ragione pratica, questa di un pubblico, che mi pare da supporsi quasi concime alla radice di ogni vigorosa vegetazione artistica.

Il rapporto di queste occupazioni con *I mari del Sud* è dunque molteplice: gli studi letterari nordamericani ponendomi in contatto con una realtà culturale in male di crescita; i tentativi novellistici avvicinandomi a una migliore esperienza umana e oggettivandone gli interessi; e finalmente la mia terza attività, tecnicamente intesa, rivelandomi il *mestiere* dell'arte e la gioia delle difficoltà vinte, i limiti di un tema, il gioco dell'immaginazione, dello stile, e il mistero della felicità di uno stile, che è anche un fare i conti con l'ascoltatore o lettore possibile. E insisto in specie sulla lezione tecnica di questa mia ultima attività, perché gli altri influssi, cultura nordamericana ed esperienza umana, sono troppo facilmente comprensibili nell'unico concetto di esperienza che tutto, e quindi nulla, spiega.

Ancora. Per un rispetto piú sottilmente tecnico le tre attività che ho detto hanno influito sui convincimenti e disegni, dati i quali ho posto mano a *I mari del Sud*. Nei tre casi, entrai variamente in contatto con l'avvenimento di una creazione linguistica a fondo dialettale o per lo meno parlato. Intendo la scoperta del volgare nordamericano nel campo dei miei studi e l'uso del gergo torinese o piemontese nei miei naturalistici tentativi di prosa dialogata; entrambi, entusiastiche avventure di giovinezza, e tali su cui fondai piú di un pensamento presto dissolto a integrato dall'incontro con la teoria identificatrice di poesia e linguaggio.

In terzo luogo, lo stile sempre parodistico della versificazione sotadica mi abituò a considerare ogni specie di lingua letteraria come un corpo cristallizzato e morto, in cui soltanto a colpi di trasposizioni e d'innesti dall'uso parlato, tecnico e dialettale si può nuovamente far correre il sangue e vivere la vita. E sempre, questa triplice e unica esperienza mi mostrava, nel groviglio donde diramano i diversi interessi espressivi e pratici, la fondamentale interdipendenza di questi motivi e il bisogno di un continuo rifarsi ai principî, pena l'isterilimento; mi preparava cioè all'idea che condizione di ogni slancio di poesia, comunque alto, è sempre un attento riferimento alle esigenze etiche, e naturalmente anche pratiche, dell'ambiente che si vive.

I mari del Sud, che viene dopo questa naturale preparazione, è dunque il mio primo tentativo di poesia-racconto e giustofica questo duplice termine in quanto oggettivo sviluppo di casi, sobriamente e quindi, pensavo, fantasticamente esposto. Ma il punto sta in quell'*og-*

gettività del divenire dei casi, che riduce il mio tentativo a un poemetto tra il psicologico e il cronistico; comunque, svolto su una trama naturalistica. Insistevo allora sulla *sobrietà* stilistica per fondamentale posizione polemica: c'era da raggiungere l'evidenza fantastica fuori di *tutti gli altri* atteggiamenti espressivi viziati, a me pareva, di retorica; c'era da provare a me stesso che una sobria energia di concezione portava con sé l'espressione aderente, immediata, essenziale. Nulla di piú ingenuo che il mio contegno di allora davanti all'*immagine* retoricamente intesa: non ne volevo nelle mie poesie e non ce ne mettevo (se non per sbaglio). Era per salvare l'adorata immediatezza e, pagando di persona, sfuggire al facile e slabbrato lirismo degli imaginifici (esageravo).

È naturale che con un tale programma di semplicità si veda la salvezza unicamente nell'aderenza serrata, gelosa, appassionata all'oggetto. Ed è forse soltanto la forza di questa passione e non la sobrietà oggettiva, che salva qualcosa di quelle prime poesie. Poiché non tardai a sentire l'impaccio dell'argomento, ossia dell'oggetto, inevitabile in una simile concezione materialistica del racconto. Mi scoprivo sovente ad almanaccare argomenti, e questo è il meno male: lo faccio tuttora con indubbio profitto. Ciò che non va, è cercare un argomento disposti a lasciarlo svilupparsi secondo la sua natura psicologica o romanzesca e prender atto dei risultati. Ossia, identificarsi con questa natura e supinamente lasciarne agire le leggi. Questo è cedere all'oggetto. Ed è quanto facevo.

Ma quantunque già allora l'inquietudine congenita a un tale errore non mi lasciasse pace, pure motivo di soddisfazioni ne avevo. Anzitutto, proprio lo *stile oggettivo* mi dava qualche consolazione con la sua solida onestà: il taglio incisivo e il timbro netto che ancora gli invidio. Si accompagnava anche a un certo piglio sentimentale di misogino virilismo di cui mi compiacevo e che, in definitiva, con qualche altro piglio compagno formava la vera trama, il vero *sviluppo di casi*, della mia poesia-racconto, che io fantasticavo oggettiva. Poiché, lodando il cielo, se sovente si teorizza bene a realizza male, qualche volta accade il contrario. E insomma, dopo anni di evanescenze e strilli poetici, ero giunto a far sorridere una mia poesia—una figura in una poesia—e questo mi pareva il suggello tangibile del conquistato stile e domino dell'esperienza.

Mi ero altresí creato un verso. Il che, giuro, non ho fatto apposta. A quel tempo, sapeva soltanto che il verso libero non mi andava a genio, per la disordinata e capricciosa abbondanza ch'esso usa pretendere dalla fantasia. Sul verso libero whitmaniano, che molto invece ammiravo a temevo, ho detto altrove la mia e comunque già confusamente presentivo quanto di oratorio si richieda a un'ispirazione per dargli vita. Mi mancava insieme il fiato e il temperamento per servirmene. Nei metri tradizionali non avevo fiducia, per quel tanto di trito e di gratuitamente (cosí mi pareva) cincischiato ch'essi portano con sé; e del resto troppo li avevo usati parodisticamente per pigliarli ancora sul serio e cavarne un effetto di rima che non mi riuscisse comico.

Sapevo naturalmente che non esistono metri tradizionali in senso assoluto, ma ogni poeta rifà in essi il ritmo interiore della sua fantasia. E mi scopersi un giorno a mugolare certa tiritera di parole (che fu poi un distico de *I mari del Sud*) secondo una cadenza enfatica che fin de bambino, nelle mie letture di romanzi, usavo segnare, rimormorando le frasi che piú mi ossessionavano. Cosí, senza saperlo, avevo trovato il mio verso, che naturalmente per tutto *I mari del Sud* e per parecchie altre poesie fu solo istintivo (restano tracce di questa incoscienza in qualche verso dei primi, che non esce dall'endecasillabo tradizionale). Ritmavo le mie poesie mugolando. Via via scopersi le leggi intrinseche di questa metrica e scomparvero gli endecasillabi e il mio verso si rivelò di tre tipi costanti, che in certo modo potei presupporre alla composizione, ma sempre ebbi cura di non lasciar tiranneggiare, pronto ad accettare, quando mi paresse il caso, altri accenti e altra sillabazione. Ma non mi allontanai piú sostanzialmente dal mio schema e questo considero il ritmo del mio fantasticare.

Dire, ora, il bene che penso di una simile versificazione è superfluo. Basti che essa accontentava anche materialmente il mio bisogno, tutto istintivo, di righe lunghe, poiché sentivo di aver molto da dire e di non dovermi fermare a una ragione musicale nei miei versi, ma soddisfarne altresí una logica. E c'ero riuscito e insomma, o bene o male, in essi *narravo*.

Che è il gran punto in esame. Narravo, ma come? Ho già detto che giudico le prime poesie della raccolta materialistici poemetti di cui è caritatevole concedere che il *fatto* costituisce nulla piú che un impaccio, un residuo non risolto in fantasia. Immaginavo un caso o un personaggio e lo facevo svolgersi o parlare. Per non cadere nel genere poemetto, che confusamente sentivo condannabile, esercitavo una vigliacca economia di versi e in ciascuna poesia prefissavo un limite al loro numero, che, parendomi di far gran cosa ad osservare, non volevo nemmeno troppo basso, per il terrore di dare nell'epigramma. Miserie dell'educazione retorica. Anche qui mi salvò un certo silenzio e un interessamento per altre cose dello spirito e della vita, che non tanto mi portarono un loro contributo, quanto mi permisero di meditare *ex novo* sulla difficoltà, distraendomi dallo zelo feroce con cui facevo pesare su ogni mia velleità inventiva l'esigenza della *virile oggettività* nel racconto. Per restare in biblioteca, un nuovo interesse fu la rabbiosa passione per Shakespeare e altri elisabettiani, letti tutti, e postillati, nel testo.

Capitò che un giorno, volendo fare una poesia su un eremita, da me immaginato, dove si rappresentassero i motivi e i modi della conversione, non riuscivo a cavarmela e, a forza d'interminabili cincischiature ritorni pentimenti ghigni e ansietà, misi invece insieme un *Paesaggio* di alta e bassa collina, contrapposte e movimentate, e, centro animatore della scena, un eremita alto e basso, superiormente burlone e, a dispetto dei convincimenti anti-imaginifici, «colore delle felci bruciate». Le parole stesse che ho usato lasciano intendere che a fondamento di questa mia fantasia sta una commozione pittorica; e infatti poco prima di dar mano al *Paesaggio* avevo veduto e invidiato certi nuovi quadretti dell'amico pittore, stupefacenti per evidenza di colore e sapienza di costruzione. Ma, qualunque lo stimolo, la novità di quel tentativo è ora per me ben chiara: avevo scoperto l'*immagine*.

E qui diventa difficile spiegarmi, per la ragione che io stesso non ho ancora esauito le possibilità implicite nella tecnica di *Paesaggio*. Avevo dunque scoperto il valore dell'immagine, e quest'immagine (ecco il premio della testardaggine con cui avevo insistito sull'oggettività del racconto) non la intendevo piú retoricamente come traslato, come decorazione piú o meno arbitraria sovrapposta all'oggettività narrativa. Quest'immagine era, oscuramente, il racconto stesso.

Che l'eremita apparisse colore delle felci bruciate non voleva dire che io istituissi un parallelo tra eremita e felci per rendere piú evidente la figura dell'eremita o quella delle felci. Voleva dire che io scoprivo un *rapporto fantastico* tra eremita e felci, tra eremita e paesaggio (si può continuare: tra eremita e ragazze, tra visitatori e villani, tra ragazze e vegetazione, tra eremita e capra, tra eremita e sterchi, tra alto e basso) *che era esso argomento del racconto*.

Narravo di questo rapporto, contemplandolo come un tutto significativo, creato dalla fantasia e impregnato di germi fantastici passibili di sviluppo; e nella nettezza di questo complesso fantastico e insieme nella sua possibilità di svilppo infinito, vedevo la *realtà* della composizione. (A questo piano si era trasferita la mania di oggettività, che ora si chiariva bisogno di concretezza).

Ero risalito (o mi pareva) alla fonte prima di ogni attività poetica, che avrei potuto cosí definire: sforzo di rendere come un tutto sufficiente un complesso di rapporti fantastici nei quali consista la propria percezione di una realtà. Continuavo a sprezzare, evitandola, l'immagine retoricamente intesa, e il mio discorso si manteneva sempre diretto e oggettivo (della nuova oggettività, s'intende), eppure era finalmente cosa mia il senso tanto elusivo di quel semplice enunciato che essenza della poesia sia l'immagine. Le immagini formali, retoricamente parlando, le avevo incontrate a profusione nelle scene degli elisabettiani, ma appunto andavo in quel tempo faticosamente persuadendomi che la loro importanza non stava tanto nel significato retorico di termine di paragone, quanto piuttosto in quel mio significato, ultimamente intravveduto, di parti costitutive d'una totalitaria realtà fantastica, il cui senso consistesse nel loro rapporto. Favoriva questa scoperta la natura peculiare dell'immagine elisabettiana, cosí piena straripante di vita, e ingegnosa, e compiaciuta di questa sua ingegnosità e pienezza come della propria giustificazione ultima. Per cui molte scene di quei drammi mi parevano trarre il loro respiro fantastico esclusivamente nell'atmosfera creata dalle loro similitudini.

La storia delle mie composizioni successive al primo *Paesaggio* è naturalmente, in un primo tempo, una storia di ricadute nell'oggettività precedente, psicologia o cronaca; come accade ad esempio per *Gente che non capisce*, tutta percorsa però anch'essa di brividi nuovi. In seguito, la traduzione in fantasia di ogni motivo dell'esperienza mi si venne facendo quasi metodica, sempre piú sicura, istintiva; e fu a questo punto che presi coscienza del nuovo problema da cui non sono ancora uscito.

Va bene, dicevo, sostituire al dato oggettivo il racconto fantastico di una piú concreta e sapiente realtà; ma dove si dovrà fermare questa ricerca di rapporti fantastici? cioè, quale giustificazione di opportunità avrà la scelta di un rapporto piuttosto che un altro? Mi impensieriva, in una poesia come *Mania di solitudine,* la sfacciata preminenza data all'io (che fin dal tempo de *I mari del Sud* era stato mio polemico vanto ridurre a mero personaggio e talvolta abolire), non tanto intendendolo argomento oggettivo, ché era ormai timore puerile, quanto perché alla preminenza dell'io mi pareva di vedere accompagnarsi un piú sregolato gioco di rapporti fantastici. Quando, insomma, la potenza fantastica diventa arbitrio? La mia defiinizione dell'immagine non mi diceva nulla in proposito.

Ancor adesso non sono uscito dalla difficoltà. La ritengo perciò il punto critico di ogni poetica. Intravvedo tuttavia una possibile soluzione, che però poco mi soddisfa perché poco chiara. Comunque, essa ha il pregio ai miei occhi di riportarmi a quella convinzione della fondamentale interdipendenza tra motivi pratici e motivi espressivi, di cui parlavo a proposito della mia formazione linguistica. Consisterebbe, il criterio di opportunità nel gioco della fantasia, in una *discreta* aderenza a quel complesso logico e morale che contituisce la personale partecipazione alla realtà spiritualmente intesa. Va da sé che questa partecipazione è sempre mutevole a rinnovabile e quindi il suo effetto fantastico incarnabile in infinite situazioni. Ma la debolezza della definizione risulta da quella *discrezione* cosí necessaria e cosí poco concludente agli effetti del giudizio sull'opera. Bisognerà dunque affermare la precarietà e superficialità di ogni giudizio estetico? Si sarebbe tentati.

Ma intanto smaniavo sotto l'assillo creativo, e faticosamente inciampando in modo vario sempre nella stessa difficoltà, mettevo insieme altre narrazioni d'immagini. Ormai mi compiacevo anche in rischi virtuosistici. In *Pieceri notturni*, per esempio, volli costruire un rapporto, a contrasto, di notazioni tutte sensoriali, e senza cadere nel sensuale. In *Casa in costruzione*, nascondere il gioco delle immagini in un'apparente narrazione oggettiva. Nella *Cena triste*, rinarrare a modo mio, a intrico di rapporti fantastici, una trita situazione.

Per ciascuna di queste poesie rivivevo l'ansia del problema di come intendere e giustificare il complesso fantastico che la costituiva. Diventavo sempre piú capace di sottintesi, di mezze tinte, di composizione ricca, e sempre meno convinto dell'onestà, della *necessità* del mio lavoro. Al confronto, talvolta mi parve piú giustificato il nudo e quasi prosastico verso de *I mari del Sud* o di *Deola* che non quello vivido, flessibile, pregnante di vita fantastica, di *Ritratto d'autore* e del *Paesaggio IV*. Eppure tenevo fede al chiaro principio della sobria e diretta espressione di un rapporto fantastico nettamente immaginato. Tenevo duro a narrare e non potevo certo perdermi nella decorazione gratuita. Ma è un fatto che le mie immagini—i miei rapporti fantastici—andavano sempre piú complicandosi e ramificando in atmosfere rarefatte.

[novembre 1934]

A proposito di certe poesie non ancora scritte

È un fatto che va osservato: dopo un certo silenzio, ci si propone di scrivere non *una* poesia ma *delle* poesie. Si giudica la pagina futura come un'esplorazione rischiosa di quello che da domani in poi sapremo fare. Parole taglio situazione ritmi da domattina ci promettono un campo piú largo del singolo pezzo che scriveremo.

Se questo slargo sul futuro mancasse di orizzonte, e cioè coincidesse con *tutto* il nostro futuro possibile, sarebbe il normale desiderio di campare e lavorare a lungo, e buona notte. Ma succede che una certa dimensione o durata spirituale gli è implicita, e per quanto non se ne vedano i limiti questi sono presenti nella stessa logica interna della novità che stiamo per creare. La poesia che stiamo per scrivere aprirà delle porte alla nostra capacità di creare, e noi passeremo per queste porte—faremo altre poesie—, sfrutteremo il campo e lo lasceremo spossato. Qui è l'essenziale. La limitatezza, cioè la dimensione, della nuova provincia. La poesia che faremo domani ci aprirà alcune porte, non tutte le possibili: verrà cioè un momento che faremo delle poesie stanche, vuote di promessa, quelle appunto che segneranno la fine dell'avventura. Ma se l'avventura ha un principio e una fine, vuol dire che le poesie in essa composte formano blocco e costituiscono il temuto canzoniere-poema.

Non è facile accorgersi quando una simile avventura finisca, dato che le poesie stanche, o poesie-conclusione, sono forse le piú belle del mazzo, e il tedio che accompagna la loro composizione non è gran che diverso da quello che apre un nuovo orizzonte. Per esempio, *Semplicità* e *Lo steddazzu* (inverno 1935–36) le hai composte con inenarrabile noia e, forse proprio per sfuggire alla noia, tratteggiate in modo cosí bravo e allusivo che piú tardi a rileggerle ti sono parse pregne di avvenire. Il criterio psicologico del tedio non è quindi sufficiente a segnare il trapasso a un nuovo gruppo, dato che la noia, l'insoddisfazione, è la molla prima di qualunque scoperta poetica, piccola o grande.

Piú attendibile è il criterio dell'*intenzione*. Per esso le nostre poesie si definiscono stanche e conclusive, oppure iniziali e ricche di sviluppo, a seconda che si sceglie noi di considerarle. Evidentemente questo criterio non è arbitrario, poiché mai ci verrà in mente di decretare a capriccio la portata di una poesia, ma sceglieremo per farle fruttare quelle appunto che non solo componendole ci hanno promesso avvenire (che sarebbe ben raro, per la ragione sopraddetta del tedio) ma che, rimeditate una volta composte, si offrono concrete speranze di ulteriori composizioni. Con che si viene a dire che l'unità di un gruppo di poesie (il poema) non è un astratto concetto da presupporsi alla stesura, ma una circolazione organica di appigli e di significati che si viene via via concretamente determinando. Succede anzi che, composto tutto il gruppo, la sua unità non ti sarà ancora evidente e dovrai scoprirla sviscerando le singole poesie, ritoccandone l'ordine, intendendole meglio. Mentre l'unità materiale di un racconto si fa per cosí dire da sé ed è cosa naturalistica per il meccanismo stesso del raccontare.

Hai intanto escluso che la costruzione del nuovo gruppo possa essere un disegno autobiografico, che sarebbe narrazione nel suo significato naturalistico.

Devi ora decidere se certe poesie sciolte (non comprese nel primo *Lavorare stanca*) sono la conclusione di un vecchio gruppo e l'inizio di uno nuovo. Che componendole tu avessi l'intenzione di superare *Lavorare stanca*, risulta per lo meno dal fatto che allora (inverno 1935) il libro era già in tipografia. L'inverno del '35–36 segnò la crisi di tutto un ottimismo basato su vecchie abitudini e l'inizio di nuove meditazioni sul tuo mestiere, che si espressero in un diario e si allargarono via via a un approfondimento prosastico della vita intera, e attraverso preoccupazioni successive (1937–39) t'indussero a tentare novelle e romanzi. Ogni tanto facevi una poesia—l'inverno 1937–38 ne produsse parecchie sotto un ritorno materiale alle condizioni del 1934, l'anno di *Lavorare stanca*—ma sempre piú ti convincevi che il tuo attuale campo era la prosa, e le poesie rappresentavano un *afterglow*. Poi il 1939 non ne vide piú. Ora che con l'inizio del 1940 ci sei tornato, si domanda se quelle estravaganti rientrano in *Lavorare stanca* o presagiscono il futuro.

Sta il fatto che riprendendo in mano il libro e rimaneggiandone l'ordine per includervene alcune censurate nel 1935, le nuove vi hanno trovato posto agevolmente e sembrano comporre un tutto. La questione è quindi praticamente risolta, ma resta che l'*intenzione* delle estravaganti ti faceva chiaramente sperare un nuovo canzoniere.

Vediamo. Queste sbandate poesie cadono in due gruppetti, anche cronologici. Inverno 1935–36, la liquidazione del confino: *Mito, Semplicità, Lo steddazzu*; inverno 1937–1938, la rabbia sessuale: *La vecchia ubriaca, La voce, La puttana contadina, La moglie del barcaiolo*. È chiaro che questi due momenti sono già in *Lavorare stanca*, e il primo mazzo si riconnette a *Terre bruciate* e *Poggio Reale*; il secondo a *Maternità* e *La cena triste*. La gran questione è se qualcosa nel loro accento giustifica l'intenzione di erogarle nel futuro canzoniere, come senza dubbio componendole speravi.

Non pare. La novità di *Lo steddazzu* era solo apparente. Il mare, la montagna e la stella, l'uomo solo, sono elementi o fantasie che si trovano già in *Ulisse*, in *Gente spaesata*, in *Mania di solitudine*. Né il ritmo del fantasticare è diverso o anche solo più ricco che in passato. Non si esce dalla figura umana veduta nei suoi gesti essenziali e attraverso questi raccontata. Lo stesso puoi dire dei ritratti di donne nel secondo gruppo (*La vecchia ubriaca* e *La moglie del barcaiolo*), che, a parte la novità tutta esteriore del sogno, ripetono la presentazione figurativa di *Ulisse* e *Donne appassionate* ricorrendo all'immagine interna (un particolare del quadro, usato come termine di paragone nel racconto) e non giungendo quindi nemmeno al nebuloso ideale dell'immagine-racconto avanzato già nel 1934. Quanto alla sobrietà di tratti della *Moglie del barcaiolo*, siamo ancora addirittura a *Deola*.

A dire il vero, in questi anni l'intenzione costruttiva più che nelle nuove poesie si esprime nelle meditazioni diaristiche che le accompagnarono e all fine soffocarono (1937–1939). E siccome solo la consapevolezza critica conclude un ciclo poetico, questo continuo insistere con note di prosa sul problema dei tuoi versi è la prova che una crisi di rinnovamento s'andava svolgendo. Diremo quindi che, se nel travaglio sei giunto insensibilmente a definirti *Lavorare stanca*, tanto che ultimamente l'hai ripreso e rimaneggiato scoprendovi una costruzione (ciò che ti pareva assurdo nel 1934), tu miravi più in là. Esaminando la poetica dei gruppi estravaganti e scoprendola coerente col resto di *Lavorare stanca*, manifestavi la velleità di una nuova poetica e ne delineavi la direzione. Qual è dunque la molla di queste ripetute e frammentarie indagini prosastiche che hai esercitato per tre anni?

Definito *Lavorare stanca* come l'avventura dell'adolescente che, orgoglioso della sua campagna, immagina consimile la città, ma vi trova la solitudine e vi rimedia col sesso e la passione che servono soltanto a sradicarlo e gettarlo lontano da campagna e città, in una più tragica solitudine che è la fine dell'adolescenza—hai scoperto in questo canzoniere una coerenza formale che è l'evocazione di figure tutte solitarie ma fantasticamente vive in quanto saldate al loro breve mondo per mezzo dell'*immagine interna*. (Esempio. Nell'ultimo *Paesaggio* della nebbia, l'aria inebria, il pezzente la respira come respira la grappa, il ragazzo beve il mattino. Tale è tutta la vita fantastica di *Lavorare stanca*).

Ora, tanto l'avventura vissuta come la sua tecnica evocativa in questi quattro anni si sono dissolte. La prima si è conclusa con l'accettazione pratica e la giustificazione della solitudine virile, la seconda con la provata esigenza e qualche scarno tentativo di nuovi ritmi e nuove figurazioni. Com'era giusto, la tua critica si è accanita soprattutto sul concetto d'immagine. L'ambiziosa definizione del 1934, che l'immagine fosse essa stessa argomento del racconto, si è chiarita falsa o per lo meno prematura. Tu hai sinora evocato figure reali radicandole nel loro campo con paragoni interni, ma questo paragone non è mai stato esso stesso argomento del racconto, per la sufficiente ragione che argomento era un personaggio o paesaggio naturalisticamente inteso. Non è un caso infine che tu abbia intravisto la possibile unità di *Lavorare stanca* soltanto sotto forma di avventura naturalistica. Quale il canzoniere, tale la singola poesia.

Sia detto chiaramente: la tua avventura di domani deve avere altre ragioni.

Questo nuovo canzoniere porterà in sé la sua luce quando sarà fatto, quando cioè dovrai negarlo. Ma due premesse risultano dal sin qui detto:

1) la sua costruzione sarà analoga a quella di ogni singolo pezzo poetico;
2) non sarà riassumibile in racconto naturalistico.

Ciò che in questi due punti è gratuito—l'esigenza di una poesia non riducibile a racconto—è tuttavia il lievito di domani. È l'elemento arbitrario, precritico, che solo in quanto tale può stimolare la creazione. È un'intenzione, una premessa irrazionale, che sarà giustificata soltanto dall'opera. Quattro anni di velleità e d'introspezione te l'impongono, come nel 1931–32 una voce t'imponeva di *raccontare* versi.

È logico che davanti a quest'esigenza scompaia quella, inconcludente, di sapere che cosa dirà la nuova poesia. Lo dirà la poesia stessa, e quando l'avrà detto sarà cosa del passato, come ora *Lavorare stanca*.

È certo che anche stavolta il problema dell'immagine terrà il campo. Ma non sarà questione di *raccontare immagini*, formula vuota, come s'è visto, perché nulla può distinguere le parole ch'evocano un'immagine da quelle ch'evocano un oggetto. Sarà questione di descrivere —non importa se direttamente o immaginosamente—una realtà non naturalistica ma simbolica. In queste poesie i fatti avverranno—se avverranno—non perché cosí vuole la realtà, ma perché cosí decide l'intelligenza. Singole poesie e canzoniere non saranno un'autobiofrafia ma un giudizio. Come succede insomma nella *Divina Commedia* —(bisognava arrivarci)—, avvertendo che il tuo simbolo vorrà corrispondere non all'allegoria ma all'immagine dantesca.

Al canzoniere sarà inutile pensare. Come s'è visto con *Lavorare stanca*, basterà di volta in volta assorbirsi nella singola poesia, superare in essa il passato. Se la prima delle due degnità è vera, basterà fare una sola poesia nuova—e forse è già fatta—e sarà assicurato l'intero canzoniere-poema. Non solo, ma dato un verso tutto vi sarà implicito. Verrà un giorno che una tranquilla occhiata porterà l'ordine e l'unità nel laborioso caos che domani incomincia.

[febbraio 1940]

To this definitive edition of my book (incorporating and replacing the first edition approved for publication by the censor in October 1935), I have appended two critical postscripts—my subsequent efforts to explain to myself the meaning and consequences of what I had written. The first piece, "The Poet's Craft," was written in November 1934 and has for me now merely documentary interest. All its assertions and proud claims are apparently withdrawn or superseded in the second piece, "Concerning Certain Unwritten Poems," which I wrote in February 1940. Whatever my future as a writer may be, I regard these two prose pieces as terminating the project of *Hard Labor*.

—C.P. *(1943)*

Postscript I: The Poet's Craft

Three years, three years of youthful discoveries, went into writing this book of poems. Naturally, during those years both my idea of poetry and my own insights gradually developed and deepened. And even now, when that depth and vigor have largely lost their charm for me, I don't believe that those three years were absolutely wasted. Not absolutely. I don't know whether I will write poetry again or not. I may busy myself with other projects, but, whatever I do, I plan to concentrate completely on putting to one side everything which has hitherto occupied me. In a word, this book of mine interests me, not because I wrote it, but because, at the time I wrote it, I regarded it as among the best poety being written in Italy. And because, as things stand now, I am the person best equipped to understand it.

There was, I suggested, a natural development from poem to poem. Others may be tempted to find here what is sometimes called a "construction," i.e., a unified formal structure of poetic "moments," governed by some idea large or small, abstract and even esoteric in nature, which is thereby revealed in particular, tangible forms. Now I don't deny that such concepts, perhaps quite a number of them, can be found in my collection; all I deny is that I put them there.

Let me be explicit. Genuine or putative structures of this sort (*canzonieri* like *Les fleurs du mal* or *Leaves of Grass*) leave me with a feeling of puzzlement; I have even managed to envy them the unity and continuity claimed for them. But, finally, despite my best efforts to understand them and justify them to myself, I had to recognize that there was no imaginative connection between one poem and the next, and, in the last analysis, no conceptual link either. At best— as in Whitman's "Halcyon Days," a series of images extending from June to September—the sequence is merely temporal. A story or poem in which the imaginative and conceptual bond is provided by the subject matter of the narrative is clearly quite another matter, since the consciousness of a single subject unifies the different aspects of an experience. But in that case, we cannot claim to create a poem simply by juxtaposing these unities; we must find the courage and strength to conceive a work of larger scale, with a sweep and breath of its own. Just as two poems don't make a single narrative (at best they are related by links between characters or similar elements), so two or more poems don't make a narrative or formal structure (except as one poem requires another to complete it). The poet's ambition should be satisfied—as mine is in this collection—if each poem, in its own brief compass, manages to create an adequate structure of its own.

So much may be obvious. Yet the technical justification of every poem in this book (whether it comes from my naïveté at the outset or from a poetic taste to which I still cling) lies in a long, painful attempt to achieve a single goal. *Every poem is meant to be a story.*

However confusedly, my taste aimed at essential expression of essential facts. I wanted to avoid the usual abstract introspection expressed in that bookish and allusive language which, with so little warrant, passes for essential. Now the mark of the specious *canzoniere*-poem is that it achieves the illusion of formal unity by linking one page to the next through the very faintness and tenuousness of its "voices" and the conceptual nature of its themes. My need to be faithful to my own taste and my desire to avoid the specious unity of the *canzoniere* amounted, then, to the same thing. That need was technical for the reasons mentioned, but it demanded complete commitment of all my faculties and skill.

Meanwhile, I was developing my own notion of something I called the "poem-story," which I failed at first to distinguish sharply from the conventional "short poem." The difference is not, of course, simply a matter of scale. Poe's reservations (still valid) about the concept of the poem have to be fused with considerations of content into a single whole, and this whole is identical with external considerations of compositional scale. It was here, right at the outset, that I failed to achieve clarity and, with a certain arrogance, flattered myself that a vigorous act of faith in poetry was enough, so long as the poetry itself was clear, precise, muscular, objective, essential, and so forth. At the beginning I spoke of this book as having "developed." And the entire development lies right here—in my growing awareness of this problem, which, for me at least, still seems far from being solved.

My first notable success in achieving my aims was "South Seas," which for that reason is the first poem in the book. I hardly need to add that, from the moment I first thought about writing poetry, I struggled with a presentiment of its difficulty. And, in point of fact, innumerable other poems preceded "South Seas." At the same time my experience in writing prose fiction or simply critical prose revealed the desperate banality of those first poetic efforts and made it impossible for me to feel any pleasure in what I had done.

I moved abruptly from a lyricism combining explosive personal feeling and self-analysis (wretched introspection which led to self-indulgent outbursts of feeling, which in turn always ended in a pathological scream) to the narrative clarity and serenity of "South Seas." I could explain this change only by recalling that it did not, in fact, happen suddenly; that for almost a year before writing "South Seas" I had not seriously thought about writing poetry. During that year I was intensely involved in a number of projects. On the one hand,

I was busily—more busily than before—translating works by American authors. On the other, I was writing short stories in semi-dialect form and, in collaboration with a painter friend, putting together an amateurish collection of pornography (or *pornotheca*, as we called it). Of this last project nothing more need be said here than that it resulted in a group of ballads, tragedies, *canzoni*, poems in *ottava rima*, all vigorously Sotadic in style. None of which matters now; what does matter is that these works were all powerfully imagined, written with gusto, and addressed to an audience of friends, some of whom were extremely appreciative. Indeed, they could hardly have been written without that audience (and, in general, the fact of such an audience seems to me to have the same invigorating effect on a writer as fertilizer on a plant's roots).

The link between these activities and "South Seas" is complex. My studies of American literature put me in contact with the reality of a developing culture, a culture "in growing pains." My experiments with fiction enlarged and sharpened my sense of human experience and rooted those interests in a real world. Finally, from a technical point of view, my work on the "*pornotheca*" was crucial, teaching me the *profession* of art, the joy of resolving problems, the limits of a theme, the play of imagination and style, and also the mystery of felicity in a given style, which means coming to terms with the possible audience or reader. I particularly insist on the technical lessons learned in this last activity, since the other influences—American culture and human experiences—are too easily subsumed under the general rubric of experience, which explains everything and therefore nothing.

Again, in a rather subtle technical way, all three projects influenced the convictions, aims, and assumptions with which I started working on "South Seas." In all three I came into contact—in each case contact of a different kind—with an emergent linguistic creation based on dialect or actual speech. By this I mean my discovery, in the course of my studies, of colloquial American, and the use of Piedmontese or Turinese slang in my efforts to write naturalistic dialogue. Both were the adventurous projects of youthful enthusiasm, to which I had devoted sustained and serious thought, and both were integrated by the encounter with a theory in which poetry and language were identified.

Third, the basically burlesque style of Sotadic verse accustomed me to thinking of all literary language as fossilized, a dead body, in which life could not quicken or the blood flow unless it received continual transfusions of colloquial, dialectal, and technical language. And this unique, threefold experience kept me constantly aware, amidst that confused tangle from which practical experience and expression branch out, of the interdependence of both, and the need to guard against sterility by continually revising my principles. These activities prepared me, in short, for the idea that the condition of every poetic stimulus, however lofty, is always scrupulous attention to the moral—which is to say the practical, experiential—requirements of the world in which we live.

"South Seas," then, was the product of this natural preparation and my first effort to write a "poem-story." The hyphenated term is justifiable, I think, insofar as that poem is a realistic development of situations, told in a straightforward——and therefore, to my mind, imaginative—way. But the crucial thing is the objectivity with which the situation is developed: and this implies that what I was in fact writing was a short poem, half psychological, half narrative, but along realistic lines. At the time I insisted on *austerity* of style as a basic premise of my poetics, the point being to achieve imaginative clarity without recourse to *all the other* expressive devices which, to my mind, had been vitiated by rhetoric. The point was to prove to myself that austere energy of conception must necessarily find apposite, spontaneous, and essential expression. Nothing could have been more naïve than my attitude toward the conventional "rhetorical" image; I wanted no images in my poetry, and (except for several oversights) I cut them out. No matter what the cost, I wanted to preserve the directness I so much admired; I wanted, even at my own personal risk, to avoid the facile and sloppy lyricism of D'Annunzio and his school. (I overdid it.)

Obviously, given a program of such stark simplicity, the only salvation was close, possessive, passionate adherence to the object. The strength of this passion in my work, not my austerity and objectivity, may be why something in these early poems can be salvaged. I soon came to feel that the plot, or the object rather, was an obstacle or hindrance—which was inevitable in a mode of narrative as oriented to subject matter as mine. I often found myself musing and puzzling over my plots. In itself this is not a bad idea; I still do so, and to obvious advantage. What is wrong is looking for a plot with the notion of letting it unfold according to its own psychological or narrative dynamic, of simply watching what happens. Or identifying oneself with this dynamic and passively letting it operate according to its own laws. That means surrendering to the plot. And that is what I did.

But although the anxiety produced by such mistakes gave me no peace, I still had reason for satisfaction. Above all, I was consoled by the solid honesty of the objective style I was aiming at; it possessed an incisiveness and tonal clarity which I still envy. A secondary effect was a certain sense of (misogynist) masculinity which I enjoyed and which, in point of fact—along with certain accompanying touches—supplied the real design, the real development of situation in my "poem-story" (which I fondly imagined to be objective). When a man is praising the sky, he frequently theorizes well and realizes badly; but sometimes the opposite happens too. The fact is that, after years of vaporizing and poetic screaming, I had managed to make one of my poems smile—a figure in a poem—and this struck me as the tangible sign of stylistic mastery and conquest of experience.

I had also created a verse of my own. This was not done, I swear it, deliberately. All I knew at the time was that free verse, with its principled chaos and exuberance—its chief imaginative claim—was unsuited to my talents. On the subject of Whitman's free verse, which I greatly admired and feared, I have expressed myself elsewhere; in any case, I already had a vague sense of the oratorical quality needed to give life to its inspiration. For this I had neither the range nor the temperament. But I had no faith in traditional meters either, because of the triteness and sloppiness inherent in them. In any case I had parodied them too often to take them seriously now or achieve a rhyming effect which was not merely comic.

I knew of course that, in an absolute sense, there are no traditional meters, that every poet re-creates in them the interior rhythm of his own imagination. Then, one day, I found myself mumbling a rigmarole of words (a couplet of "South Seas") in the same stress cadence which I had used as a boy, when reading novels, to note down phrases which particularly haunted me, murmuring them over and over. This was how, quite unconsciously, I discovered my own verse—a verse which, throughout "South Seas" and several other poems, was wholly instinctive (traces of it remain in several verses of the earliest poems, still in traditional hendecasyllabics). By means of murmuring, I gave a rhythm to my poems. As I gradually discovered the implicit laws of my own metrical practice, the hendecasyllabics vanished and my verse assumed one of three constant forms, which I could somehow anticipate in the act of composing. But I was careful not to let it tyrannize me, and I was always ready, when necessary, to adopt other stress patterns and syllabic groupings. For the most part, however, I kept fairly close to my scheme, and this I regard as the real rhythm of my imagination.

There is no point, now, in saying why I think this mode of writing poetry is advantageous. I need only say that, by and large, it met my wholly instinctive need for long lines. I felt I had a good deal to say and that my verse should not be cramped by some metrical exigency but should satisfy its own natural needs. In this effort I succeeded, and, for better or worse, I *told* my poems in this rhythm.

Which brings me to the main point. I *told* poems, but what does this mean? I have already admitted that I regard the early poetry in this collection as basically realistic short poems, of which it can be charitably said that the *fact* is nothing more than an obstacle, a residue which the imagination has left unresolved. I imagined an incident which I developed, or a character to whom I assigned words. In order to avoid the genre of the "small poem," I practiced a niggardly economy and determined in advance the number of lines in a given poem. I put considerable stress on keeping this number, and I was wary of setting the total too low out of fear of being epigrammatic. (Such are the miseries of a rhetorical education.) At this juncture too I was saved by a certain temperamental silence and other interests in matters of life and the mind. These interests did not so much influence my work directly as allow me to meditate *ex novo* on the problem; in this way they distracted me from the ferocious zeal with which I imposed on every creative task the requirement of *muscular objectivity* in the story. Finally, so far as literature is concerned, one of those outside interests was my wild passion for Shakespeare and the other Elizabethans, all of whom I had read and annotated in the margins of the text.

I was trying one day to write a poem about an imaginary hermit, with the idea of showing how and why he had become a hermit, but the attempt failed. In its place, by dint of innumerable scrapped drafts, reworkings, doubts, self-ridicule, and agony, I composed a "landscape" ("Landscape I") about a hill, contrasting the summit with the lower slope, and moving back and forth between them. The energizing focus of this landscape was a hermit who, as a kind of "sublime joker," embodied both "high" and "low," and whom, in violation of my own negative convictions about imagery, I described as being "the color of burnt bracken." My choice of words makes it quite clear that my fantasy was grounded in pictorial feeling. And, in point of fact, just before writing "Landscape I" I had been looking at a group of new canvases by a painter friend, work of such astonishing clarity of color and compositional skill that I envied it. But whatever the original stimulus, the novelty of my effort at the time is now quite apparent to me. I had discovered the image.

Since I have not yet exhausted the possibilities implicit in the technique of "Landscape I," explanation at this point becomes difficult. But I had discovered the value of the image. And this new image of mine (*here* was my reward for my stubborn insistence on concrete narrative) was not imagery in the familiar rhetorical sense, i.e., a more or less arbitrary decoration imposed on a realistic narrative. In some obscure sense, my image *was* the story itself.

The fact that the hermit appeared to be "the color of burnt bracken" did not mean that I had established a parallel between hermit and bracken in order to give prominence to either. It meant that I had discovered an *imaginative relationship* or *link* between hermit and landscape (I could go on: links between hermit and girls, city visitors and peasants, girls and vegetation, hermit and she-goat, hermit and dung, high and low), and *that this relationship itself was the subject of the story*.

I was *narrating* this relationship, studying it as a significant whole created by the imagination and so imaginatively "seeded" that it could be further refined and developed. Both in the precision of this imaginative cluster and in its potential for infinite development, I saw the *reality* of the poem. (My passion for objectivity, now clarified as the need for concreteness, had become a passion for this new kind of reality.)

I had worked my way back (or so I thought) to the primal source of all poetic activity. I might have defined poetry as the effort to create a self-sufficient whole out of a cluster of those imaginative relationships in which the proper perception of a particular reality consists. I went right on evincing my dislike of traditional rhetorical imagery by avoiding it, and my narrative style remained straightforward and objective (I am speaking of course of my *new* objectivity). Still, I had finally made sense—my own sense—out of the simple but elusive dictum that imagery is the essence of poetry. I had of course encountered formal rhetorical imagery in rich abundance in Elizabethan plays, but at the time I was laboriously involved in persuading myself that its importance lay not so much in the rhetorical meaning of the term of comparison as in my own newly perceived meaning, i.e., as components of a total imaginative reality whose true meaning was their interrelationship. My discovery, I felt, was supported by the distinctive nature of Elizabethan imagery, with its stunning exuberance and ingenuity as well as its final sanction—the delight which the dramatists took in their own richness of invention and ingenuity. This was why many scenes in Elizabethan plays struck me as deriving their imaginative life from an atmosphere created by their own metaphors.

What happened with the poems written after "Landscape I" is naturally, at least at first, a story of lapses into my earlier form of psychological or narrative realism. This is the case, for instance, with "People Who Don't Understand," though it too everywhere exhibits the effects of my new discovery. Later on, I found I could translate experience into imaginative terms almost methodically; my technique became surer, almost instinctive. And it was at this point that I became conscious of a new problem, which I have not yet solved.

What I was doing was substituting an imaginative account of a more concrete, more informed reality for the event itself. All very well, I told myself, but at what point does the search for imaginative links stop? What, after all, is the proper criterion for preferring one imaginative link to another? In "Passion for Solitude," for instance, I felt apprehensive about the shameless prominence assigned to the first-person speaker (from "South Seas" on, it was part of my poetic program to reduce this "I" to mere character or to abolish him altogether). Not because I wanted to use this "I" for realistic personal narrative (by now that worry seemed childish), but because its prominence seemed to involve me in too many imaginative links, too richly related. When, I asked myself, does the imagination's power become merely arbitrary? My definition of the image gave me no answer to this question.

As of now I have still not solved the problem. And for that very reason I regard it as the crux of my poetics. While I do have a glimmering of a possible solution, it is still too unclear to satisfy me. Yet it does have the advantage of taking me back to my long-standing conviction of a fundamental interrelationship between the needs of experience and expression (a problem at which I glanced earlier when speaking of the development of my linguistic sense). The test of propriety in the interplay of imaginative links would seem to lie in a *discerning* loyalty to that moral and rational complex which defines personal participation in reality (in the larger sense of the word). Needless to say, this participation is subject to change and renewal, and for this very reason its imaginative effect can be embodied in innumerable situations. But the weakness of the definition is the very *discernment* so necessary to judgment of the work, but so inconclusive where the effects of judgment are concerned. Must we therefore say that all aesthetic judgment is precarious and superficial? It would be tempting.

Meanwhile I was working like a madman, in a creative frenzy; and although I was constantly, in different ways, running into the same difficulty, I put together more of these "narrated images." By now I had come to enjoy the risks of virtuosity. In "Night Pleasures," for instance, I wanted, by means of contrast, to link together a series of wholly sensory perceptions, but without lapsing into sensuality. In "House under Construction" I wanted to conceal the play of imagery in an outwardly realistic narrative. In "Sad Supper" I wanted to take a hackneyed situation and, by carefully interweaving its imaginative links, retell it in my own way.

In each of these poems I re-experienced the anxiety of my besetting problem: how to understand and explain the imaginative complex out of which it was made. I became more and more skilled in my use of elliptical hints, delicate shading, dense composition—and less and less convinced of the honesty and *necessity* of what I was doing. By comparison, the naked, almost prosaic verse of "South

Seas" or "Deola Thinking" seemed at times more convincing than the vivid, flexible poetry, dense with imaginative life, of "Portrait of the Author" and "Landscape IV." Still, I remained steadfastly loyal to the clear principle of direct, austere expression of an imaginative relation accurately and precisely perceived. I held stubbornly to narration, and I refused to lose myself in decorative effects for their own sake. Yet the truth is that my images—those imaginative links of mine—became constantly more complicated, constantly branching out into ever thinner air.

It is worth noting that, after a period of silence, a poet proposes to write, not *a poem*, but *poems*. The unwritten page is viewed as a risky exploration of something which, in the future, he will have the knack of doing. As of tomorrow morning, words, form, situation, rhythms all promise him a much wider horizon than the particular poem he will actually write.

If this widening future were boundless, if it had no horizon and were synonymous with his *whole* possible future, the poet's normal urge would be to keep on working, to muddle along and think no more about it. But the future is limited, it has a spiritual size and dimension; and although the limits may not be visible to the poet, they are present in the inward logic of the poem he is about to write. The poem he *will* write is like a door, it opens out to his ability to create; and he will go through that door—he will write other poems, he will exploit the ground and leave it exhausted. This is the essential point—the limitation, i.e., the extent, of this new territory. The poem he will write tomorrow will take him through several doors, not through all possible doors. The day will come when he will write tired poems, poems without promise, the kind of poem that tells him that that particular adventure is over. But if the adventure has a beginning and an end, that means that the poems written during that period form a single group and make up a lyric whole—i.e., the dreaded *canzoniere*.

It is hard to know when such an adventure is over. The tired or "terminal" poems may, after all, be the loveliest of the group, and the feeling of depression or boredom connected with writing them is not markedly different from that which reveals a fresh horizon. For instance, I wrote "Simplicity" and "Morning Star" (winter 1935–1936) in a state of indescribable boredom; it was perhaps precisely to escape my own boredom that I handled them so boldly and allusively that, rereading them now, they seem full of promise. Which means that the test of boredom is inadequate proof of a transition to a new phase, though boredom and dissatisfaction are admittedly the chief stimulus of any poetic discovery, great or small.

A sounder criterion is that of *intent*. A poet's poems are described as "tired" or "terminal," or as "fresh" and "promising" because he himself chooses to consider them that way. This criterion is clearly not arbitrary, since it would never occur to a poet to make a capricious decision about a poem's import. He will choose to write not simply those poems which struck him as promising when he wrote them (something which, because of the boredom already mentioned, rarely happens), but those which, upon later reflection, offer him the promise of future poems. It must also be noted that the unity of a group of poems (*the* poem) is not an abstract idea already present in the draft, but an organic flow of meanings and approaches which very gradually define themselves in concrete form. Besides, even after the poet has finished a group of poems, he sometimes cannot discern their unity and has to discover it by carefully analyzing every poem, changing their arrangement, and understanding them better. But the effective unity of a narrative is as it were self-created, and it is the very machinery of narration that makes it realistic.

The new group, my future poems, could of course be structured along autobiographical lines, which would mean narrative in the realistic sense of the word. For the time being, I have excluded this possibility.

I must now decide whether a number of homeless poems (not included in the 1936 edition of *Hard Labor*) are the end of an old group or the beginning of a new one. By the very act of writing them, I obviously meant to move beyond *Hard Labor*, since at the time (winter 1935) the book was already at the printer's. The winter of 1935–1936 was for me an acutely critical time. A long period of optimism and self-confidence was beginning to break down, and I was trying to rethink my attitude toward my profession from scratch. My reflections were committed to my diary and gradually turned into a lengthy examination of my entire life which, combined with subsequent anxieties (1937–1939), finally convinced me to try my hand at short stories and novels. Now and then I wrote a poem; in the winter of 1937–1938, during an effective return to the conditions of 1934, the year of *Hard Labor*, I wrote several. But I became more and more convinced that my real field was prose and that these poems were in fact an "afterglow." Then, in 1939, I wrote no poetry at all. In early 1940, when I once again returned to poetry, it was to ask whether these unassigned poems belonged to *Hard Labor* or indicated a new departure.

The fact is that, when I picked up the book and adjusted the order so as to include several poems deleted by the censors in 1935,* the later poems fell naturally into place and seemed to form a whole. Practically speaking, then, I had the answer to my question, but the fact remains that the direction of these unassigned later poems gave me clear hopes of writing a whole new group.

Let us see. These later poems fall into two natural groupings,

---

* The poems deleted by the Fascist censor were: "The Goat God," "Ballet," and "Fatherhood." Characteristically, the censor's displeasure was visited, not on the political poems, but on those that offended the almost puritan propriety of Fascist "morality."—W.A.

which are also chronological. Winter of 1935–1936, the winding up of my political detention in Calabria: "Myth," "Simplicity," and "Morning Star"; winter of 1937–1938, sexual passion: "The Old Drunk," "The Voice," "The Country Whore," and "The Boatman's Wife." Clearly, these two thematic groupings were already present in the 1936 edition of *Hard Labor*. The first group is linked to "Sultry Lands" and "Prison: Poggio Reale"; the second group is connected to "Motherhood" and "Sad Supper." The crucial question is whether anything in their tone justifies my intention of assigning them to a new book of poems—which is obviously what I hoped when I wrote them.

It seems doubtful. The novelty of "Morning Star" was an illusion. The sea, the mountain, the star, the solitary man—these elements or themes are already present in "Ulysses," "Displaced People," and "Passion for Solitude." And the rhythm of imaginative movement is not different from, or even significantly richer than, earlier poetry. The reader is left with nothing but the human figure seen in his essential gestures and narrated by means of those gestures. The same thing could be said of the women's portraits in the second group ("The Old Drunk" and "The Boatman's Wife") which, apart from the outward novelty of the dream, repeat the figurative pattern of "Ulysses" and "Women in Love"; both make use of the internal image (a detail of the picture, used as a term of comparison) and both fail to achieve even the hazy ideal of the "image-story" I advanced in 1934. As for the austerity and economy of "The Boatman's Wife," it takes us right back to "Deola Thinking."

The truth of the matter is that during those years of personal crisis (1937–1939), my artistic purpose expressed itself, not so much in these new poems as in the reflections I was making in my diary at the same time—reflections which finally suffocated the poetry. Since periods of poetic activity usually end with critical awareness, and since my diary constantly stressed the *problem* of my poetry, a crisis —a crisis of renewal—was clearly in the offing. Put it this way. In the actual work of writing *Hard Labor* I had succeeded in defining what I was doing, and when I recently went back to the book and rearranged it, I discovered that it had a formal structure (an idea which in 1934 struck me as ludicrous). And this very discovery shows that I intended to go beyond *Hard Labor*, to strike out in a new direction. By the very act of examining the poetics involved in the poems I had written after 1936, by my discovery that they were compatible with the rest of *Hard Labor*, I indicated my desire to work out a new poetics and suggested the direction it might take. Why, then, these constant, fragmentary critical inquiries which occupied me for three long years?

Hard Labor can be defined as the adventure of the adolescent boy who is proud of the countryside where he lives and who imagines that the city will be like the country. But in the city he discovers loneliness and tries to cure it with sex and passion; but they only uproot him and alienate him from city and country alike, leaving him in a more tragic loneliness which marks the end of adolescence. In this *canzoniere* I discovered a formal coherence—the evocation of completely solitary figures who are imaginatively alive insofar as they are bound to their brief time and place by means of the *internal image*. (Example: in "Landscape VI" the foggy air *intoxicates*, the beggar breathes the air as if it were *grappa*, the boy *drinks in* the morning. The entire imaginative life of *Hard Labor* is based upon this kind of imagery.)

For four years I lived that adventure, and now it is over, along with the techniques created to evoke it. The adventure itself ended with my practical acceptance and understanding of male loneliness; I finished with the techniques by demonstrating a need for new rhythms and new forms (and a few meager efforts to achieve them). My criticism has fallen, as it should, with special severity on my idea of the image. My ambitious definition of 1934—that the image was identical with the plot of the story—was shown to be false or at least inadequate. More recently, I have created real figures by rooting them in their background by means of internal metaphors, but this metaphor itself has never been the subject of the story for the simple reason that the subject was a character or a real landscape. It is no accident, after all, that I saw that the only possible unity of *Hard Labor* was a real human adventure. As is the *canzoniere* as a whole, so is the individual poem.

Let me say it clearly: tomorrow's adventure, my future poetry, must have different reasons, different motives.

This future collection, this new *canzoniere*, will clarify itself only when it has been written—by which time I will be obliged to repudiate it. In what has been said there are two premises which concern this future work:

1. Its general structure will be analogous to the structure of each poem in it.

2. It will be incapable of prose paraphrase.

The second premise—my requirement of a poetry that cannot be reduced to narrative—is optional; nothing requires it. Yet it is the yeast of tomorrow's poetry. It is the arbitrary, the precritical factor; only insofar as it is, can it stimulate poetry. It is an intention, an irrational premise, which only the work itself will justify. Four long years of self-questioning and aspiration impose this need on me now —just as in 1931 and 1932 a voice required me to *tell* my poetry.

Obviously the need to write a different kind of poetry brings with it the need to know what this new poetry will say. But only the new poetry will say what it is, and once it has said it, it will be a thing of the past, as *Hard Labor* is now.

And this time too, no doubt about it, the question of the image will be crucial. But this time it will not be a matter of *narrating images*—an empty formula, as we have seen, since nothing whatever distinguishes the words which evoke an image from those which invoke an object. It will be a question of describing—whether directly or by means of images is irrelevant—a reality which is not realistic but symbolic. In these future poems events will take place—if they take place—not because reality wishes it, but because intelligence so decides. Individual poems and the *canzoniere* as a whole will not be autobiography, but judgment. Which is what happens, after all, in *The Divine Comedy* (we had to get around to Dante sooner or later) —always bearing in mind that my symbol will correspond not to Dante's allegory but to his imagery.

There is no point in thinking about the book of poems as a whole. As we saw in the case of *Hard Labor*, all one can do is immerse himself in the individual poem and overcome the past within the limits set by the poem. If the first of my two premises is correct, all that is needed is to write a single new poem—it may already be written—and the whole *canzoniere*, the entire poem, will be assured. Not only that: once a single verse exists, everything will be implicit in it. A day will come when one calm, peaceful glance will bring order and unity to the laborious chaos which begins tomorrow.

Translator's Notes*

The present translation of Cesare Pavese's *Lavorare stanca* is based upon the edition published by Einaudi in 1943. This edition, however, was not the first. In 1936 the Florentine review *Solaria* had published a collection of forty-five poems under the same title. When Pavese revised and regrouped his book for the Einaudi edition seven years later, he excised six of the original poems and added twenty-one additional poems.

Lavorare stanca. Literally translated, it means simply "Work is wearying" (or "tiring" or "wearing"), which hardly makes good English: either too alliteratively "poetic" or pleonastic. *Hard Labor* puts a different emphasis—a prison emphasis—on P.'s title perhaps, but insofar as a term in prison implies eventual release (or at least the hope of it), and a whole section of the book ("Green Wood") is devoted to the theme of imprisonment, it comes, I think, passably close. Still, P. lavished great pains on his titles (which often provide the crucial access to the work) and, despite the *apparent* banality, *Lavorare stanca* is a title which deserves much more than a cursory note. It contains, in fact, the dominant—or recurrent—themes of the book.

What P. means by his title is, I am convinced, a rhythm or balance between two opposed poles or spiritual conditions. *Lavorare stanca* is intended to suggest the exhaustion of willed work, the boredom of consciousness and routine, the fatigue of merely compulsive labor, even the weariness of overworked intellect—and this state of psychical exhaustion *implies* its opposite (i.e., carefree freedom, the exhilaration of release, the vagabond existence and the "open road," the instinctual life, free from conscious duty and constriction, living like a child, *in* and *for* the moment). But P.'s effective general stress clearly falls on fatigue, on pain and suffering; the emphasis is undeniably tragic, even bleak. Joy is only implied; suffering is dominant. Poem after poem moves between these poles; each poem is in its own way a product of the *labor* whose aim is release, balance; the *joy* of an *accurate* poem, even accuracy in suffering and grief. The poems move according to a dynamic which for P. has the character of psychological law, of necessity. The city necessarily seeks the country;

* I acknowledge, as any translator of Pavese must, my indebtedness to Italo Calvino, who scrupulously and intelligently edited the complete edition of Pavese's poetry (*Poesie edite e inedite* [Turin, 1962]). I have drawn heavily and repeatedly on Calvino's work for information and elucidation; when I cite him directly, I have so indicated by adding "[I.C.]." Otherwise the notes are my own.

the country requires the city. Those numbed by excessive compulsion and the strain of consciousness are driven toward unconscious compensations—to drunkenness, vagabondage, instinctual release, annulment of will, to primitive or wild behavior, and so forth. Denial of consciousness, the "wilderness" in turn point back toward the city, responsibility, history, consciousness, the engaged and striving will, the *joy* and *discipline* of work.

For P. the essential problem of living—*il mestiere di vivere*, the "life-craft" he feared he did not possess—was to find a balance, or at least a rhythm of movement, between these opposed poles; an existential skill which enabled a man to keep his *human* balance, to honor his divided nature, part animal and part god, to become himself. Thus the peasants in *The Goat God* know how to keep the precarious human and civil balance, combining work with joy, discipline with release, in a life which makes their world and themselves human, *beautifully* human:

> They make their women pregnant, the peasants, and go on working
> just the same. Day or night they wander where they like.
> They aren't afraid of hoeing by moonlight, or making a bonfire
> of weeds and brush in the dark. And that's why the ground
> is so beautifully green, and the plowed fields at dawn
> are the color of sunburned faces. . . .

The dangers of lost balance are made visible in the hermit in "Landscape I," who, like the "goat god" in the poem above, has gone wild ("he's the color of burnt bracken"; see Postscript I); or the city girls who come, on their "day off," to "celebrate the she-goat." So too, in *People Who Don't Understand*, P. gives us his own polar geography: the faceless, exigent, desiring city from which (in part) Gella seeks release; then the *paese* of Gella's mother, with its human scale and balance; and finally the compensatory wilderness, the zero-world of instinct toward which Gella is most deeply driven.

For P. himself, an extremely lonely man with a corresponding hunger for community, friends, and transcendence, the dangers of losing balance were particularly acute. The price of lost balance was death, human death; a man could die as a man by immuring himself in desperately compulsive work, using work as an anodyne against suffering, or, alternatively, by abandoning everything in a rage for release, the extinction of consciousness, the joy of transcendence. All his life P. struggled—heroically, I believe—to keep his balance, and finally the passion for transcendence overwhelmed him, the passion to extinguish himself in a larger life, to *become* sky, sap, leaves, rain, the hill, earth.

All his life he moved—often violently, compulsively, quietly—between the poles implied in his title, right to the end. (Even when he was renting the hotel room where he had decided to die the death of a stranger in his own city, he demanded a room with a phone, still hoping that he could reach someone who might dissuade him by proving to him that he was not alone.) In the title *Lavorare stanca* the fatal imbalance is already visible, the torment of a man who, in Calvino's words, could not achieve integration: "a child in the world of adults, a man without a profession in a working world, without a woman in the world of love and the family, defenseless in a world of bloody political battle and civil duties." Now and then perhaps there was a brief reprieve or parole, but in most respects P.'s sentence was simply a harsher version of the common human fate: solitary confinement and hard labor. And *Lavorare stanca* (with *Il carcere* and other works) is in some clear sense part of the great Italian prison literature that runs from Silvio Pellico to Gramsci.

There were models and influences as well. Behind the terms implied in P.'s title and spiritual landscape, informing and clarifying it, are the influences of his own "province" of Piedmontese culture and the exotic world of American literature. The central Piedmontese influence was Augusto Monti (see note below on "South Seas"), in whose novel *I sansossi* (Piedmontese for *sans souci*), P. found a fully developed version of the antitheses expressed in *Lavorare stanca*. Central to Monti's work was an elaborate contrast between two traditional Piedmontese "types": on the one hand, the *sansossi* of his title, carefree, nonchalant, spontaneous, uninhibited; on the other, the stolid, hard-working, stoical, and laconic Piedmontese peasant (see Pavese's "Ancestors" or "Landscape III"). Beyond Piedmont lay America, and America confirmed for P. the polar geography he had already discovered in Monti and in his own village of Santo Stefano Belbo. Whitman above all; not Whitman the poet-orator (whose example Pavese tended to eschew), but rather Whitman's *attitude* toward his world, Whitman as champion of the vagabond life and the open road, but also the celebrator and evangelist of work. "Truly," P. wrote, "Whitman *was* an idler [*fannullone*] in the sense in which every poet is an idler when instead of working he prefers to wander about, turning over in his mind, *with great labor and the rare joys that compensate all such labor*, his lines. . . . He was an idler at every ordinary task, because he had other business in hand."* [My emphasis.]

p. 2. "South Seas." Augusto Monti, to whom the poem is dedicated, was perhaps the single most decisive literary and intellectual influence in P.'s life. A professor at the Liceo Massimo d'Azeglio in Turin, Monti was at first P.'s revered teacher, then his mentor, and finally

---

* "Interpretation of Walt Whitman, Poet," in Cesare Pavese, *American Literature*, trans. Edwin Fussell (Berkeley and Los Angeles, 1970).

his close friend. A real moving force in the intellectual life of Torino and the region, he was also the respected spokesman of traditional Piedmontese liberalism; and it was around Monti that the young anti-Fascists of P.'s circle rallied. P.'s dedication of his first important poem (and his longest) was a homage in the deepest sense of the word: literary, political, cultural, personal. Without Monti's example, it is doubtful the poem would have been written, certainly not *as* it is written.

For P.'s own estimate of "South Seas," see Postscript I. In his diary (November 10, 1935), P. wrote: "If there is a figure in my poems, it is the figure of the runaway who returns home, joyously, to his native village; he has seen many things, colorful things, he has very little desire to work, takes great pleasure in the simplest things, is always expansive and good-natured, incapable of deep suffering, content to follow nature and enjoy a woman, but no less content to keep to himself, free of all obligations, ready to start each morning afresh. As in 'South Seas.' "

P.'s "cousin" in the poem had served aboard a Dutch whaler in the Pacific and seen the world; so too P.—whose poetic development parallels the career of the "cousin"—had spent several years prior to writing the poem translating *Moby Dick*.

p. 13. "Landscape I." See Postscript I ("The Poet's Craft') for Pavese's account of the genesis of this important poem and its significance in the development of his poetry and his "image-poem." The "Pollo" of the poem's dedication is the "painter-friend" Mario Sturani, remembered in the same appendix.

p. 17. "The Goat God." Deleted by the Fascist censor—on the grounds of moral indecency—from the *Solaria* edition (1936) of *Lavorare stanca*.

The god if the title is, of course, a rural Italian version of Pan, whose epiphany as god of the wild and wild places the poem is designed to evoke—and, if possible, cope with, come to *human* terms with. (For the resonance of "wildness" and "wilderness" in P.'s work, see the remarkable late essay "*Il selvatico*"). But, such is P.'s elliptic reticence that the word "wild" is never mentioned in the poem, though constantly, insistently, in detail and contrast, implied and evoked. For the translator the problem lies in P.'s poetic situation— the fact (conveyed by the word *caprone*) that a domestic billy goat has escaped and gone wild. Since English lacks pejorative suffixes like *-one*, the translator can only convey the sense by the clumsy phrase "the wild billy." ("He-goat" tells us nothing about the fact that the goat in the poem has *gone wild, reverted*). But the intrusion of the word "wild" means that the translator cannot honor P.'s scrupulous reticence and ellipsis; that he *must*, even though he would rather not, name what P. has carefully *not* named.

p. 25. "August Moon." In his diary for November 24, 1935, Pavese wrote: "I seem to be discovering a new vein. The gist is *restless meditation* on things, even Piedmontese things. I notice that at first I wrote in *dreamy meditation* ('South Seas'; 'Landscape IV'; 'Portrait of the Author'); the change occurred not only after May 15, but in work done earlier this same year ('Hard Labor, Getting Tired'; 'Ulysses'; 'Love Affairs'; 'Outside')—a note of anxiety, sadness, pain, hitherto unrecognized or sternly repressed. After May and August, of course, this tone became the general rule. . . . In any case, to get a clear sense of the transition, compare 'Landscape II' with 'August Moon.' What in the former was entirely descriptive spiritualization of a scene becomes in the latter the creation of a natural mystery around human pain."

p. 29. "Landscape III." My translation of the final line of this poem may raise eyebrows, but I am convinced that the meaning is correctly rendered. P. was an early and enthusiastic reader of Frazer, and in the cadence and thrust of the peasant's "reported" thought, we are meant, I believe, to hear something like *Ci vuole forza!* He is saying, that is, not only that his field needs a display of *strength* to protect it from thieves, but it could use a *dressing* (i.e., a manuring of blood and flesh, a sacrifice) in order to stimulate growth. For P.'s express familiarity with the idea, see Lityerses' words to Heracles in P.'s *Dialogues with Leucò*: "You've eaten with us, you've drunk our wine, and now these fields of ours will drink your blood. There'll be a bumper crop in the Meander Valley next year. . . . You'll fertilize these fields all right. . . ."

p. 37. "Passion for Solitude." On the reverse side of a typescript of this poem, P. wrote in longhand: "My work consists in putting together a structure which, through correspondence between its parts, is self-sufficient; the subject matter is made of a *reality* which lives by means of animated relationships—not of external images, but identities and combinations between various emergent and created aspects of this reality. For the colorful or musical—the fanciful—image, I substitute the *perceived structure* of the very reality I am dealing with."

p. 53. "Sultry Lands." The Italian title of the poem is *"Terre bruciate"* (literally, "burnt lands" or "scorched lands"). What P. clearly intends is an ambiguous term (*bruciate*) which will cover the two opposed perspectives: Piedmont and Calabria, city and country. As

Turin is *bruciata* by sexual passion, so Calabria is *bruciata* by the sun, a "scorched" land. Neither "burnt" nor "scorched" adequately convey the ambiguity in English, so I have reluctantly altered the title to "Sultry Lands." "Tropical" would have done nicely, except for the afct that the Calabrian landscape hardly satisfies the lush, paradisal green promised by "tropical."

p. 75. "House under Construction." P.'s poems tend to be organized around a key word or idea, everywhere suggested but nowhere explicitly stated. Reticence and ellipsis as well as constant understatement are the most persistent features of P.'s poetry, and the translator's most ticklish task, I think, is respecting this reticence. The danger, of course, is allowing the American reader, deceived perhaps by the realistic narrative and low-keyed diction, to conclude that the poems lack tension and depth. The "hidden" idea in this poem is the word "blood," around which most of the action revolves, and a persistent secret violence, *primal* violence. With considerable trepidation, for reasons that I hope will be clear to the reader, I have introduced the word "blood" into the final line, where in the original it is obviously evoked but is left unstated. The literal Italian reads: "Once a stone ended up on the head / of the boss, and they all stopped work / to carry him down to the stream and wash his face."

p. 95. "Lack of Discipline." Despite his considerable erudition, P. rather scrupulously avoids the show of learning, of bookish and allusive references. The reason was not, I think, mere populist pedantry (of whose dangers P. was well aware), but the poet's conviction that a poem had to earn its own meaning, that (apart from cultural commonplaces) it could not depend upon the props of polite culture. This remarkable poem, I believe, probably derives its basic idea (the drunk as an intruder *from another dimension*, from another world, "submarine and profound") from Plato's *Phaedo* (a dialogue of which P. was extremely fond). The pertinent passage is that in which Socrates is metaphorically contrasting the world of reality with the world of sublunary change, flux, and perishing particulars —the world in which most men actually live:

> We do not realize that we are living in the hollow places of this earth, but assume we dwell on the earth's surface. Imagine someone living in the depths of the sea. He might think he was living on the surface, and seeing the sun and the other heavenly bodies through the water; he might suppose that the sea was the sky. . . . Now we are in the same position. Although we live in a hollow of the earth, we assume that we are living on the surface, and call the earth heaven, as though it were the heaven through which the stars move. . . . [109 c-d]

Plato's point of view is, needless to say, not Pavese's; indeed, P. seems to be asserting that the quotidian complacency of ordinary consciousness is shattered by the drunk's presence, revealed in its fragility and precariousness by the drunk's "submarine" perspective. The drunk brings with him the threat of a "husky" voice (always in P. the voice of our origins, of instinctual memory), the sense of a *real world* (which he inhabits effortlessly and naturally) suppressed by urban certainties and routines. Hence the drunk's power to intimidate, embarrass, to excite fear, to "touch" us where we live—that part of us which is "oceanic" too.

p. 97. "Portrait of the Author." Alternative draft titles of this poem were "Two Hobos" and "The Blue of Summer." The various drafts clarify the poem's opening situation: two hobos sitting on the ground; one of them has taken off his pants, the other his sweater; together they compose a single nude body. The poem then proceeds to develop the links between the images skin-smell-sexual potency, seen from the viewpoint of someone who identifies himself with smoothness of skin and an absence of odor; who sees himself as resembling the boy, and who has not yet proved himself sexually. [I.C.]

p. 99. "Grappa in September." Grappa is a strong, cheap, colorless ("the color of water") Italian brandy made from the residue of pressed wine, especially common in the North.

If this poem is obviously P.'s own "Ode to Autumn," it is also an exceptionally beautiful example of P.'s "image-story" (see Postscript I). Thus in the first stanza the key imaginative "links" (the clear morning, the dawn fog, tobacco, and grappa) are introduced realistically, and then "narrated" (i.e., developed in likeness and contrast) in the succeeding stanzas. The women *ripen* like fruit, *drink in* the foggy air, and so forth. Because their relation to the world is wholly natural and integrated, they neither drink nor smoke; the men, by contrast, are excluded from the universal process: they can participate in it only at a metaphorical remove, by simulation. Their tobacco gives off a bluish haze, like fog; they absorb the ripening world in the grappa they drink. Thus, by the end of the poem ("So it seems/ the women aren't the only ones enjoying the morning"), there is a kind of resolution in enjoyment, as the men manage to merge, if always at a remove, in the world which excludes them.

The act of smoking (and drinking) is P.'s way—at once realistic and metaphorical—of indicating the *observer's* stance as against the *participant's*. See also "Mediterranean" and "Portrait of the Author."

p. 101. "Ballet." One of the three poems deleted by the Fascist censor —on moral, not political, grounds—from the *Solaria* edition (1936) of *Lavorare stanca*.

p. 103. "Fatherhood." Also deleted by the Fascist censor from the *Solaria* edition.

p. 121. "Night Pleasures." See Postscript I: "In 'Night Pleasures' . . . I wanted, by means of contrast, to link together a series of wholly sensory perceptions, but without lapsing into sensuality."

p. 123. "Sad Supper." In "The Poet's Craft" (Postscript I), P. remarks: "In 'Sad Supper' I wanted to take a hackneyed situation and, by carefully interweaving its imaginative links, retell it in my own way."

p. 143. "Workers of the World." The Italian title is *"Fumatori di carta"* (literally, "smokers of paper"). After World War I and during the Depression, tobacco in Italy became very expensive, and those who could not afford it made (I am told) an ersatz out of shredded newspapers. But the word *fumare* has connotations of hazy, vaporous dreaming (cf. English "pipe dreams"), and in this sense "paper smokers" would be as it were doctrinal visionaries, that is, political dreamers whose visions are based upon printed abstraction and "party line" ideology. P.'s title thus conveys his characteristic ambivalence: on the one hand, sympathy and solidarity with the poor and oppressed; on the other, a skeptical literary man's distrust of dialectical abstractions which scanted or obscured human tragedy. "Workers of the World" is my effort to suggest something of the ambivalence of the (untranslatable) Italian title and, perhaps, a sense of P.'s ironic detachment. If it is generally known that P. was a Communist, it is less well known that he was, at least in the period of *Hard Labor*, often detached from and even diffident toward official ideology.

p. 147. "A Generation." Davide Lajolo, in his biography of P. (*Il vizio assurdo*, p. 38) informs us that P. made two annotations on this poem in Lajolo's copy of *Lavorare stanca*. At the fifth line P. wrote "Dec. 18th, 1922. Remember: Torino massacre . . ." At the fourteenth line P. wrote down the names of all fourteen, men and boys, who had been shot down, adding, "I was 12 years old at the time."

p. 149. "Green Wood." P.'s title for this poem (and the section in which it occurs) is clearly meant to suggest both adolescent immaturity and early tragedy (or premature death), and its source is Dante's figure at *Inferno* 13, 40 ff.:

Come d'un stizzo verde che arso sia
      dall' un de' capi, che dall'altro geme
      e cigola per vento che va via:
sì della scheggia rotta usciva insieme
      parole e sangue. . .*

The poem, written in 1934, is dedicated to Massimo Mila, a friend
who had been imprisoned briefly for anti-Fascist activities in 1929
(and who, in 1935, would again be sentenced to prison, this time for
seven years). It may be, as Calvino suggests, that P.'s title is meant
to glance ironically at the visionary romanticism of the young anti-
Fascist resistance (see note on "Workers of the World"), but the
more natural reading seems to me elegaic, a lament for the tragic
waste of youthful lives. "Words and blood . . ."

p. 153. "Prison: Poggio Reale." In certain details the poem does not
quite fit the environment of the Neapolitan prison of Poggio Reale,
and is apparently a composite of the various prisons in which P. was
detained after his arrest for anti-Fascist activities and en route to his
confinement in Calabria; namely, the Carceri Nuove in Torino, Regina
Coeli in Rome, and Poggio Reale in Naples.

p. 161. "Landscape VI." See P.'s remarks on this poem in Postscript
II ("Notes on Certain Unwritten Poems") and also in his diary for
December 16, 1935 and February 16, 1936.

p. 165. "Paradise on the Roofs." Written in 1940, this poem is an
uncannily exact anticipation of P.'s suicide ten years later in the
fourth-floor room of the Albergo Roma in Torino. The poet was not
of course simply enacting his poem; both poem and suicide derive
from an older, deeper fatality, with its own tonal and symbolic structure, its recurrent pattern of loneliness and passion for transcendence.
Alternative titles of the poem were "The Last Room," "The Last
Ceiling." In the drafts occur these discarded lines: "in the warmth of
the last sleep,/ and the sky will be the same sky that once filled the
streets./ There are no more streets. There will be a window/ —a
great window—will fill the room. . . ." And these lines, as Calvino
observes, clarify the basic image: the disappearance of the world in
a sky seen through a skylight overhead. A window opening onto a
blank sky, pure nothingness, is P.'s most persistent symbol of infinity—and transcendence of the lonely personal "I" in that infinity.
In a late essay ("State of Grace") P. wrote: "A simple staircase win-

---

* "As a green brand that burns at one end, and at the other end oozes sap and
hisses with the wind escaping; so from that broken splint, words and blood
came forth together."

dow opening on a blank sky puts a man of my acquaintance into a
state of grace. . . . Why, out of all the possible images of the infinite,
did he choose this particular image? . . . Symbols are . . . our instinctual response to the claims of culture The staircase window may be
the one in the school where we spent our first years and made our
first, perhaps reluctant, acquaintance with poetry. But what mattered,
what still matters, is the empty and immemorial sky."

p. 171. "Fatherhood." In the ms. of the poem is the alternative title
"Sad Love" ("Amore triste"). The first version of lines 15 ffff. gives:
"in the bed is the woman who would make a boy,/ if she weren't far
away, beyond the clouds,/ beyond the great mountains."

The title "Fatherhood" is best understood in contrast with another
poem entitled "Motherhood." In the latter, the woman's *motherhood*
is present in her children even after she has died; in the former,
fatherhood is unrealized in "the man alone," the man who has no
children of his own. Since the titles of the two poems are also titles
of two sections of the book, the contrast was obviously important to
P. Implicit in it are two themes constantly present in P.'s mythical-
agricultural sense of all aspects of human life: the sense of the
woman-as-earth, who transmits life, and the sterility of "the man
alone," excluded from the natural cycle of procreation. It is worth
noticing that in much of P.'s work the sea is a symbol of sterility,
contrasted with the earth-woman. Only in the poems written after
Hard Labor do the two symbols of the sea and the earth-as-woman
converge. [I.C.]

p. 173. "Morning Star." This intensely lonely poem, almost Sapphic
in its poetics, is dated January 9–12, 1936, and is the last poem written by P. during his period of political confinement at Brancaleone
Calabrese. To North Italian ears, attuned to companionable and
"civil" Tuscan, the exile's loneliness would have been significantly
heightened by P.'s simple device of using Calabrian (*Lo steddazzu*)
rather than Italian for the "morning star" of the title.

At the time of his tragic death by suicide in 1950, **Cesare Pavese** was —as he still is—regarded as Italy's greatest contemporary writer. In addition to his novels (*The Devil on the Hill, The Moon and the Bonfires,* and others), his classic essays on American literature, his autobiography (*The Burning Brand*), and his prose masterpiece, *Dialogues with Leucò,* Pavese was also a poet of major importance, whose poetry, long eclipsed by the fame of his fiction, is only now receiving its due recognition. Both in Italy and abroad, Pavese's poetry is regarded as true pioneer work, decades ahead of its time, and Pavese himself is recognized as essentially a poet—and an extremely important one—in everything he wrote.

William Arrowsmith is both poet and translator. He has translated six plays of Euripides, four of Aristophanes, and the *Satyricon* of Petronius. In addition, he has translated from Italian, French, Japanese, and German. He is the author of *Image of Italy* and the editor of *Six Modern Italian Novellas.* With D. S. Carne-Ross, he translated Pavese's major work, *Dialogues with Leucò.* He was a founding editor of the *Hudson Review, Chimera,* and *Arion* and is now contributing editor of the *American Poetry Review* and *Mosaic.* Educated at Princeton and Oxford, where he was a Rhodes Scholar, Arrowsmith currently holds joint appointments as professor in the Writing Seminars and the Classics Department at The Johns Hopkins University. In 1978, in recognition of his work as translator and writer, he received the Award for Literature from the American Academy and the National Institute of Arts and Letters.

The Johns Hopkins University Press

This book was composed in Linotype Palatino text and display type by the Maryland Linotype Composition Co., from a design by Charles West. It was printed on 50-lb. No. 66 Eggshell Offset Cream paper and bound by Universal Lithographers, Inc.

Library of Congress Cataloging in Publication Data

Pavese, Cesare.
  Hard labor.

  Translation of Lavorare stanca.
  Poems.
  Reprint of the 1976 ed. published by Grossman
Publishers, New York.
    I. Arrowsmith, William, 1924-   II. Title.
[PQ4835.A846L313 1979]   851'.9'12   79-2371
ISBN 0-8018-2180-0